Intersecting Film, Music, and Queerness

Palgrave Studies in Audio-Visual Culture
Series Editor: **K. J. Donnelly**, University of Southampton, UK

Advisory Board: **Philip Brophy**, Australia, **Michel Chion**, University of Paris III: Sorbonne Nouvelle, France, **Sean Cubitt**, Goldsmiths, University of London, UK, **Claudia Gorbman**, University of Washington Tacoma, USA, **Lev Manovich**, Graduate Centre, CUNY, USA and **Elisabeth Weis**, Brooklyn College, CUNY, USA.

The aesthetic union of sound and image has become a cultural dominant. A junction for aesthetics, technology and theorisation, film's relationship with music remains the crucial nexus point of two of the most popular arts and richest cultural industries. Arguably, the most interesting area of culture is the interface of audio and video aspects, and that film is the flagship cultural industry remains the fount and crucible of both industrial developments and critical ideas.

Palgrave Studies in Audio-Visual Culture has an agenda-setting aspiration. By acknowledging that radical technological changes allow for rethinking existing relationships, as well as existing histories and the efficacy of conventional theories, it provides a platform for innovative scholarship pertaining to the audio-visual. While film is the keystone of the audio-visual continuum, the series aims to address blind spots such as video game sound, soundscapes and sound ecology, sound psychology, art installations, sound art, mobile telephony and stealth remote viewing cultures.

Titles include:

Anna Katharina Windisch and Claus Tieber (*editors*)
THE SOUNDS OF SILENT FILMS
New Perspectives on History, Theory and Practice

Danijela Kulezic-Wilson
THE MUSICALITY OF NARRATIVE FILM

Aimee Monaghan
THE VISUAL MUSIC FILM

K. J. Donnelly and Ann-Kristin Wallengren (*editors*)
TODAY'S SOUNDS FOR YESTERDAY'S FILMS
Making Music for Silent Cinema

Jack Curtis Dubowsky
INTERSECTING FILM, MUSIC, AND QUEERNESS

Palgrave Studies in Audio-Visual Culture
Series Standing Order ISBN 978–1–137–42975–9   hardcover
Series Standing Order ISBN 978 1–137–42976–6   paperback
(*outside North America only*)

You can receive future titles in this series as they are published by placing a standing order. Please contact your bookseller or, in case of difficulty, write to us at the address below with your name and address, the title of the series and one of the ISBNs quoted above.

Customer Services Department, Macmillan Distribution Ltd, Houndmills, Basingstoke, Hampshire RG21 6XS, England

---

Intersecting Film, Music, and Queerness

Jack Curtis Dubowsky

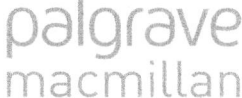

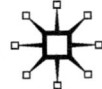
First published 2016 by
PALGRAVE MACMILLAN

The author has asserted his right to be identified as the author of this work in accordance with the Copyright, Designs and Patents Act 1988.

Palgrave Macmillan in the UK is an imprint of Macmillan Publishers Limited, registered in England, company number 785998, of Houndmills, Basingstoke, Hampshire RG21 6XS.

Palgrave Macmillan in the US is a division of Nature America, Inc., One New York Plaza, Suite 4500, New York, NY 10004-1562.

Palgrave Macmillan is the global academic imprint of the above companies and has companies and representatives throughout the world.

Hardback ISBN: 978–1–137–45420–1
E-PUB ISBN: 978–1–137–45422–5
E-PDF ISBN: 978–1–137–45421–8
DOI: 10.1057/9781137454218

Distribution in the UK, Europe and the rest of the world is by Palgrave Macmillan®, a division of Macmillan Publishers Limited, registered in England, company number 785998, of Houndmills, Basingstoke, Hampshire RG21 6XS.

Library of Congress Cataloging-in-Publication Data

Names: Dubowsky, Jack Curtis, author.
Title: Intersecting film, music, and queerness / Jack Curtis Dubowsky.
Description: Houndmills, Basingstoke, Hampshire ; New York : Palgrave Macmillan, 2016. | Includes bibliographical references and index.
Identifiers: LCCN 2015038165 | ISBN 9781137454201 (hardback)
Subjects: LCSH: Homosexuality in motion pictures. | Homosexuality and motion pictures. | Motion picture music—History and criticism. | BISAC: ART / Film & Video. | MUSIC / Genres & Styles / Musicals. | SOCIAL SCIENCE / Gay Studies.
Classification: LCC PN1995.9.H55 D83 2016 | DDC 791.43/6526642—dc23
LC record available at http://lccn.loc.gov/2015038165

A catalogue record for this book is available from the Library of Congress.

A catalogue record for the book is available from the British Library.

Typeset by MPS Limited, Chennai, India.

Contents

List of Figures

Acknowledgements

I would like to thank series editor K. J. Donnelly for being a staunch advocate for my work. Without Kevin's interest and encouragement, this book would not have happened.

Librarians, researchers, and bookworms provided invaluable assistance in locating and accessing various rare and obscure resources. I am especially grateful to Kali Freeman, Alicia Byer, Jason Gibbs, and James Wintle for their help. I would also like to thank the Library of Congress for preserving and allowing access to Eugene Ormandy's hand-marked conductor copy of Virgil Thomson's *Louisiana Story* full orchestral score.

For generously giving their time to read my work in progress and provide valuable feedback, I would like to thank my colleagues Harry Benshoff, John Richardson, Stephen C. Meyer, Norm Hirshy, Daniel Goldmark, Colin Roust, Mitchell Morris, Robyn Stilwell, K. J. Donnelly, and Helen Hanson.

Other colleagues suggested resources or ideas for me to consider, and for their expertise I wish to recognize Ben Winters, Kay Kalinak, Paul Cote, Emilio Audissino, Susan Stryker, Deborah Cohler, and Jonathan Rhodes Lee. James Wierzbicki provided encouragement and memorable tautological advice on how to sit down and write.

I would like to thank Chris Penfold and the people at Palgrave Macmillan for welcoming this monograph. I would like to thank Eric Arnold Sylvain Kahn for introducing me to so much music, my parents for their support, and numerous directors, especially David Lewis and Jim Tushinski, for giving me opportunities to compose so much music for film, experiences that provided a practical context and framework for my thoughts and research here.

I am extremely grateful to people who generously gave of their time to be interviewed or answer questions for this book, including directors Rose Troche and Kimberly Peirce, visionary studio executive Marcus Hu, Michael Matson, John Munt, my colleagues at Pixar David Slusser and Torbin Xan Bullock, and Christine Parker.

'Musical Cachet in New Queer Cinema' was originally published in *Music, Sound, and the Moving Image* 8.1 (Spring 2014) published by Liverpool University Press (http://msmi.liverpooluniversitypress.co.uk) and is reprinted with their kind permission.

Many easy listening, ambient, and electronic phonographic long-playing records were auditioned during the writing of this monograph.

Introduction

'Film music' and 'queerness' were, for many years, marginalized areas of academic interest, relegated to ignoble statuses such as 'low art' or 'underground' culture. This book looks at ways that queerness intersects film and its synchronized musical audio tracks. Recent developments in scholarship have encouraged, if not demanded, this interrogation. Books such as *Feminine Endings*, *The Queer Composition of America's Sound*, *Queering the Pitch*, and *Queering the Popular Pitch*, to name a few, have pursued lines of inquiry into music that take into account queerness, gender, and sexuality. *Music, Sound, and the Moving Image* published a special issue on 'Gender, Sexuality, and The Soundtrack' (2012: 6.2). The *Journal of the American Musicological Society* published a colloquy on 'Music and Sexuality' (2013: 66.3: 825–72). James Buhler's essay 'Gender, Sexuality, and the Soundtrack' (2014), published during the writing of this book, proffers challenges and directions that a book such as this one might tackle. By now it must be accepted, even by detractors within the academy, that current discourses in musicology and cinema studies regard gender and sexuality as essential facets of human identity and culture that create new ways of critically analyzing cinema and music.

Discerning 'queerness' within film – even within mainstream cinema – can involve applying models of allegory, affinity, identity, cachet, interpretation, and community. Queer perspectives, and 'queer films' themselves, operate as hothouses for issues affecting wider mainstream culture: cultural marginalization can exacerbate common challenges such as budgets, production practices, and the acquisition of cultural cachet. Recent examinations such as *The Culture of Queers*, *Club Cultures*, *Queer Pollen*, and *Impossible Dance* look at interactions between queerness, culture, identity, and the mainstream. This inquiry needs to be

1

applied to the motion picture soundtrack, to how music creates identity and positions a film within niche markets and mainstream culture, and to how music interacts with cachet and modes of interpretation, whilst taking gender and sexuality into special consideration.

Existing scholarly analyses of film music have come from disciplines of literary analysis, cinema studies, musicology, psychology, communication studies, and music theory, to name but a few. Each of these disciplines has particular interests at heart, and many of those interests overlap, yet scholars frequently favor study of the composer or the composer's final recorded musical output. Bringing queer theory into the discussion enables a deeper level of discourse, especially in regard to interactions between audience, production practice, meaning, and message.

This book uses independent and Hollywood films, from the 1930s to the current decade, as case studies to investigate deeper narratological meanings, messages, and histories embedded in film music and the soundtrack. It takes into consideration queer composers and queer films, but it also examines select mainstream composers, filmmakers, and films with a queer perspective. To this aim, I understand and interpret 'queer' broadly, in accordance with contemporary queer theory, to encompass all types of non-heteronormative and non-homonormative sexualities and genders: not only male cisgender homosexuals, but lesbians, transgender people, bisexuals, and heterosexuals whose partnering, fetish, or lifestyle interests fall beyond dominant patriarchal paradigms. Sexuality, gender, and identity are best appreciated with acceptance of their potential fluidity and hybridity; these factors, given the strictures of society, can provide a unique queer perspective and sensitivity to unspoken aspects of characterization and narrative. This queer perspective can unlock layers of meaning in a wide variety of films where such insights are particularly relevant in how the music functions or in how an alternative interpretation of surface narrative is communicated.

The idea of the 'intersection' is not new. Borrowing a principle from set theory,[1] this book addresses the overlap of three growing areas of critical inquiry – film, music, and queerness – within a framework of humanities research and theory. This intersected area may appear esoteric, but the fields of media studies, musicology, and queer theory are themselves expanding, and the area they intersect will likewise grow.

Joseph Kerman, a leading and early proponent of the 'new musicology,' in discussing competition between the fields of musicology, music theory, and ethnomusicology, wrote, 'It is often where two or even all three systems can be said to compete for the intellectual control of territory that we will find the most promising fields of study' (Kerman 1985: 15). This thinking may be extended to the intersection of cinema studies, musicology, and queer theory. Binary intersections of these three fields have been accepted in academia since the 1990s at least and, in the case of film music, much earlier. Briefly I will describe the three distinct binary academic intersections that occur between these fields.

Music and film

The academic study of film music, its composition, history, and theory, has grown sufficiently large that a comprehensive overview is difficult to undertake in a few paragraphs. The field has splintered into various divisions: extension classes, scoring programs, and vocational music colleges that offer a 'practical' approach to aspiring practitioners; musicologists who wish to add the film scores of choice composers to the canon of twentieth-century compositional masterworks; and humanities scholars of all stripes who regard the cinema as an arrow in their quiver of critical expertise. There are film music appreciation courses, as well as 'handbooks,' 'readers,' 'histories,' 'guides,' and numerous anthologies of film music scholarship on academic presses by authors with a wide variety of academic credentials. Any historicgraphy of the field of film music, therefore, tends to reflect personal biases and favoritisms, as well as an obligatory nod to its implicit futures: music for television, music for advertising, music for gaming, music for the Internet, and the catchall, music for media.

Film music composition, criticism, theory, and compendiums of suggested 'cues,' such as Erno Rapée's *Encyclopedia of Music for Pictures* (1925), date to the 'silent' period, as described in Rick Altman's authoritative *Silent Film Sound* (2004), for even if the *films* were silent, the *cinema* was not. This existing body of work expanded to match the success and eventual domination of the sound film. Frankfurt School philosopher Theodor Adorno and German composer Hanns Eisler published an influential midcentury book of film music theory, *Composing for the Films* (1947), a touchstone for further theoretical discourse in the creation and analysis of film music. In 1957, Roger Manvell and John Huntley co-wrote *The Technique of Film Music*, part of a 'technical series' on film production for the British Film Academy, a book 'addressed to everyone interested in the film, as well as to composers and professional film-makers' (1957: dust jacket). The 1970s saw a growth in professional 'how-to' books, such as composer Earle Hagen's *Scoring For Films* (1971) and music editor Milton Lustig's *Music Editing for Motion Pictures* (1980). Others followed, such as composers Fred Karlin and Rayburn Wright's heavy tome *On the Track: A Guide to Contemporary Film Scoring* (1990), which 'includes a complete click book' so the budding composer can calculate tempos and correlate them to celluloid's sprocket-lock mag synchronization systems.[2]

In 1977, New York University Press released sound and music editor Roy Prendergast's *Film Music: A Neglected Art*. Subsequent film music books in an increasingly 'academic' style began to snowball in the early 1990s. These include Claudia Gorbman's *Unheard Melodies: Narrative Film Music* (1987), Michel Chion's books *L'Audio-Vision* (1990) and *La musique au cinema* (1995), Kathryn Kalinak's *Settling the Score: Music and the Classical Hollywood Film* (1992), Caryl Flinn's *Strains of Utopia: Gender, Nostalgia, and Hollywood Film Music* (1992), and Royal S. Brown's *Overtones and Undertones: Reading Film Music* (1994). These books were largely created within a humanities framework, outside a musicological establishment still struggling to integrate the interests and approaches of the 'new musicology.' But musicologists soon followed with their own rigorous work, as perhaps best exemplified by Scarecrow Press's 'Film Score Guide' series, in which each volume is dedicated to a single film, painstakingly researched, and robust with detailed musical transcriptions. Academic journals in a variety of disciplines became increasingly welcoming of work devoted to film music, and new, specialized journals joined the fray: *The Soundtrack*; *Music and the Moving Image*; *Music, Sound, and the Moving Image*; and *The Journal of Film Music*. Omni Music Publishing recently published limited edition, full orchestral scores of Hollywood blockbusters including *The Matrix*, *Batman*, and *Back to the Future*. Today there are an increasing number of film music concerts, festivals, documentaries, and specialized conferences.

Queerness and film

Using a broad, contemporary definition of 'queerness,' one that encompasses an inclusive spectrum of alternative sexualities and gender identities, challenges us to locate precisely when studies of queerness *and* film may have began, but it encourages us to consider sources such as George De Coulteray's *Sadism in the Movies* (1965). According to its own dust jacket, it is 'the book that shocked a nation,' published by the reputably-named Medical Press of New York, also home to

The Sadist: An ABZ of Love (illustrated), and *The Kama Sutra of Vatsyayana*. De Coulteray's is not a pulp book; it boasts 256 illustrations in a durable hardback, accompanied by thorough analyses that consider desire, cruelty, rape, spanking, slavery, bondage, whips, and torture chambers, as well as 'sexual assassins' and vampires.[3] I am certain more books like this were once in circulation, but are now out of print, ignored or forgotten by the academy. I hope such books will be rediscovered and reevaluated for their contributions to scholarship and evidence of progressive thought, proof that an appreciation of 'queerness' is not a post-modernist phenomenon.

Overall, the study of the intersections of alternative sexualities and film predates our current academic construct or label of 'queerness,' and begins instead with studies of 'homosexuality,' typically weighted, however well intentioned, towards *male homosexuality*. In 1972, author and film critic Parker Tyler published his comprehensive book *Screening the Sexes: Homosexuality in the Movies*. Tyler was grounded in experimental and underground film, as well as Hollywood motion pictures, and so is able to document a queer connection to the avant-garde (Jack Smith, Jean Genet, Kenneth Anger) as well as to the fabulousness of Hollywood glitter and intrigue. Tyler makes a distinction between the 'sex organ,' the 'sexual personality,' and 'gender,' in order for the book to aspire to 'all-inclusiveness' (1972: xi).

In 1977 the British Film Institute released the first of several printings of *Gays & Film*, edited by cultural theorist Richard Dyer, a shorter but more academic and theoretical work that pioneered an application of queer theory to cinema studies. Therein Dyer looks at 'ideology' and 'stereotyping,' Caroline Sheldon ventures into the 'politics of lesbian-feminism,' and Jack Babuscio considers 'gay sensibility' and various readings of 'camp.'

In 1981, historian, activist, and cinephile Vito Russo published his landmark book, *The Celluloid Closet*, an influential compendium of observations and innuendos intending to establish irrefutable evidence of homosexual 'visibility' in Hollywood cinema. One of the book's most valuable contributions is a catalogue or 'necrology' of morbidly homophobic films; many of these gay deaths arguably were encouraged by the strictures of the Motion Picture Production Code, or 'Hays Code,' that allowed for moral turpitudes to be depicted as long as the perpetrators were adequately punished.[4] Russo's book and public lectures were a starting point for further research and public interest. *The Celluloid Closet* also achieved greater visibility than Tyler or Dyer's earlier works largely because of Russo's connection to the growing New York activist community; his profile was raised considerably through involvement with ACT UP and GLAAD, groups that sought media attention for their work.

In the early 1990s, Alexander Doty, Corey Creekmur, D. A. Miller, B. Ruby Rich, and others published new, influential work on film from a queer analytical perspective. Books such as Doty's *Making Things Perfectly Queer: Interpreting Mass Culture* (1993) coincided roughly with the explosion of the 'New Queer Cinema' on screens in film festivals and urban centers. While the New Queer Cinema celebrated fresh voices and overt queer content, scholars were also encouraged to revisit and reevaluate historic, canonical films like *Bride of Frankenstein* and *Mädchen in Uniform*, and narrowed their focus with books such as *Monsters in the Closet* (1997), Harry Benshoff's monograph that looks specifically at the horror genre. 'Queer studies' would make further inroads into the academy: today there are university departments and degree programs associated with the field, whose research often thrives on studies of cinema and media culture.

Concerns of the intersection of queer and cinema studies include how sexual and gender diversity is presented; how morality and deviance are projected; how subcultures and marginalized communities are represented, misrepresented, or kept invisible; how stereotypes and clichés are propagated or challenged; how audience sympathies are manipulated; and how legal and marketing concerns affect these issues.

Queerness and music

Beginning in the 1970s, Joseph Kerman and other musicologists began to question the field's dominant positivist leanings that favored an approach of music theory and analysis over interdisciplinary approaches that would consider sociological and anthropological factors as well as the notion that music could signify cultural meanings and messages.[5] Kerman believed new critical approaches would not supplant musical analysis, but 'should be joined with analysis to provide a less one-dimensional account of the artistic matters at hand' (Kerman 1980: 331). Kerman and his like-minded colleagues became the proponents of what came to be called the 'new musicology.'

The application of queer theory within musicology generated controversy and heated argument, enlivening debates about Handel, Schubert, Tchaikovsky, Britten, German cabaret, and Stevie Nicks, to name but a few. These contentious debates, often between established scholars, helped revolutionize musicology itself, propelling the 'new musicology' into uncharted (yet familiar) territory, and pushing academic journals to publish arguments and rebuttals, claims and counterattacks.

Some scholars were aware that these 'new' perspectives had long been around, even if they had been obscured by positivism's stranglehold.

> Musicological explorations of the intersection of music and sexuality have a long history, if we include such writing as Edward Lockspeiser's 1945 coded commentary of Tchaikovsky's music as 'shameless in its sensuousness and splendor.' In 1977, Philip Brett's article 'Britten and Grimes,' which appeared in the *Musical Times*, inaugurated a serious and antihomophobic sub-discipline of musicological scholarship that explores the ways in which sexual orientation affects musical expression. (Peraino and Cusick 2013: 826)

Mainstream recognition of this intersection was hard-fought and did not happen overnight. Proponents of a queering of musicology risked jeopardizing their standing within the academy and, for new faculty, their attainment of tenure: 'Many of the texts in the first generation of queer musicology carry traces of defiance or trepidation in the face of personal risk. Now, however, the approaches in question have gained a measure of institutional acceptance' (Whitesell, 2013: 836).

Part of the academy's initial resistance to a 'queering' of musicology related to a perceived subjectivity of such an approach. Susan McClary, in *Feminine Endings: Music, Gender, & Sexuality* (1991), argues for recognition that music *can* signify: music is more than a music theorist's crossword puzzle, but communicates meanings and significations that can be unpacked. McClary insists that associations between music and gender are not recent inventions, but have been prescribed by canonical composers:

> Beginning with the rise of opera in the seventeenth century, composers worked painstakingly to develop a musical semiotics of gender: a set of conventions for constructing 'masculinity' or 'femininity' in music. (McClary 1991: 7)

Musical tropes for constructing 'masculinity' or 'femininity' surely date earlier than the seventeenth century, but are certainly present and obvious in opera.[6] The use of such tropes in opera extends to their use in film music. Even more fascinating is McClary's argument that Western art music itself bears a metaphorical relationship to coitus, not by sub-limation, but by principles inherent in music theory.

> Not only do gender and sexuality inform our 'abstract' theories, but music itself often relies heavily upon the metaphorical simulation of sexual activity for its effects. I will argue [...] that tonality itself – with its process of instilling expectations and subsequently withholding promised fulfillment until climax – is the principal musical means during the period from 1600 to 1900 for arousing and channeling desire. (McClary 1991: 12)

This argument that music can be a metaphor for sexuality is founda-tional groundwork for the intersection of queerness and musicology. McClary presages how queerness and musicology might intersect, but cautions, 'before we can address the questions concerning gender and sexuality [...] it is necessary to construct an entire theory of musical signification' (McClary 1991: 20). But it may *not* be necessary to con-struct an 'entire theory' of musical signification, since such significa-tions depend upon cultural literacy and assimilations tied to time and place. Different cultures and subcultures read signs and significations differently, making a single 'entire' theory unlikely. What are most important are valid correlations between music and meaning that are constructed within the music itself. That is to say, *musical* details affect responses, not merely learned associations or personal favoritisms that elicit a response. McClary forecasts how this line of inquiry into musical signification connects to the study of film music.

> Composers of music for movies and advertisements consistently stake their commercial success on the public's pragmatic knowledge of musical signification – the skill with which John Williams, for instance, manipulates the semiotic codes of the late nineteenth-century symphony in *E.T.* or *Star Wars* is breathtaking. (McClary 1991: 21)

Many contemporary audience members who might not recognize even one nineteenth-century symphony will still understand the musical semiotic codes employed in a John Williams film score. McClary's argument that music signifies is bedrock for the foundations of further film music analysis, a position that the uninitiated take for granted.[7] McClary's arguments on feminism and music paved the way for schol-ars to further consider queerness and music.

Of course, 'queerness' is not simply 'homosexuality.' Trails blazed by scholars of queerness and musicology helped encourage new scholarship around Australian composer Percy Grainger (1882–1961), who copiously detailed in photographs and letters his own sexual interest in sadomasochism and incest (Bird 1999; Gillies 2006). There is little controversy around the *nature* of Grainger's interests, as he documented them himself, but groundbreaking is the exploration that Grainger's fetishes and paraphilias might be *relevant to his music*. This is the most promising area for further research: not that any particular composer liked men or women or whipping or their own mother or whatever else might be unusual or titillating, but how might such interests connect with the composer's music and musical significations.

An extension of such queerness brings us to the short but fascinating life of French Canadian composer Claude Vivier (1948–1983), a homosexual man with an avid interest in sadomasochism (Gilmore 2014: 184–5, 227). Vivier also dabbled as a filmmaker himself (Gilmore 2014: 196–8), a likely next step for contemporary composers. As the means of producing motion pictures becomes increasingly accessible at low cost through inexpensive filming equipment, video editing software, and online distribution, inspired creative people such as composers have an added incentive to make their own films.

All three together

The previous three sections looked at the unique binary intersections of the fields of queer theory, musicology, and cinema studies. If we consider these three fields together, we have a sizable overlap rich with potential and opportunities for scholarship. Scott Paulin considered these possibilities in 'Unheard Sexualities? Queer Theory and the Soundtrack' (1997).

> A conversation is indeed possible between queer theory and film sound criticism, for music often participates directly in constructing onscreen representations of desire and sexuality, usually encouraging the audience to identify with a (hetero)sexual relationship and to desire its consummation. (Paulin 1997: 37)

Paulin sees that a conversation between these fields can yield information about audience identifications; this is certainly a useful tool in understanding how film music works. 'Onscreen representation' has been a longstanding concern of queer theorists and advocates for social justice. McClary sees the possibilities of musical significations, tropes, and features in the musical score itself that can be unpacked and analyzed. So, there are actually a lot of places the overlap of the three fields can take us. Catherine Haworth, in her introduction to the *MSMI* special issue on 'Gender, Sexuality, and the Soundtrack' notes

> Regardless of genre, content, media, and stated or assumed intent, the soundtrack impacts directly upon issues of gendered and sexual identity, both in its engagement with the narrative and its characters, and in our own engagement with it as active and individual subjects. (Haworth 2012: 130)

Haworth asks us to consider how the soundtrack impacts not only the narrative and onscreen world, but also our own engagement with the film. This proposes a kind of dialectic, where music interacts with the film itself but also with the audience directly. This is often why music is employed in motion pictures anyway, to promote or enhance audience engagement. When the audience is not engaged, as is often observed in a studio 'test screening' for instance, music will be brought in or adjusted to help the film. Many times music is called upon to 'fix' unconvincing acting or stilted dialogue; bringing 'queerness' into this particular interrogation increases the possibilities of analysis.

James Buhler's essay, 'Gender, Sexuality, and the Soundtrack,' suggests another line of inquiry that the overlap of these three fields is ideally situated to follow: a political, Marxist, and activist role that can expose entertainment industry power structures and colonialist, capitalist power motives.

> Like feminist and postcolonial theory, [queer studies] seeks not only to unmask stereotypes but to analyze their discursive functions in order to displace and destabilize the social structures and power relations that support them. (Buhler 2014: 370)

These social structures and power relations are inherent in mass media and multinational corporate entertainment businesses.[8] The histories behind queer communities inform an activist perspective well suited to incisive readings of politicized and manipulated sociological situations. These power relations, as Buhler notes, occur at the societal level and at the personal level; they are signified through music.

> Queer theory [...] is oriented around identifying and analyzing the process of subjectification embedded within the representations of sexuality proffered by film, around looking at those representations

less as reflecting power relations of the society than of signifying them. (Buhler 2014: 371)

This perspective adds to the existing mix of musicological and representational issues the complications of signifying societal power relations; music can do that too. Buhler's essay charges scholars who undertake a study of the intersection of queerness, music, and film with several ambitious tasks.

> A critical theory of the soundtrack informed by gender and queer theory would be concerned with the 'articulation of power and sexuality' on the soundtrack, how desire is made audible on it, for whom, by whom, and to what purpose. It might ask whether and to what extent the soundtrack enforces a compulsory heterosexual code, examining, for instance, how the soundtrack imposes normative gender roles and lines of sexual desire on the film's characters and our apprehension of them. [...] One can certainly imagine, at a first stage, analytical studies of how, say, gay or lesbian characters are scored, the way the soundtrack reinforces or resists engaging cultural stereotypes, whether it chooses to demonize, complicate, or valorize the character types the film presents, and so forth. (Buhler 2014: 370–71)

Buhler has outlined a number of topics he would like to see addressed. By intersecting the established academic fields of musicology, film studies, and queer studies, we have a potential to gain deeper understandings in these areas Buhler has mentioned. Some scholars warn of risks involved in interdisciplinary work, should the rigor of the fields involved become diluted. This is especially of concern in highly technical fields, such as cinema or music.

> When music becomes the object of academic disciplines as it is today, discourse can become a site of struggle among the factions and interest groups that compete for the cultural authority to speak about music. The expert critical and technical languages that these groups invent can foster a social bond among those who share them, but they can also alienate and exclude outsiders. (Korsyn 2003: 6)

Scholars and practitioners of film music have seen this invention of 'expert' critical and technical languages happen. As humanities scholars rushed into the alluring and burgeoning field of film music in the 1990s, they created new jargon while avoiding the existing language of music theorists, claiming their own territory. Media scholars and philosophers, who lacked ear training and knew little of, say, Schenkerian analysis, functional harmony, or serial operations, eagerly pontificated about film *music* within their own newly invented cultural concepts. Scholars who knew little about the 'field' or actual production practices would speak a new critical language where terminology sometimes already existed, albeit with differing 'nuance.' Film music scholars gushed effusively about 'diegesis,' 'sound advance,' the 'fantastical gap,' and 'liminal space.' Industry professionals outside of academia had different words, and often different concerns, discussing 'source,' 'prelap,' 'perspective,' and 'procedural' music.[9] The one term all camps seemed to enjoy was 'needle drop,' with its charming visual reference.

Of course, everyone had something to bring to the table: many of the arguments that inform film music scholarship today come from the cultural studies area and were proffered by scholars without musical training. Indeed, philosophical approaches allow us to look at production and musical practices from outside the stresses of the field environment.

There is an inherent risk involved in intersecting multiple fields or specializations: to pretend to know something about all of them, while really knowing very little about anything. This book similarly teeters on an academic precipice where my own shortcomings and biases will be apparent to many scholars and practitioners. In the process of researching and writing this book, I have adhered to approaches that I find interesting and compelling. I have tried to privilege primary sources and information that has an informed relationship to production practices, filmmakers, and composers.

This book looks at how select examples of musical, cinematic, and queer 'texts' or queer 'readings' coincide, and what observations can be made when they do. I hope that these intersections will indicate what *we have been missing* when scholars and critics have looked at these films, and their musics, in the past.

Larger issues

The arguments contained in this book should be further understood within and contextualized by certain broader discourses. These include debates about audition, audience perspectives, gender, historiography, authorship, auteur theory, cultural cachet and 'street' credibility, the new musicology, and queer and trans identities and politics.

It has, on occasion, been argued that film music is 'unheard' or is not meant for active listening; that it is some kind of remote, unessential, cinematic subtext. An opposing view insists that for music to be 'unheard' defies both logic and production practice; critical analyses of music rely on its audition, even if it is considered only a subtle reinforcement of narrative. There are fan communities who do *actively* listen to film music, and fans who will see a movie simply because a specific composer wrote its music. These spectators might even listen to the music and ignore superimposed dialogue; they may not lose any understanding of the film in doing so. And yet some absolutists argue that 'film music' is not truly music at all, in the strictest sense, since it is governed by an exterior logic, that of the motion picture, rather than its own internal logic, and therefore loses any substance or validity, becoming a kind of quasi-musical sonic wallpaper.[10]

This epistemological debate, on whether or not we 'hear' music in film, springs from an older debate on the role of music within broader artistic and performance traditions.[11] This debate has included the role of music in theatre, where it bolsters interludes and distracts during set changes; music in restaurants or soirées, where it is offered to delight guests, facilitate conversation, and aid in gustation; music for dance, where it establishes tempo but takes a back seat to beautiful dancers; and arguably even music for opera, where a typically reduced orchestra becomes a backdrop for vocal calisthenics and the parade of costume.[12] Questions concerning the importance, centrality, or obsequiousness of music are questions that solicit answers that expose the *perspective* of the responder. At a wedding, all eyes are typically on the bride, not the organist, but how can you be sure? What might we surmise about the wedding guest who is more interested in the organist than the bride?

The argument that film music is 'unheard' makes for a curious connection to queerness. It is often said that queer voices are unheard, queer images unseen, and the very presence of queers ignored or denied.[13] Vito Russo fought this notion in *The Celluloid Closet* when he insisted that queers were visible in Hollywood film despite suppression and homophobia. Even in cultures that actively suppress queer voices, there is often a powerful underground culture. This might be a good analogy to the film music fan community's underground culture of championing 'unheard' music.

Proceeding in the absence of a uniform queer politic

Academia, activists, and popular culture all negotiate a continually shifting queer politic, focusing on what is queerly 'owned' or rejected in language, history, or social structures. In the 1960s and 1970s, a 'gay liberation' movement was organically connected to a broader social movement of sexual liberation, where wife swapping, swingers' parties, and promiscuity were all the rage among some heterosexuals, as parodied in the Mike Myers' *Austin Powers* films, for example. The rise of the AIDS pandemic in the 1980s and 1990s elicited a reactionary sexual conservatism that may have encouraged interest in monogamy and binary relationships. Nevertheless, many queers remain highly sexually active today; consider the ethos and politic of *The Ethical Slut*, and ongoing debates on appropriate behavioral responses to the AIDS crisis and prevention. At the same time, gay 'promiscuity' is considered a dated cliché among many in an assimilationist, 'mainstreamed' homonormative gay culture that has fought to promote 'marriage equality,' to access a civil convention that many in the age of sexual liberation rejected. There is still a broad body of queer literature that argues against marriage; this debate is too entangling to be presented here as anything other than an example of the complexities of shifting queer politics (Benderson 2014; Bernstein and Taylor 2013; Conrad 2010).

Another issue at the forefront of homosexual concerns until the mid 1980s was the 'age of consent.' Socio-political new wave dance band Bronski Beat even titled their 1984 debut album *The Age of Consent*; the LP's full color inner sleeve had information on the age of consent in different countries worldwide. While this remained a concern due to such issues as entrapment and police harassment, the main issue became AIDS, a mysterious, new, fatal disease that shook the queer community into a new level of activism. There were ties between queer activism and queer academics; as this was a life-or-death situation, more people came out, lived openly, and brought queerness into their professional lives.

> Queer Nation, like ACT UP, also happened to be closely intertwined with the forms of Cultural Theory then underway. [...] Queer Theory transposed an activist style into a more abstract key in hopes of unlocking and dislodging an assortment of intellectual complacencies in the study of gender and sexuality. (Morris 2013: 834)

Queer theory did not go unquestioned, even by many queers themselves, trying to make sense of it all. Although it seemed to be new territory, it had a presumed history, going back millennia, of course; since there always had been queers, this could not be a new phenomenon. Right?

The moment that the scandalous formula 'queer theory' was uttered, however, it became the name of an already established school of theory, as if it constituted a set of specific doctrines, a singular, substantive perspective on the world, a particular theorization of human experience, equivalent in that respect to psychoanalytic or Marxist theory. The only problem was that no one knew what the theory was. And for the very good reason that no such theory existed. (Halperin 2003: 340)

A complication of proceeding with the inquiry of the intersection of film, music, and queerness is that queer theory itself, its history, canon, and politic, are still in flux. Although the academic field has its established scholars, they are not always names known and lauded by the everyday queer-on-the-street. As a contrast, Harvey Milk, a politician and activist who built bridges between gays, seniors, minorities, and labor interests, whom he notably called 'the usses,' is recognized as a universal civil rights hero, while queer studies risks becoming an increasingly specialized and rarefied field. As the field progresses, scholars balance interests and omissions, inclusions and exclusions.

I endeavor to use a broad definition of 'queerness,' that may include people of all sexual persuasions, interests, and genders, anyone bullied or cast outside for who they 'are' or might be presumed to 'be.' Queer communities will continue to negotiate their political postures; there is still dissention among the ranks with issues such as assimilation versus liberation, marriage versus other possibilities, and how queerness encourages certain geopolitical alliances in transnational struggles, to name a few.

The book's three sections

The first section of this book, 'Mad About the Boy: Male Homosexuality and Music in Film,' contends with male homosexuality, which has been the subject of much existing research and argument in cultural studies. Robert Flaherty's *Louisiana Story* (1948) is rich with inference, innuendo, and subtext normative for its period; the histories of the director, composer, and film are intertwined with perceptions and misperceptions of Virgil Thomson's orchestral score. Gregg Araki's *The Living End* (1992), a watershed New Queer Cinema film, uses songs from the Los Angeles industrial club scene to capitalize on audience affinities. Ang Lee's *Brokeback Mountain* (2005), an audience favorite with a prolific and outspoken fan community, puzzled scholars and critics for perpetuating regressive tropes, while Gustavo Santaolalla's guitar score clenched the Oscar.

The second section, 'Fighting the Patriarchy: Dykes, Misogyny, and Gender Fear,' deals with representations and anxieties in films in which a male paradigm is challenged. As far back as classical Hollywood, music informed the audience of gender roles, as it does in contemporary cinema, inviting layered critical analysis. The use of popular music can help a mainstream audience to identify with outsider characters, and can be employed to make overt textual references. The compilation score became commonplace in American cinema, especially in road movies, a genre that creates many opportunities for typification and subversion. As cinema told stories involving the trans community, gender stereotypes in text and music add further complications and nuance to the soundtrack.

The third section explores the 'Queering of Genre,' and how music is an integral part of the creation and subversion of film genres. Music helps situate film within particular genres and satisfy audience expectations, but it can also navigate liminal spaces between genres in films that defy simple categorization. Horror movies, monster movies, musicals, comedies, Westerns, road movies, virtually every type of film there is, can be queered or given a queer reading. Genres such as musicals and horror films became queer favorites, but queers also see representations of themselves in melodramas, Westerns, cartoons, and action films. Music can indicate and suggest various readings, providing subcultural signs and characterizations that inform audience sensibilities. With this, music and queerness give us much to explore in cinema.

Part I
Mad About the Boy:
Male Homosexuality and
Music in Film

1
Louisiana Story, Homoeroticism, and Americana

Homoeroticism has a long and colorful history in art and literature.[1] Frequently this homoeroticism is more tangible when it involves an appreciation and idealization of youth, often from a safe distance or through sublimation, directing the viewer's gaze upon romanticized depictions of the body at rest or in action, sport, combat or dance, for instance. This tradition of homoeroticism naturally extends to cinema as well, where the direction of the camera's gaze is under complete control of the filmmaker. This chapter examines male homoeroticism in *Louisiana Story* (1948) and the contributions that music makes towards the romanticizing of male youth.

Louisiana Story is a rustic, languidly poetic film, commissioned by Standard Oil to quietly support the public image of the oil industry. It was made during a conservative postwar period marked by the height of the 'Golden Age' of Hollywood film music and the strictures of the Motion Picture Production Code or 'Hays Code.'[2] This period was also characterized by vibrant activity on the part of American midcentury modernist homosexual composers, including the iconic Virgil Thomson who scored *Louisiana Story*.[3] The complexities of the time period both restricted and encouraged queer aesthetics and codes.

The film obsessively follows a barefoot adolescent boy through the scenic bayous of Cajun Louisiana. There is an oil derrick blowout and an alligator, but otherwise the film is remarkably devoid of conflict. The boy loses and finds his pet raccoon, Jo-Jo. The film won awards at the British Academy of Film and Television Arts (BAFTA) and the Venice Film Festival; the National Film Registry of the Library of Congress has preserved the film. Thomson won the 1949 Pulitzer Prize for Music for this score, the only film score to ever win the award.

This chapter situates *Louisiana Story* as a queer text through examination of Robert Flaherty's personal life and preoccupations; Virgil Thomson's personal life; the subversive context of the film; and the imagery, symbolism, fetishism, and use of screen time within the film. This chapter then examines existing explanations of the music, from Virgil Thomson himself and others. Period explications of Thomson's score exaggerate its position as a preservation or representation of Cajun folk music, and overlook its conventional romantic tropes that romanticize and fetishize the boy. While one can only speculate Flaherty's inner desires and motivations, Thomson's score to *Louisiana Story* reinforces a homoerotic reading of the film. The music is an emotive, romantic nostalgia, not a stylized Cajun portrait or exotica; it focuses more on the *boy* than on the titular Louisiana.

Situation of *Louisiana Story* as a queer text

While *Louisiana Story* can be read as an industrial film, a documentary film, or a poetic visual essay, *Louisiana Story* can also be situated as a queer text. Contemporary standards may facilitate this reading, but it is corroborated by existing scholarship and a careful study of the historical record.

Tracking the obsessive gaze of the camera and following the 'eye trace' – 'the concern with the location and movement of the audience's focus of interest within the frame' (Murch 2001: 18) – yields insight into the film's homoeroticism.

Flaherty took his time shooting Joseph 'JC' Boudreaux, the twelve-year-old who played the boy in *Louisiana Story*, lingering over his face, physique, and feet. Editor Helen van Dongen recalled, 'Bob had to be pushed in completing shots of J.C. who was growing rapidly from a dreaming small boy into a young adolescent' (1998: 28). Van Dongen noted that Flaherty always got good coverage of the boy, while missing footage of other things, like showing where the raccoon had got to when it was lost. Bob shot ample footage of the boy simply looking around for his lost pet. 'Though he has a beautiful face, should not be reason to have all sequences same' (1998: 39) noted van Dongen.

The film's gaze must be contextualized through the queerness of Flaherty and Thomson; this queerness may not be perfectly coincident with today's homonormative constructs and conceptions of what it means to be 'gay' culturally, sexually, and otherwise. Rather than reduce Flaherty and Thomson to stereotypes that may not apply, or that may be inappropriate for their time period, I relate their queerness to their status as outsiders and to their personal lives and erotic preoccupations.

Robert Flaherty

Director Robert J. Flaherty (1884–1951) achieved fame with *Nanook of the North* (1922), a worldwide critical and box-office success that depicted Eskimo life in northern Canada's wintry Hudson Bay area. In 1914, Flaherty married Frances J. Hubbard, who became both wife and collaborator, and he fathered three children. But Flaherty's filmmaking as a director and producer was consistently homoerotic, in spite of his life as an ordinary heterosexual family man.

Flaherty's obsession with boyhood and boy actors was noted by his wife Frances, editor van Dongen, and biographers and scholars including Richard Griffith, Paul Rotha, Eva Orbanz, and Richard Barsam. Rotha is of particular importance, since he was a leader in the British documentary film movement, a personal friend and colleague of Flaherty, and devoted years to writing an authoritative academic biography of Flaherty. Rotha notes, 'After *Nanook*, all of [Flaherty's] films [...] are haunted by the image of a youth or boy' (Rotha 1983: 278). These films, like *Nanook, Elephant Boy* (1937), *Louisiana Story*, and F. W. Murnau's *Tabu: A Story of the South Seas* (1931), focus on stories about exotic places with a boy as the central figure though which the story is told. Rotha states, 'as his life went on, Flaherty began to dislike grown-ups (other than his closest friends) and tried to lose himself in the world of childhood' (1983: 278–9).

These boys, from 'exotic' cultures, had striking appearances and athleticism. There is a deliberate use of casting; while Flaherty was considered a documentarian during his day, he used recreations, imposed storylines, sets, and careful casting to create illusions of magical worlds that nevertheless preserved elements of endangered and disappearing cultures. The selection of these boys is never accidental; they are idealized representations or fantasies of male youth. The way Flaherty treated these boys and the chemistry he developed with them has been documented in firsthand accounts and production stills.

Sabu Dastagir (1924–1963), star of *Elephant Boy*, was young and charismatic. Frances Flaherty recalled, 'Sabu, his little brown body in nothing but a tight-fitting breech cloth, was a perfect thing of beauty' (Griffith 1953: 120). Robert Flaherty's camera lingered over the boy's face, physique, and feet in this film also. Flaherty marveled at Sabu's ability to control the elephant with his bare feet: 'the elephant, as soon as he had felt the touch of the child's feet' (Griffith 1953: 121–22) responded to the boy's command. Dastagir rode the success of Flaherty's film to a mainstream acting career, becoming a gay icon and representation of white male fantasy, as evidenced by resultant popular commentary even years later.

> The majority of Sabu's roles were that of a dominated native, usually a sidekick to the white hero adventurer [...] [T]here was always a hidden homoerotic subtext which made the half-naked, well-built Sabu appealing to gay audiences. On the screen, Sabu would usually be scantily clad, his bare skin glistening with sweat on his muscular body [...] Sabu also seemed to have had an effect on director Robert Flaherty who was said to have been strongly possessive towards the boy, and who frequently shot the semi-nude youth being caressed by the dangling proboscis of the elephant Kala Nag (whose name means 'black snake'). (Gray 2009)

The 'black snake' assertion comes from Kipling's *Jungle Book* story 'Toomai of the Elephants' (1894–95) that provided inspiration for *Elephant Boy* (Barsam 1988: 75). Gray's explicit discourse has been excluded from academia; Rotha tiptoed around such explanations of Flaherty's known fascinations. Whereas Rotha, writing from 1957 until publication in 1983, must bite his tongue, Gray may speak freely.

Flaherty was 'strongly possessive' of not just Sabu, but of Joseph 'JC' Boudreaux, the twelve-year-old who plays the boy in *Louisiana Story*, a role extravagantly named 'Alexander Napoleon Ulysses Latour.' Photographer Arnold Eagle's production stills from *Louisiana Story* show a physical proximity and body language between Flaherty and Boudreaux that would confirm Flaherty's preoccupation with male youth.[4] Flaherty could also be jealous of the boy's attentions. Ryan Brasseaux describes Flaherty's manipulation of the young actor:

> Flaherty's working relationship with Boudreaux was also contrived. The director ordered his crew to avoid intimate contact with the boy. Instead, as Frances Flaherty recalled, 'Bob was insistent that no one should show any affection for the boy except himself. He wanted sole control over him.' By forging a paternalistic relationship with the fatherless Boudreaux, Bob Flaherty found the key to manipulating his young star's behavior on and off screen. (Brasseaux 2009: 27)

Flaherty's well-documented preoccupation with male youth was so pronounced that, to Rotha, as an academic biographer, it demanded explanation. But satisfying this demand was problematic during a time period when conjecture or discussion of alternative sexuality was markedly uncomfortable. These cultural circumstances encouraged only obtuse psychological hypotheses and euphemistic references to ancient Greek mythology.

> From the psychological point of view we could say, with Jung and Wilhelm, that the boy represents an archetype deeply embedded in Flaherty's subconscious and the center of the mandalas he constructed in the form of films. It would be difficult, however, to speculate on the archetypal myth – Atthis, Adonis, Ganymede, the infant Dionysus. On the other hand there is Freud's thesis that 'the goal of mankind is childhood.' Newton Rowe [... believes ...] that by the time Flaherty left Savaii his character was fixed and did not change further. [...] According to Rowe, Flaherty was unconsciously but instinctively in search of Freud's Nirvana principle and its forerunner in Tahitian life. He believes that Flaherty was in search of perpetual happiness and that he found happiness among the Eskimos. (Rotha 1983: 279)

Biographer Rotha squirms and trips over himself to avoid stating the simplest, easiest explanation: maybe Flaherty just liked adolescent boys. It seems reasonable to suggest that artistic fascinations and observed behaviors indicate that Flaherty may have had a particular 'erotic age orientation' (Bering 2013: 169) that otherwise did not interfere with his life and work. I do not mean to suggest or imply anything nefarious here, nor is there any evidence to suggest any kind of untoward behavior on the part of Flaherty, nor is there any reason to demonize Flaherty for such an idée fixe.[5]

Coupled with this potential erotic age orientation is prudishness uncharacteristic for a lifelong world traveler who, at the age of twelve, 'went into the Canadian gold fields with his father, where he lived for years among gamblers, miners, prostitutes, gunmen, and Chippewa Indians' (Taylor 1949a: 32). By all accounts, Flaherty was bold and adventurous even in his youth, and coming of age amongst such people would suggest knowledge of and liberal attitudes towards, if not even actual experience with, sex. But biographer Rotha relates, 'of all his hundreds of stories and anecdotes not one was about sex' (Rotha 1983: 278). Ernestine Evans, a longtime friend, recalled that the evening a final work print of *Louisiana Story* was screened for Standard Oil, Flaherty had a small group to dinner. 'The main topic of conversation across the dinner table, she recalls, was the Kinsey Report, which had just been published. Flaherty was disgusted' (Rotha 1983: 252).

Flaherty's dislike of grown-ups later in life, as described by Rotha, might suggest a 'lost childhood.' Flaherty's prudishness might suggest a cover for his own interests, or a discomfort with sexuality overall, given his own possible predilections. We cannot really know. But knowledge of Flaherty's background and familiarity with his other films encourages a reading of *Louisiana Story* as a queer text.

Virgil Thomson

Virgil Thomson (1896–1989) belonged to a generation of gay American composers that also worked in film, such as Aaron Copland, Leonard Bernstein, Paul Bowles, and David Diamond, who together were highly influential in creating a distinctive and original compositional sound in the United States. Their work in film did not tarnish their primary reputations as composers of serious 'art' or 'concert' music, even if other composers who worked more regularly in film had difficulty establishing concert careers. This circle of gay composers is explored in depth in musicologist Nadine Hubbs' book, *The Queer Composition of America's Sound* (2004). Hubbs looks at how these composers helped forge a unique 'American' sound, one that proved useful for many films as well. Virgil Thomson, who studied with Nadia Boulanger in Paris, was part of a 1920s American expatriate circle that included many queers. He worked with Gertrude Stein on two operas, *Four Saints in Three Acts* (1928) and *The Mother of Us All* (1947). Thomson was able to leverage his position as a powerful music critic for the *New York Herald Tribune* from 1940 to 1954 to advance his career, as well as his position in society. Although he kept a decorous public image, he was privately known as 'a campy homosexual whose personal identity fell under the rubrics of "pansy" and "fairy"' (Hubbs 2004: 14). This dichotomy would yield awkward results in Thomson's conservative 1966 autobiography, *Virgil Thomson*.

In 1922, at the age of 26, Thomson began a frustrating, unrequited, yet mushy love-relationship with Briggs Buchanan, who was 18. Briggs had entered Harvard University in 1920 at the tender age of 16, befriending writers and majoring in fine arts. Virgil met Briggs at the Liberal Club. Briggs looked up to Thomson, eight years his senior, and they became fast friends. But Virgil wanted more, and became increasingly frustrated, as Briggs knew how to tease and lead Virgil on. This is documented in correspondence that begun in 1923:

> They describe their struggles with euphemisms and metaphors. Virgil seldom stated his desires explicitly. Sometimes they taunt each other with accounts of indiscretions with other men, indiscretions that, particularly in Briggs's case, may not have amounted to much more than collegiate 'experimenting.' But the taunts stung. (Tommasini 1997: 112)

Things with Briggs did not work out romantically, and Virgil moved to Paris to pursue his music. Briggs became a stockbroker and married Florence Reynaud in 1936, 'a path to married respectability that Virgil could not follow' (Tommasini 1997: 120). Thomson would remain friends with the couple. Briggs' and Virgil's correspondence provides evidence that Thomson, perhaps like Flaherty, had an appreciation for a younger male. This was not an uncommon interest; consider the political issue of 'the age of consent' and the resultant entrapment of homosexuals that concerned the homophile movement well into the 1980s. Thomson's relationship with Briggs also suggests that the composer would have likely appreciated Flaherty's inclusion and foregrounding of handsome male youths in his films.

But Thomson, also perhaps like Flaherty, was never fully comfortable with sexuality, especially his own.

> Thomson didn't want to be queer. He would eventually have to concede that he was. [...] Even during his Paris days, and certainly after he returned to New York in 1940, Thomson maintained two circles of friends. He had many gay friends with whom he loved being catty, outrageous, and affectionate. [...] But he also had a circle of 'proper' friends, mostly heterosexual, with whom he never talked about 'being queer.' (Tommasini 1997: 70)

Thomson would not permit his sexuality to be discussed in print, even in his own autobiography; he pressured his friend, the composer and prolific memoirist Ned Rorem, to refrain from clearly exposing him as a homosexual. But one might not judge Thomson too harshly, given his ambitions, the time period, and the circumstances in which he lived and worked.

In 1942, Thomson was arrested in a raid on a gay bordello in Brooklyn that attracted young sailors (Tommasini 1997: 355–57). To provide some context, consider that in 1936, Thomson's colleague, Henry Cowell, at age 39, went to prison for four years for performing oral sodomy on a 17-year-old male (Tommasini 1997: 357). At the local precinct, Thomson was questioned for several hours and frightened; he was able to call Geoffrey Parsons, his editor at *The Herald Tribune*, and was bailed out. Thomson's arrest record stands, but no charges were filed. This repressive context, as well as Thomson's high society aspirations, led Thomson to a lifetime of discretion and secrecy. Even his 1966 autobiography minimizes the importance of Maurice Grosser, Thomson's longtime lover and companion.

The Brooklyn bordello was a place where a 'cross section of New York professional men' could meet 'young military men who flocked to the place, mostly sailors, but also marines, soldiers, and merchant seamen' (Tommasini 1997: 355). There were bedrooms upstairs that could be rented by the hour, to facilitate assignations. Thomson, who was 45 years old at the time of his arrest, would have fallen into the category of the older, professional man who was interested in the younger men.[6]

Flaherty was not part of Thomson's New York queer, cultural, or high society social circles, although both men lived at the Chelsea Hotel. Flaherty admired Thomson's scores for director Pare Lorentz's documentaries *The Plow That Broke the Plains* (1936) and *The River* (1938), and Thomson had previously worked with Flaherty's film editor, Helen van Dongen, on *The Spanish Earth* (1937, dir. Joris Ivens). In December of 1947, Flaherty screened a rough cut of *Louisiana Story* for Thomson in New York. According to Kathleen Hoover and John Cage, 'Thomson was ravished by its beauty and engaged himself with joy to compose music for it' (Hoover and Cage 1959: 104). The subtext of 'ravished by its beauty' suggests an appreciation of the film's young star, a fixation that would have been understood by John Cage, also a homosexual composer.[7] Thomson's appreciation of the boy in *Louisiana Story* helps explain how his score romanticizes the boy, and reinforces a reading of the film as a queer text.

Context and subversion

The broader production and finance context of *Louisiana Story* also supports a queer reading of the film. Standard Oil wanted a goodwill film, and, arguably aware that *Nanook of the North* had been quietly and privately financed by fur traders Revillon Frères, thought that Flaherty could be persuaded to represent and document their own industry – in a positive light, of course. Flaherty professed interest, negotiated a generous contract, and promptly made a film following a boy around. The oil company approved Flaherty's draft script, but the subversion of the film's implied mission shows both sublimation of male desire and the 'queering' of corporate PR.

Standard Oil's involvement included some approvals and screenings, but Flaherty was able to make the film he wanted. 'Standard Oil provided complete finance for Flaherty's next film but left him its sole owner, with no obligations to repay the negative cost and with distribution rights entirely in his hands' (Griffith 1953: 148). Standard Oil didn't even want their name in the credits, in order to better legitimize the film's planned editorial stance. Yet Flaherty's film subverts corporate intentions: the encroachment of the oil industry into the bayou is somewhat sanitized but is clearly shown as an invasive, capitalist intrusion into a delicate, untamed environment. *The New Yorker* observed, '*Louisiana Story* is one of the subtlest commentaries ever set forth on the inevitable advance of machines, their shock and roar, their unknown effect on the destiny of man' (Taylor 1949c: 42). The machines are loud, disruptive, and unpredictable; while they symbolize capitalist 'progress,' it is implied their effects will be irreversible. Flaherty's subtle commentary queers the industrial film; he sends his own message, and reaps the financial rewards himself.

In addition to the subversion of the film's ostensible pro-oil industry slant, the use of screen time is also subverted: far less screen time is devoted to oil and drilling than might be expected. Most of the film's screen time is spent gazing upon the barefoot Cajun boy.

Image and screen time

Flaherty's films nearly always orbit around the gravitational pull of an attractive boy.

Cinematographer Richard Leacock, in a letter written between April 1946 and June 1947, describes their discovery of Joseph 'JC' Boudreaux.

> Last night we were eating in a café at Cameron, and Mrs. F[laherty] noticed a hell of a nice boy sitting at the counter. We got talking with him, and found he spoke with a good Acadian accent, had done some trapping with his father, could handle a pirogue, and was twelve years old. Oh, perfect. *He's good looking, nicely built, good dark pigment, wonderful smile.* (Leacock 2003, emphasis added)

Leacock was married and I do not doubt his heterosexuality, but I think he understood what Flaherty was looking for, and he appropriated the director's enthusiasm. 'The boy,' as the role is listed in the film's credits, is the most important image of the film, more so than bayou, derrick, or alligator. Leacock understood that the boy needed to be 'good looking' and 'nicely built.' His 'dark pigment' aligned with both Flaherty's apparent existing tastes and likely expectations of Acadian ethnicities and appearances.

As far as screen time goes, no one comes close to 'the boy,' played by Joseph 'JC' Boudreaux, whose image dominates the film. There are no other major characters. Flaherty himself told Rotha, 'In *Louisiana Story* again nothing really remains but the boy. The adults are almost banished' (Flaherty in Rotha 1983: 279). The boy's father and Tom the oilman support the boy's adventures and contextualize an obligatory spoonful of information about the oil business. The boy spends time with his pet raccoon, Jo-Jo, who goes missing for much of the film, but reappears safely at the end. In screen time, advertising, and marketing, the image of the film is the image of the boy.

Symbolism and fetishism

The boy is used as a fertility and virility symbol. He is superstitious, wary of mermaids and werewolves. His rituals involve spitting, fondling a bag of salt, and fertilizing the drillers' hole with it (Figure 1.1). Naturally, it is this fertilization that causes the well to yield oil. Just as JC's salivary ejaculate provides success in the Hunt, it also proves effective with the drillers' oil well. The film elevates JC's ritualistic fertilization to a religious level. Leacock wrote:

> Yesterday we did the enormously important scene of JC spitting in the hole and looking at his frog. [...] JC coming in and kneeling at the hole, so solemnly and beautifully. His perfect grace, it adds up to a purely religious scene. (Leacock 2003)

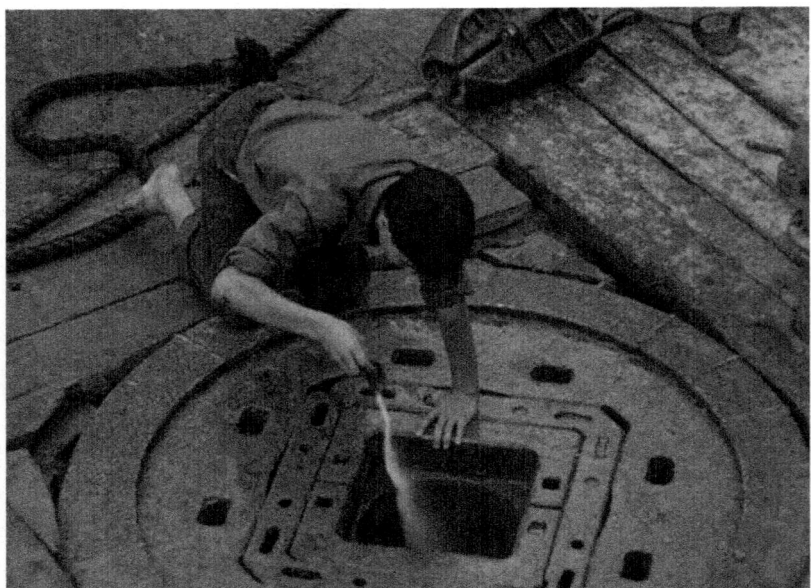

Figure 1.1   JC seeds the driller's hole with salt

This scene couches JC as both a religious and sexual symbol. The boy's superstitious relationship with his frog, hidden in his shirt, paints him as a kind of 'primitive' or 'shamanistic' figure; cast in an 'indigenous' role, symbiotically connected with the land and nature, he is permitted or expected to easily access such symbolic representation.[8]

In one shot, JC is awkwardly and stoically posed after Oscar Roty's *La Semeuse*, the symbolic and archetypal French sower of seeds (Figure 1.2). Roty's iconic design dates to 1886, originally used for a medal for France's minister of agriculture. It was used on French coins from 1898 and on stamps from 1903 (Figure 1.3), and likely inspired the 'Walking Liberty' half dollar coin issued by the United States from 1916–47; these coins and stamps were in circulation at the time of filming. The explicit symbolism of La Semeuse and the awkwardness of this pose for a live actor emphasize connections between the boy, his spitting, his pouch of salt, the land, and fertility rituals. This pose reinforces JC's positioning as a 'primitive,' 'indigenous' 'sex symbol.'

JC is eroticized through the camera's gaze, which often lingers upon the boy's bare feet (Figure 1.4). This gaze forces audience attention, with or without their complicit awareness, wherever the filmmaker desires,

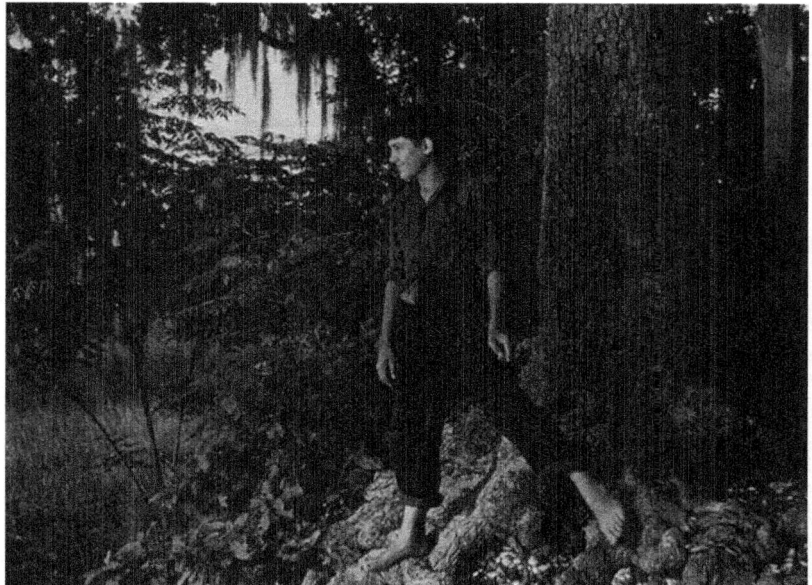

Figure 1.2 JC Boudreaux posed as Oscar Roty's *La Semeuse*

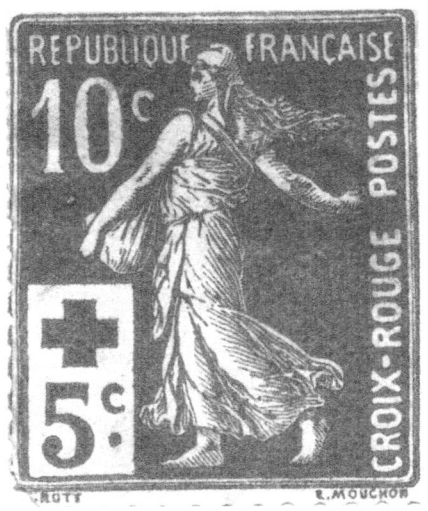

Figure 1.3   Oscar Roty's *La Semeuse* on a French postage stamp

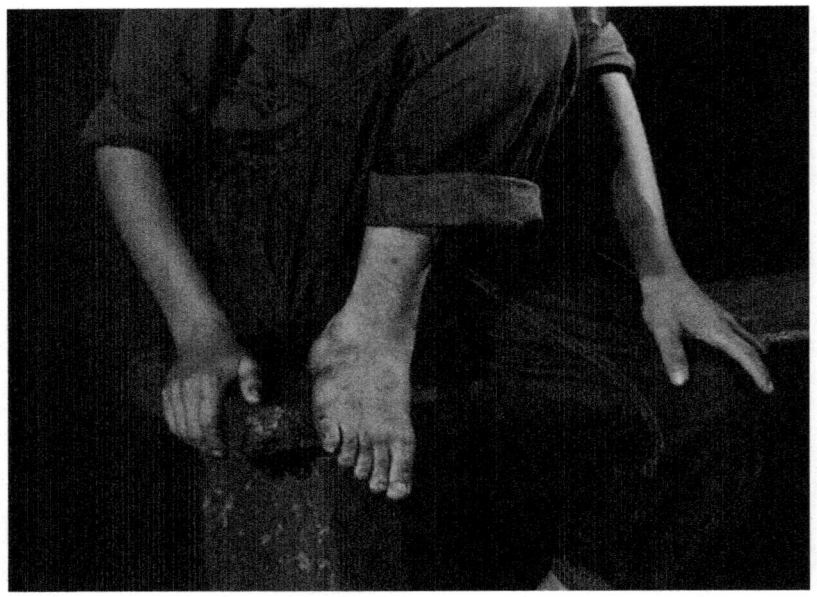

Figure 1.4   The camera's gaze upon JC's bare feet

with the power to eroticize and objectify. Much work has been done in the area of the 'male gaze,' a critical discourse initiated largely through the work of Laura Mulvey (1975). Naturally, the cinematic gaze extends to homoeroticism:

> The location of the erotic male image in a context of heterosexual masculinity serves to establish the homoerotic gaze as a secretive source of pleasure for the male spectator. The homoerotic gaze depends neither on the screen characters' actual engagement in homosexual acts nor on the spectator's individual sexual orientation. (Schuckmann 1998: 677)

Louisiana Story's cinematic gaze returns time and again to highlight or fixate upon the boy's bare feet, a common erotic target, especially in men. 'Podophilia, or "foot fetishism," is by far the most common manifestation of what sexologists refer to as a sexual "partialism," which is an erotic pre-occupation with a nonreproductive body part' (Bering 2013: 36). JC's bare feet also underscore his boyishness, sensuality, connection to the earth, as well as poverty and 'primitive' qualities Flaherty likely associated with his characterization of the local Acadian bayou population.

Flaherty was appreciative of the boy's feet, remarking in admiration that 'Joseph had gone to the nearest town for an ice cream cone, walking the twelve miles barefoot' (Flaherty in Griffith 1953: 150). Flaherty was not ashamed or disturbed by feet. Flaherty himself appears barefoot, at his desk, on the telephone, in a late photograph taken in his home office at the Chelsea Hotel in New York (Barsam 1988: 114). During filming of *Nanook of the North*, Flaherty and an Eskimo hunting party became trapped by a ferocious storm and holed up in an igloo for eight days; 'The Eskimos kept Flaherty from freezing by holding his bare feet against their bare stomachs' (Taylor 1949b: 29). In *Louisiana Story*, the focus on the boy's feet is not accidental. Although various meanings can be ascribed to the camera's lingering gaze, the eroticization of JC's feet is, whether intentionally or unintentionally, part of the film as a queer text.

A symphony of sound and steel

Tom the oilman invites the curious boy into the exclusively male area of the oil derrick. In this male space, topped with its tall, phallic, metal tower, the drillers all wear protective hard hats, gloves, and boots. In contrast, the boy remains barefoot throughout the film (Figure 1.5). Tom lures him in, never offering any protective gear, and promptly does

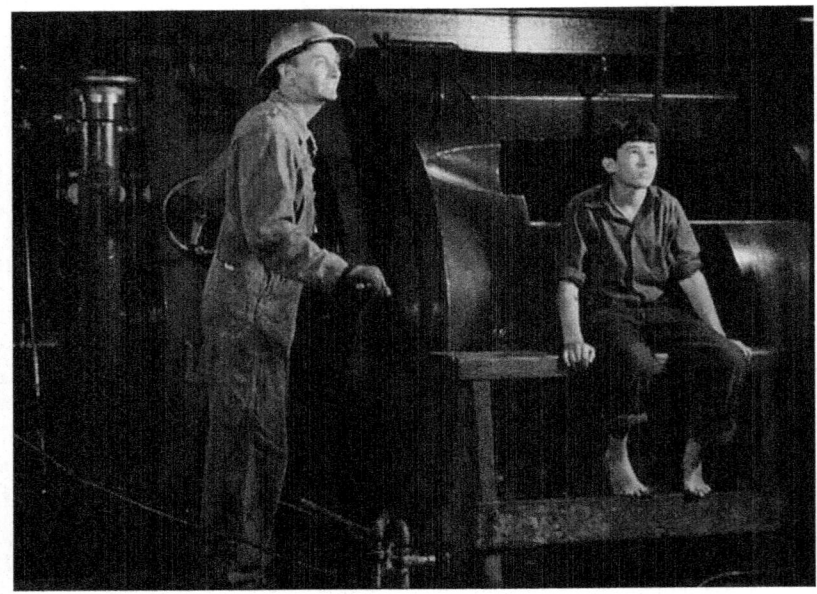

Figure 1.5   Tom, in hard hat, boots, and gloves, invites JC into the derrick

what might be described as a weird humping dance with the equipment (Figure 1.6). This section of the film is devoid of Thomson's music, giving it a dry, cinéma vérité quality. The intricacies and procedures of the equipment are not explained, and the audience must interpret the machinery in real time much as JC might be observing and experiencing it for the first time himself.

The industrial sounds and rhythms nevertheless make this section strikingly musical. These sounds were recorded by sound man Benjamin Doniger and his assistant, Lennie Starck, on the derrick itself, capturing both overall noise and individual sounds with multiple microphones at the request of film editor Helen van Dongen. These sounds were recorded using a disc recorder, due to problems with electrical instability, and re-recorded onto mag film later (Achtenberg and van Dongen 1976: 51; Orbanz 1998: 106–7).[9] This gave van Dongen a unique and authentic collection of raw material from which to construct an original sonic composition tailored to the onscreen action:

> By separating sound into separate elements, recreating each component artificially, recording these again in many different ways,

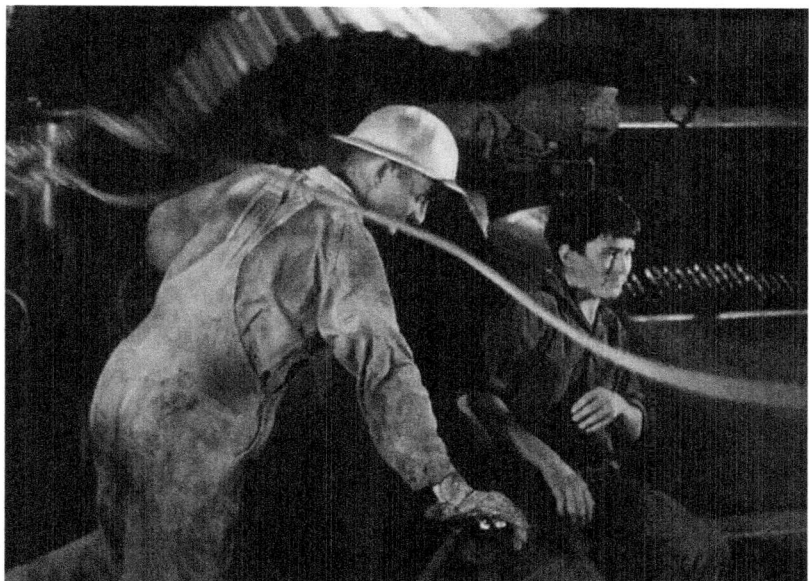

Figure 1.6 Tom dances with machinery and cables

through filters or echo chambers, further away from or closer to the microphone, too loud or too soft, to judge the effects this would make, re-recording them faster or slower to increase or decrease pitch, etc. etc. then orchestrating each individual element or component as if it were an instrument and re-recording the many individual tracks as one would plan an orchestra. (van Dongen 1998: 107)

Van Dongen's sonic construction underscores the entire oil drilling section. Thomson was impressed, and lauds van Dongen's work, calling it 'music' without reservation.

The noise-music used is the recorded sound of oil-well-digging machinery. I call it music because, as compounded and shaped by Helen Van Dongen into a rich and deafening accompaniment for a passage of well digging one whole reel (nine minutes) long, these noises make a composition. Also, I find this composition more interesting to follow than almost any of the industrial evocations, including my own, that musicians have composed with tonal materials. (Thomson 1966: 394)[10]

Likewise, Flaherty compares the sonic collage to a 'great symphony.'

> From the very first we had been fascinated with the sound a derrick makes. The mighty clash and ring of the steel pipe, the clatter of the block and the cables, with the steady throb of the engines running underneath it all, had the qualities of a great symphony. This sound proved to be an inspiration to Virgil Thomson, too, when he came to write the music for the film. (Flaherty in Griffith 1953: 152)

During this oil derrick sequence, with the orchestral score gone, the romanticizing of the boy is reduced. The boy, taken out of his idyllic element, is overshadowed by machinery and the sounds of man. The industrial sound collage brings the viewer inside the derrick and, by providing a temporary but major shift in the overall sound design, helps structure the film overall. Critic and musicologist Frederick W. Sternfeld, reviewing Thomson's score in 1948, notes how, in the oil drilling scene,

> Flaherty accompanies his wonderful photography with a symphony of sound and steel, not of musical notes. In its integration and shape, the result compares well with many a work of the concert hall and the sound track in its clarity is a delight to the ear. Flaherty used seven single tracks to compose it. At all screenings which I attended the level of the volume was sufficiently high to bring out nuances of suspense, the massiveness of the climax, the gracefulness of the tapering off, and the quiet motor beat that opens and closes the scene. (Sternfeld 1948: 9)

Sternfeld should have given credit to van Dongen,[11] but this omission aside, his praise for the 'symphony of sound and steel' is right on the money. These sounds are carefully organized within an aesthetic system; the structure assigned (the quiet motor that opens and closes the scene, the massive climax, and so on) ensures that these sounds function as music, just as they function simultaneously as sound effects. Michel Chion argues that one must recognize the practical realities of the tri-partite dialogue/sound effects/music division within the film production environment, but at the same time appreciate that all sound can be analyzed or appreciated purely as sound, where classifications are boundless or open to interpretation (Chion 2010: 65). Van Dongen's sonic collage, an enjoyable fulfillment of expectations of sound effects, environmental noise, and music, transcends categorization. As a pure sensory experience, linked with the visual image, it deserves Sternfeld's positive evaluation; I am certain Chion would agree.

> The feeling of sonic beauty is tied to a perception that certain sonic criteria are harmoniously combined, are adapted to their context. The study of film sound aesthetics should rely upon sensory criteria, criteria that reduced listening can understand, while surpassing traditional musical criteria, which are often inapplicable. (Chion 2010: 79, my translation)

The industrial noises of van Dongen's sonic composition underline potential dangers of working in the derrick. The stark contrast between protected men and naïve vulnerable boy represents loss of innocence. The boy has now seen what goes on in this place, and he correctly intuits that the derrick will stay. The blowout's soiling of the purity of the bayou provides further symbolism of defilement. The erotic subtext, the removal of orchestral score in favor of industrial sound collage, the blowout's explosive ejaculation of filth, and the boy's continued fascination with the derrick and 'that hole,' as described by the father, all queer the film on many levels, erotic as well as political.

Existing explanations of the music

To source Cajun tunes, songs, and melodies, Thomson relied upon Irene Thérèse Whitfield's 1939 compendium *Louisiana French Folk Songs*, as well as Lomax records from the Library of Congress (Sternfeld 1948: 6; Hoover and Cage 1959: 251). For other projects, Thomson had already used *The Sacred Harp* and *The Southern Harmony*, both classic texts with multiple nineteenth-century editions. For *Louisiana Story*, Thomson had some Lomax recordings, but primarily he had lyrics and diatonic transcriptions from Whitfield's book. Thomson, having lived in Paris, would have been able to understand the transcribed lyrics, provided only in French, filtered through Whitfield, who additionally supplied phonetic pronunciations of Cajun dialect. Thomson's choice of folksong (a handful out of dozens offered by Whitfield) reflects particular lyrical choices that reinforce onscreen action and characterizations of the boy. The audience would have been unaware of the original French lyrics and their meanings, but Thomson made choices for witty commentary, even if it was for his own pleasure.

Existing musical analyses of Thomson's *Louisiana Story* score focus on theme source identification, conventional music theory, and the way the score suggests location and environment. To date, analyses have overlooked questions of authenticity, representation, erotic subtext, and conventional Hollywood romanticism; instead, they describe the score as Cajun Americana situated outside of Hollywood's normal musical purview. There are four significant period analyses or commentaries on the score: Frederick W. Sternfeld (1948), Roger Manvell and John Huntley (1957), Kathleen Hoover and John Cage (1959), and Thomson himself (1966).

Sternfeld, a music professor at Dartmouth and the first to analyze the score, identifies many of Thomson's themes right out of Whitfield's book. He gushes with admiration, and many of his observations and analyses are repeated in Manvell and Huntley, and Hoover and Cage. Manvell and Huntley comment, 'Use is made of folk music but the original material has been re-set in the manner of *The River* and *The Plow That Broke the Plains*' (1957: 100), pushing to frame *Louisiana Story*'s music as Americana, but distance or differentiate it from affective Hollywood dramatic film scores, even though it largely functions to romanticize and eroticize the boy, rather than offer realistic Cajun music.[12] Manvell and Huntley specifically use the *Louisiana Story* score as an example of 'Scenic and Place music' (1957: 92).[13] While Thomson's score does provide this function to some artificial extent, this overlooks how the score romanticizes the boy, who is the center of the film.

Virgil Thomson discusses *Louisiana Story*'s music in an expectedly chaste manner, but accurately attributes more credit to classical influences than Sternfeld and others have. This attribution is important, because late romantic classical composers also fueled Hollywood's contemporaneous 'Golden Age' symphonic sound.

> *Louisiana Story*'s music is of three kinds – folk music, scenery music, and noise-music. The Cajun people are represented by their waltzes and square dances and the tunes of the songs they sing. Natural scenery is depicted through musical devices adapted from Mendelssohn, Debussy, and other landscape composers. The noise-music used is the recorded sound of oil-well-digging machinery. (Thomson 1966: 394)

Thomson's simple explanation of his music balances his folkloric approach and appropriation of melody with a rightful credit to the late romantic sound of Claude Debussy, whose orchestral style he adopts throughout the score. Mendelssohn did write geographically inspired music, such as the 'Italian Symphony,' the 'Scottish Symphony,' and the 'Hebrides Overture,' but I believe that the French orchestration technique of Debussy is the real touchstone here.

Thomson's orchestration

Thomson's score is a typically modernist symphonic fantasia that uses standard late romantic techniques to develop simple raw material. The resulting lush romantic score complements the romanticized, homoerotic view of the boy. While certainly the score and orchestrations lean more towards French than Germanic orchestral style, it is nevertheless not far afield from Hollywood's 'Golden Age' symphonic style.[14] Thomson employs Hollywoodesque 'Americana' conventions to romanticize the boy.

Some have emphasized that *Louisiana Story* features an 'American' sound that can be differentiated from typical period Hollywood dramatic music. The score was not recorded in Hollywood with a studio orchestra. Thomson and Flaherty, who both lived in New York City at the Chelsea Hotel, decided to hire conductor Eugene Ormandy and the Philadelphia Orchestra, with a total of 41 players, recorded by engineer Robert Fine (Orbanz 1998: 107–8).

> Far from being a musical background in the conventional Hollywood style, the music grew with the film as it assumed its final shape in the cutting room and projection theatre. (Rotha 1983: 251)

I am not sure what Rotha means precisely by 'grew with the film' or how this would differentiate the score from Hollywood styles; arguably, every score is composed with sensitivity to picture changes, synchronized in a cutting room, and viewed in a projection theatre. There was one 'test run of the music with the cut with Flaherty present' on 6 April 1948 (Orbanz 1998: 108), and the score was recorded in one day, from 9:30 a.m. to 6:00 p.m., on 22 April. Rotha may wish to emphasize the director's independence or unconventional career path since Flaherty had 'been excommunicated from Hollywood since 1929' (Rotha 1983: 260; see also Griffith 1953: 159). There are other arguments used to differentiate Thomson's score from typical Hollywood music. To some, Thomson's 'American' sound is associated with documentary films.

> The 'American influence' can also be heard in the music used for nonfiction films of the period, especially that of Virgil Thomson (*The Plow that Broke the Plains, The River,* and *Louisiana Story*), Aaron

Copland (*The City* and *The Cummington Story*), Douglas Moore (*Power and the Land*), and Marc Blitzstein (*Native Land*). (Barsam 1988: 95)

In spite of any 'American influence,' in a broader context, Thomson's score is quite representational of typical period American Hollywood film music. Consider that this Americana sound, created in large part by the queer modernist circle described by Hubbs, found its way into many Hollywood films and Westerns. Aaron Copland, also a proponent of 'Americana,' could be called a Hollywood composer with studio films like *Of Mice and Men* (1939) and *The Heiress* (1949) to his credit. Certainly, Virgil Thomson's *Louisiana Story* score bears more in common with cinema music of the time than it does with authentic Cajun music.

While Thomson uses simple melodic material, he manipulates and develops it in the manner of a composer of Western art music. The finished score shows Thomson's skill as a master orchestrator. Overlaps and switch offs in two flutes seamlessly extend the duration of a line beyond what can humanly be played by just one flutist. Thomson uses many careful doublings and delicate balances; in many cases, the subtleties and detail of the score far exceed the limited audio fidelity of the film's monophonic optical track. Thomson uses many string techniques and effects including mutes, fingered tremolos, and sul ponticello bowing. To achieve a strident, ardent string sound, he scores violas and cellos *above* the violins in [1D] mm 179–183 (0:07:24).[15] In [1E] (0:08:20), Thomson uses the entire string section to imitate a massive harp in an ornate staggered pizzicato effect. In textures with harp and glockenspiel, he uses glock to accent the top line of the harp's arpeggio.

In a further indication of Thomson's Parisian training and stylistic influences, there is a smattering of French in the score: at [1B] m 110, double basses are marked 'sans lourdeur' instead of the more common Italian 'non pesante' or 'not heavy.' Other effects and voicings are idiomatic of the French orchestral style of Debussy and Ravel: chromatic, swirling clarinet runs at [1C] m 158 (0:06:58) overlap with asynchronous swirling arpeggios in the harp, creating a mélange of sonic ripples. Parallel fifths in the trombone parts, at [1D] mm 179–183 (0:07:24) and also during various statements of the 'Derrick Chorale,' trace how this supposedly 'American' sound can be seen to stem from the use of parallel fifths in the extended harmony of Debussy and Ravel. While parallel fifths became a part of the Americana sound of the open West, through Virgil Thomson, his studies with Nadia Boulanger, and his tenure in Paris, we have a direct connection back to French composers and an evolving French art music tradition. This French school itself borrowed from earlier and contemporaneous 'jazz' voicings and parallel motions, as seen in imitative pieces such as Debussy's 'Golliwog's Cakewalk' (1913), making the 'Americana' circle complete.

Existing analyses of Thomson's score favor identifying Acadian folk tunes, sourced through Whitfield and Lomax, and tend to overlook the score's lush orchestration. But even these Acadian folk tunes have been musically sanitized, simplified into diatonic transcriptions and rhythmic regularities. I do not fault Thomson for this, and in no way do I believe Thomson tasked himself with any kind of adherence to ethnomusicological authenticity. Instead, Thomson's music romanticizes and eroticizes the boy, and he took melodies as they were presented in Whitfield's book, often even preserving Whitfield's key.

Whitfield's musical transcriptions reflect recurrent issues in early 'song collecting,' notably musical simplification, conformation to preexisting expectations of rhythm, modality, regularity, and ornamentation, and the limitations of the standard music notation system used to preserve the songs. The benefit of Lomax's sound recordings is that we can hear exactly what was performed, as well as the relative skill or ease of the performer. Australian composer Percy Grainger collected English and Danish folksongs; what appealed to Grainger was to notate and preserve 'the tunes as they were really sung without watering them down to suit the rhythmic and modal preconceptions of the academic world' (Bird 1999: 157). This resulted in complex, irregular transcriptions that proved controversial among collectors. While Whitfield's transcriptions are far more rudimentary, in a way they allow Thomson even greater freedom to manipulate and develop this melodic material as he wishes.

Musical examples

Thomson's score relies heavily on 'absolute' musical structures that follow an established form or 'musical logic,' although he does incorporate much of the rhythmic breathing or unevenness of the Cajun folk music, as preserved in the Lomax audio recordings. The film's languid pace and sparsity of dialogue and action allow for significant musical structural freedom. Thomson's score avoids 'mickey mousing,' or cartoon-like mimicry of onscreen action, and maintains a pleasant flow.

In presenting musical examples from the score, I wish to focus attention upon three significant areas: lyrical significance, manipulation of thematic melodic material, and orchestration. These factors help decode Thomson's score and its meaning.

Thomson did not choose folk tunes arbitrarily. He chose them for lyrical content, even if the audience would not know the lyrics themselves. Thomson chose tunes with particular lyrical significance that reflected how he saw the narrative. He manipulated this chosen musical material using classical techniques within traditional forms, and orchestrated the score within the tradition of late romantic French symphonic music, as exemplified by Claude Debussy and Maurice Ravel.

'Je m'endors'

Whitfield calls 'Je m'endors' by the title 'French Blues' and says her source is 'From a Lomax record' (Whitfield 1939: 100). Lomax's recording of 'Je m'endors' is an unaccompanied male vocal, sung in F# minor, performed by Jesse Stafford, recorded in 1934 by John and Alan Lomax (Traditional 1934a).

Whitfield simplifies the Cajun inflections into a diatonic, metrically regular version. Whitfield transcribes it in D minor, and Thomson, as he often does, preserves Whitfield's key (Figure 1.7); but Jesse Stafford's

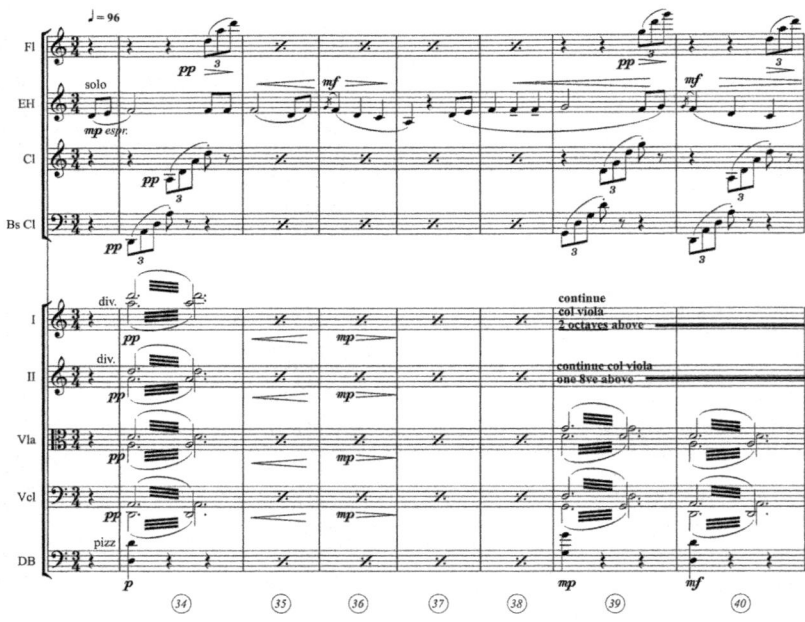

Figure 1.7   *Louisiana Story* [1A] mm 34–40 (0:03:12). Thomson's incorporation of 'Je m'endors'

characteristically Cajun bending of notes and rhythmic flexibility are discarded.

We hear 'Je m'endors' in a plaintive English horn solo at [1A] m 34 (0:03:12) when we are introduced to 'Alexander Napoleon Ulysses Latour' paddling around alone in his pirogue in the placid bayou, bubbles from 'mermaids' rising up around him in the water. The lyrics of 'Je m'endors' are poetic and suggest the poverty and difficulty of life in the bayou.

> I'm going to sleep, I'm going to sleep,
> And I'm thirsty and I'm hungry.
> The sun is set, you've come far from home.
> Whatcha got, yeah, pretty blonde?
> Whatcha got, yeah, pretty brunette?
> It's all for the blonde,
> And nothing for the brunette.
>
> (Whitfield 1939: 100, my translation)

Given that actor 'JC' Boudreaux was chosen for his 'good dark pigment,' it's easy to see him cast in the role of the song's brunette. The bayou is dimly lit, covered by vegetation; the lyrics further imply that he's paddled 'far from home,' and is therefore a bit of an adventurer.

Thomson uses very subtle, decorative, French-styled orchestration, with fingered tremolos in the strings, giving a quiet, shimmering quality. Frilly, swirly, split woodwind arpeggios rise up – perhaps they are the 'bubbles,' their triplet eighths blurring against the straight eighths of the English horn's doleful melody. These textures are idiomatic French romantic orchestration; similar fingered tremolos can be heard prominently in symphonic works such as Ravel's *Daphnis and Chloé* (1913).

Manvell and Huntley correlate and graph the film's opening music, [1A] mm 1–72 (0:02:10), which includes this excerpt, to the picture cut (1957: 101–9), creating an illustration similar to a 'bar chart' or 'bar sheet' commonly used in early animation, for purposes of analysis.[16] (A preceding [Prelude] underscores the film's main title sequence.) But beyond simply supplying this graph, the authors fail to offer any meaningful analysis of it.

Thomson's orchestration subverts the folk tune qualities of the melody and turns it into a sensitive, beautiful romantic music cue, evocative of both the scenic bayou and the Cajun boy in his pirogue.

'La Valse de la Grand'Chénier'

A tune closely associated with the boy is 'La Valse de la Grand'Chénier' or 'Grand'Chénier Village Waltz.' It's a quirky love song that characterizes and romanticizes the boy. It appears at [1C] (0:06:15) and again at [10D] (1:17:01).

> You are small, you are cute, you are jealous,
> but I love you anyhow.
> Oh beauty, you aren't washed.
> Oh beauty, you could go wash.

> (Whitfield 1939: 73, my translation)

These lyrics eroticize the boy, and the rough-and-tumble, muddy, dirtiness that boyhood represents. This simultaneous love and disdain of the unwashed is a bit like the fascination with sailors and 'trade' that can be imagined in haunts like the gay bordello in Brooklyn. In an archetypal way, the boy is dirty and gritty; always barefoot, and although eroticized in the lingering gaze of the camera, he is never neatened or cleaned up, but left an endearing, earthy scamp.

'La Valse de la Grand'Chénier' is related by melodic contour to another tune, 'Mon amour est barré,' that appears at [5J] (Figure 1.8).

By choosing tunes with similar melodic contour, Thomson gives the score a greater structural unity. While Thomson used a variety of melodies throughout the film, he maintains a musical and structural unity by choosing similar tunes that often act as variations of each other, and kept orchestrations relatively stylistically uniform in a late romantic style.

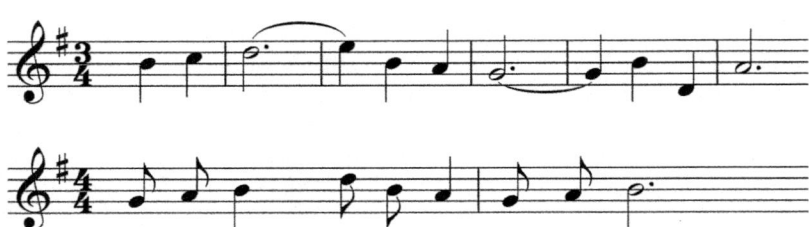

Figure 1.8 Comparison of melodic contour: 'La Valse de la Grand'Chénier' above. 'Mon amour est barré' below

'Mme Baptiste, tirez-moi pas' and 'Qui est-ce qui passe?'

The boy's pet raccoon, Jo-Jo, untamed and quite independent, cavorts with danger by swimming too close to the Alligator Mother, lurking quietly. When raccoon and alligator appear to sense each other's presence, Thomson uses the happy, playful little tune 'Qui est-ce qui passe?' or 'Who Goes There?' in the bassoon at [5F] m 1(0:41:15). This chirpy tune was previously introduced to accompany Jo-Jo's swimming and antics in cue [3C] at 0:16:43 and 0:17:07.

> Who goes there? It's the Voorhies.
> Where are they going? To Saint Martin.
>
> (Whitfield 1939: 108, my translation)

The 'Who goes there?' text suggests that the raccoon and the alligator are each aware that there is another animal in the neighborhood. Although the music is happy, the situation could become dangerous for Jo-Jo. The Alligator Mother is already agitated, having just scared off the boy, who had been investigating and disturbing her nest of alligator eggs. As Jo-Jo continues cavorting, the music shifts to another happy tune, 'Madame Baptiste, tirez-moi pas,' on xylophone, about a chicken thief who playfully and humorously begs not to be shot [5F] m 17 (0:41:30).

> Madame Baptiste, don't shoot!
> It's just me stealing your chickens.
>
> (Whitfield 1939: 107, my translation)

Thomson uses this happy tune with its dark but playful lyric to imply that Jo-Jo is a bit of a daredevil, misbehaving and laughing in the face of danger. The chickens can be seen as a reference to the alligator eggs. There is also a history of young men being referred to as 'chicken' in gay culture; it is pure speculation if this would have appealed to Thomson's camp sensibilities as well.

'Qui est-ce qui passé?' reappears later in the film, in jolly bassoon at [10B] mm 1–17 (1:15:00) and in gleeful xylophone at [10C] mm 25–32 (1:15:32), when the boy at last finds and is reunited with Jo-Jo. The question 'Who goes there?' is now free from the threat of danger, and refers to their happy reunion.

'Mon amour est barré' and 'Quoi je t'ai fait'

Jo-Jo's disappearance, suspiciously following their adventures with the alligator, greatly upsets the boy, who goes searching for his beloved pet, pleading and shouting through the bayou, 'Jo-Jo, where are you?' Thomson matches this moment with 'Mon amour est barré dans l'armoire' at [5J] m 1 (0:43:26).

> My love is locked in the closet
> And the key is hidden in my heart.
> Last night I had you in my arms,
> But I discovered it was a dream.

(Whitfield 1939: 79, my translation)

These lyrics dramatize the boy's distress over the loss of his pet. These lyrics can also be seen as emphasizing the boy himself as a love object. A further possible layer is the invocation of the 'closet,' which may have appealed to Thomson's camp sensibilities, and whose own love was locked in the closet. The word 'closet' is my own translation of 'armoire,' which is more closely translated as 'armoire' or 'wardrobe'; I admit to conflating these words, but I believe such a translation would have occurred to Thomson as well.

Thomson harmonizes 'Mon amour est barré dans l'armoire' in the relative minor, leaving the melody intact (Figure 1.9). 'Mon amour'

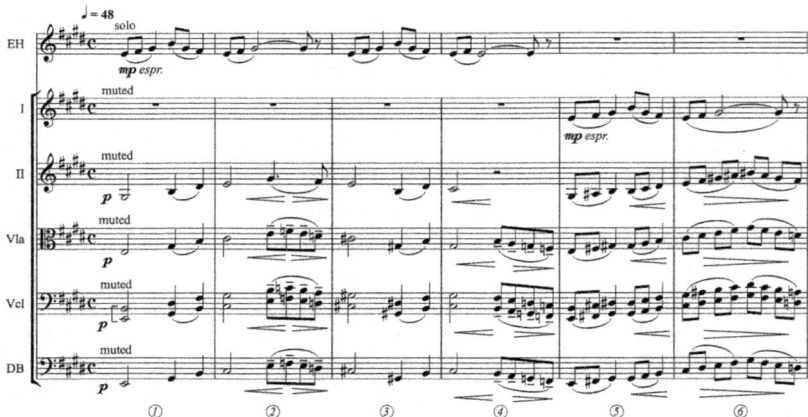

Figure 1.9 [5J] mm 1–6 (0:43:26). 'Mon amour est barré' harmonized in the relative minor

can also be seen as a variation of the opening theme 'La valse de la Grand'Chénier' ('You are small, you are cute, you are jealous, but I love you anyhow') by melodic contour (Figure 1.8). In both excerpts, the English horn takes the tune. In bar 6, accompanying cellos, double basses, and violas add Thomson's descending fifths motive from the 'Derrick Chorale.' The use of reharmonization and contrapuntal accompaniment that references other themes and motives are 'classical' techniques of compositional manipulation.

As the boy continues searching for Jo-Jo, at [5J] m 17 (0:44:39), a muted viola solo takes the tune, 'Quoi je t'ai fait, malheureuse?' Here we see nature photography: a bunny, bird, skunk, deer, the boy, and an amazing spider web shot which Flaherty had famously sacrificed a day's shooting schedule in order to capture. 'Quoi je t'ai fait, malheureuse?' is a lover's desperate plea to his beloved.

> What did I ever do to you, unhappy one?
> What did I ever do to you, you big meanie?
>
> (Whitfield 1939: 75, my translation)

These lyrics imply that the boy fears that Jo-Jo has left him for good.

'Mon amour est barré' also opens the film, [Prelude] mm 1–8 (0:00:22) during the title sequence, also with these parallel fifths, although transformed in the manner of a slow, grandiose fanfare.

'Creole Blues'

Thomson also borrows instrumental Cajun music. The composer takes a solo fiddle piece, 'Creole Blues,' from a Lomax record performed by Wayne Perry, recorded in 1934 by John and Alan Lomax (Traditional 1934b). At [3A] m 33 (0:14:41), the tune accompanies the boy and Jo-Jo in the pirogue on a large open river. In the orchestra the rough, scratchy Cajun fiddle tune becomes akin to a massive Irish jig, alternating loudly and softly with a complementary accordion-like theme. Thomson's creative orchestration evokes an acoustic guitar accompaniment at [3A] m 57, when the harp part specifies 'quickly rolled chords, guitar style, near the soundboard.' These types of imitative effects are again idiomatic for late romantic orchestration.

'Alligator Fugue'

Thomson bases his 'Alligator Fugue' [7A] (0:49:25) on his own original, angular melodic material, not found folk material (Figure 1.10). This cue,

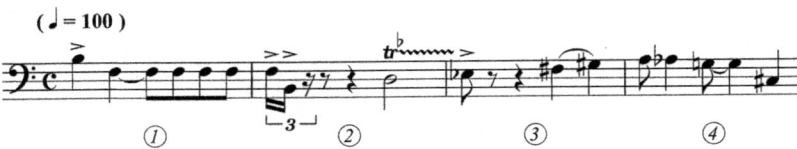

Figure 1.10   [7A] 'Alligator Fugue' first subject

running four minutes and eleven seconds in duration, is an example of the use of 'classical,' and particularly baroque, forms. As such, it defies general notions and expectations of film music, employing an absolute form, albeit with modifications and sensitivities to onscreen action that can be seen in the timing and placement of episodes and breaks.[17]

The fugue has two subjects and two countersubjects; Sternfeld calls it a 'quadruple fugue.' The fugue opens with the first subject at [7A] m 1, followed at m 13 by an episode and fragmentation of the subject. At m 17, violas and clarinets, with contrasting cellos and bassoons, introduce the second subject and its countersubject. There's a break in the music for the father to search for the boy and speak. At m 33 the fugue re-enters with first violins taking the first subject. At m 57 there is a stretto on the second subject.

Sternfeld praises the 'contemporary' quality of the piece: 'This is not the decadent chromaticism of Nineteenth Century Romanticism, nor the Hollywood cliche [sic] and synonya [sic] for evil; rather it is an expression of struggle immortal in contemporary terms' (1948: 10). The angular, jerky first and second subjects contribute to the modern quality of the piece, and the inherent dissonance of the material arguably allows for easier construction of an effective fugue, encouraging or allowing 'real' rather than 'tonal' responses.[18] This fugue is a demonstration of effective modernism that incorporates both established compositional forms and techniques and a contemporary, dissonant, twentieth-century sound.

Claims of dodecaphony: the 'Derrick Chorale'

Thomson employs a similar but less dissonant midcentury modernist sound in the 'Derrick Chorale,' which reappears throughout the score in connection with the drillers' oil derrick. This chorale first appears during the film's main titles, [Prelude] mm 9–22 (0:00:55). It next appears in a brief statement in the strings at [4B] mm 33–36 (0:20:30), when we, through the eyes of the boy, first see the tall derrick tower. The 'Derrick Chorale' is introduced in trumpets and trombones at [4D] m 78

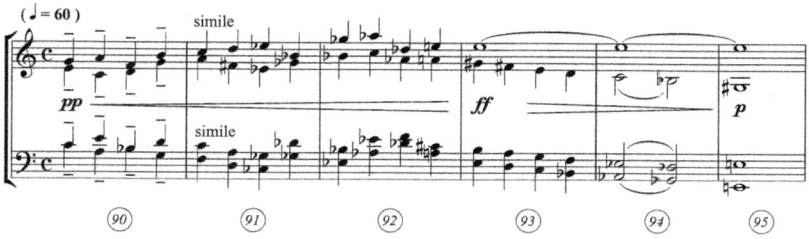

Figure 1.11 [4D] mm 90–95 (0:22:06). 'Derrick Chorale' finale tutti. Orchestra reduction by the author

(0:21:17) as the boy excitedly tells his parents to come and look at the arrival of the derrick, being towed by tugboat to its marker. The chorale builds to a climactic tutti at [4D] mm 90–95 (0:22:06) (Figure 1.11).

Towards the end of the film, at [10C] mm 1–22 (1:15:33), the chorale appears in augmentation, stretched to make it longer, as the boy's father writes a 'Dear Friend' letter explaining that the derrick is going away, to be replaced by a 'Christmas Tree' device that caps the well. Additionally, a whole-tone descending open fifths motive, borrowed from the 'Derrick Chorale' (Figure 1.11 mm 93–94), is used in [5J], in the accompaniment to 'Mon amour est barré,' and in [6B] m 7(0:47:00) in trombones, cellos, and basses as the boy sets a trap for the alligator.

Sternfeld describes this chorale as 'twelve-tone' in its construction:

> The chorale which is first stated briefly in the Prelude represents a different strand in Thomson's art, for it expresses a modern phenomenon in a modern idiom. The casual listener may be unaware of its twelve-tone construction, but he will sense that this music reflects and expresses the world of today. [...] A glance at the first two staves [...] will show that the treble and bass of measures one, two, and three touch on all of the twelve semitones within the octave. (Sternfeld 1948: 7)

Sternfeld's description of this chorale as 'twelve-tone' is really pushing it, as I will discuss below, but Hoover and Cage eagerly agree:

> The chorale itself is the composer's second intentionally dodecaphonic work. [...] Here [dodecaphony] is employed for leading of the outer voices in a four-part harmony of root-position triads. (Hoover and Cage 1959: 209)

Sternfeld, Hoover, and Cage offer detailed twelve-tone analyses of the chorale, but I would like to offer my simpler, rock-and-roll harmonic analysis. We start in the key of C major in m 90 (Figure 1.11) and stay there until we get to the D major chord in m 91, which can easily be heard as a 'V of V' secondary dominant that should resolve to the dominant, G major. But here we pivot, using the F# note in the D major chord, to resolve deceptively to B major. Bar 92 can easily be heard as a ii–V–I–bVI progression in the key of Db major; the bVI chord (A major) becomes IV of I in the key of E, which is where we resolve. For those not well versed in music theory, the redux is this: Thomson's triadic, root-position harmony means this sounds pretty, a little grandiose, and it does not obscure the anchor of tonality as Schoenberg might have done.

This raises the question, why are Sternfeld, Hoover, and Cage so concerned with praising and framing Thomson's tonal, triadic chorale as an attempt at dodecaphony? It's as much a twelve-tone composition as Bach's 'Fugue 24 in B Minor' (from *The Well-Tempered Clavier Book I*) whose subject also contains all twelve pitches, arguably making it a 'tone row.' But the manner in which the 'Derrick Chorale' and Bach's Fugue are handled compositionally has naught to do with serial operations or the freedom from tonality that was the stated goal of the twelve-tone system.

Sternfeld, Hoover, and Cage's analysis is not about advocacy for twelve-tone composition, but apologist hysteria, a response to anxieties over how the academy was lauding serial composition and deriding tonal work. In the mid-twentieth century, the academy situated itself in opposition to late romantic tonal composition, a situation described by Nadine Hubbs and others (see also the discussion of Wendy Carlos in Chapter 4). Thomson's tonal modernist circle was positioned against a 'serialist avant-garde' in a 'dualistic struggle between vying musical powers circa 1953–60' (Hubbs 2004: 154). The growing influence of serial composition championed by the academy put pressure on composers such as Thomson, Copland, and Stravinski to create their own 'twelve-tone' compositions. Thomson's 'Derrick Chorale' is only a tiny nod to serialism and twelve-tone technique. Sternfeld, Hoover, and Cage take pains to emphasize its connection to dodecaphony as a means of legitimizing Thomson's work.

Conclusion

Existing musicological explanations of Virgil Thomson's *Louisiana Story* score are incomplete or reductive; the music, while derived from folk melodies, is spun into a romantic fantasia that travels far afield from accurate representation of Cajun music. The score does not realistically set place and scenery; the bayou was never bursting with late romantic French styled symphonic music. Alan and John Lomax's 1934 audio recordings of genuine Acadian music make this clear.

Existing scholarly analyses of *Louisiana Story*, the film and its score, are good foundational work, but contemporary scholarship demands more. Flaherty's biographer Paul Rotha noticed the director's fixation with boys, but intentionally avoided confronting the obvious, offering obtuse psychological explanations. Likewise, Robert Christopher's more recent *Robert and Frances Flaherty: A Documentary Life, 1883–1922* (2005) also avoids parsing sexuality. Issues of personal obsessions, screen time, cinematic gaze, and homoeroticism need to be addressed and correlated with the film's musical score.

Flaherty romanticizes the bayou, the mighty derrick, and, most of all, the boy: a superstitious, barefoot Cajun boy with his frog, his bag of salt, his salivary ejaculations, his pet raccoon, and a belief in mermaids and werewolves. Thomson's musical score takes transcribed, sanitized Cajun tunes as raw melodic material, and treats them romantically, just as Flaherty has romanticized and eroticized the boy. Thomson's sensuous French treatment of melodic material adheres closer to Hollywood romanticism than to Lomax's field recordings. The music is an emotive, romantic nostalgia, not a stylized Cajun portrait or exotica; it focuses more on the *boy* than on the titular Louisiana. Analysis of Thomson's score elucidates subcultures of homoeroticism and layers of narrative. While one can only speculate on Flaherty's inner desires and motivations, Thomson's score to *Louisiana Story* reinforces a homoerotic reading of the film.

2
Musical Cachet in *The Living End* and the New Queer Cinema

This chapter examines how music supervision and budgetary concerns influence the soundtracks of niche market cinema, using as a primary example the classic New Queer Cinema film, *The Living End* (1992). This film exemplifies a conscious balance between budget, cachet, and effectiveness that drives music placement decisions.

Scholarly analyses of film music have come from a broad range of disciplines, including literary analysis, cinema studies, musicology, psychology, communication studies, and music theory, to name but a few. Each of these disciplines has particular interests at heart, and many of those interests overlap, yet scholars frequently favor study of the composer or their final recorded musical output at the expense of production practice and its influence upon film scoring and filmmaking.

I have worked as a composer, and I realize that there is a broad industry context for our work. For this reason, I welcome research and theory that removes the pedestal and accurately describes the production environment. Scholars including James Wierzbicki, Miguel Mera, Rick Altman, Daniel Goldmark, Jeff Smith, and others have given careful attention to production practices and technologies involved in film scoring, as well as business practices and business environments.[1] However, many scholars and theorists find it expedient to overlook these aspects. For one thing, they require deep and arcane knowledge of actual production practices that can require time-consuming research. Second, information from production practice can undermine or contradict common knowledge, sophisticated theories, or accepted analyses of film music. For example, Michael Slowik's painstaking research into 1929–1931 dubbing technology and practices debunks anecdotal claims by Max Steiner that re-recording was impossible at the time. (Slowik

2012). Histories that seem neat and tidy become complicated by technical realities and practicalities.

Often, the truth is that something was done a particular way because it was *cheap* or *expedient*. This reality need not negate other explanations of film music, but does need consideration. Study of production and business practices are a necessary part of analyzing commercial art forms such as cinema, even in cases where films are considered 'independent.'

The New Queer Cinema is a group of films recognized as a culturally important example of independent cinema from around 1989 to the mid-1990s. In 1992, in *Sight and Sound*, critic B. Ruby Rich coined the term 'New Queer Cinema' to describe a wave of independent queer films that garnered prestigious festival screenings (Sundance, Toronto, Amsterdam) and unexpected cultural attention (Rich 1992: 31–32; 2013: 16–21). The films of the New Queer Cinema were a coincidental collection of works from an unapologetic queer perspective that put strong, iconoclastic images of lesbians and gays onscreen; these films were all made with the usual budgetary constraints facing independent and outsider cinema. In many cases, they made use of preexisting music with established cachet to help situate and identify community and audience.

It is widely held as a colloquial adage in professional circles that film music can be plotted on a 'good–fast–cheap' triangle (Figure 2.1), whereby a filmmaker can *never have all three*. The purpose of this generalization is to stimulate thought and to keep decisions realistic and reasonable. If you want it *now*, it will cost you. If you want it *good*, it will cost you. If you want it *cheap*, you must sacrifice either time or quality.

This triangle has sometimes been called the 'project triangle,' and has been elaborated upon in many books and blogs. These sources frequently pertain to video game development (Bethke 2003: 65–67), to engineering,[2] to a growing white-collar, middle-management field called 'project management,' and very often to the filmmaking process overall.

This triangle analogy has long been used in the professional world of film production and post-production. Blain Brown's 1996 text on motion picture and video lighting claims, 'There is an old saying in the movie business: "Good, fast, cheap, pick any two." Nothing could be more fundamentally true' (Brown 1996: 87). While it is difficult to substantiate how old the saying actually is, Brown suggests it was well established by the time of the New Queer Cinema. The good–fast–cheap balancing act was one of many obstacles facing New Queer Cinema;

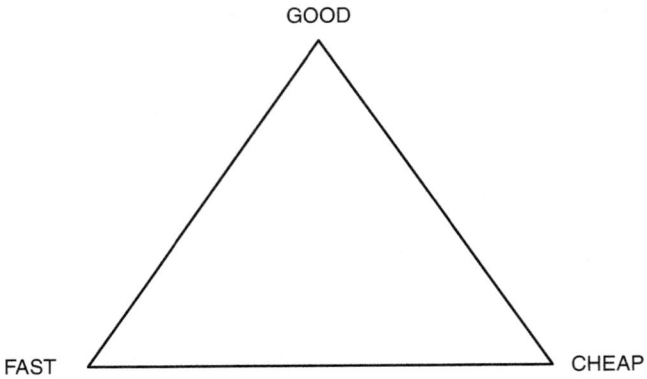

Figure 2.1 Good–fast–cheap triangle

not a glamorous aspect, but nevertheless a crucial part of the development of these films. Colin MacCabe, producer of Isaac Julien's *Young Soul Rebels* (1991), wrote 'creative decisions get made in an atmosphere where time and technique are money' (Julien and MacCabe 1991: 11). While MacCabe's observation sounds similar to 'time is money,' his inclusion of 'technique' in the equation, read here as an interpretation of 'good,' is a close evocation of the good–fast–cheap triangle.

While 'good–fast–cheap' may have already been an 'old saying' in 1996, as an expression it may postdate the classical Hollywood studio system, when expenses and budgets were dictated by executives, and music was supervised by music department heads dealing with contractual employees (Adorno and Eisler 2007: 61–62). In the Hollywood studio system, most work was done in-house, on the lot, and filmmakers typically lacked freedom to balance these corners on their own: 'The production process became quite routine as similar crews worked together under the supervision of a single production head or a few key producers' (Miller and Shamsie 1996: 529). As long as directors stayed within preset budgets, there was no triangle.

As independent and self-financed filmmaking grew, the triangle would gain relevance, becoming, certainly by the time of Brown's book, a meaningful algorithm for an increasing number of low-budget or self-financed films, including queer and other independent films in a variety of niche markets. The ability to make films cheaply on digital video stoked niche market filmmaking that includes not only queer films, but also 'reality' programming, zombie films, films about golf, cooking, travel, and so on.

Within the world of independent cinema, music for niche market film can be regarded on a similar nominative triangle: *cachet, budget,* and *effectiveness* (Figure 2.2). These three concerns must be balanced because a filmmaker cannot have all three to her advantage.

Music found at low cost may have some audience cachet (for example, culturally appropriate pop songs by emerging artists), but it may be awkward or ineffective as music for cinema. Consider the pop soundtrack for *Shallow Hal* (Bobby and Peter Farrelly, 2001): this score has vocal tracks under dialogue, resulting in speech overlaps and a jerky sound mix. Other music that fits a low budget may be *effective* (for example, an original score by a young composer), but it may have no particular cachet or audience recognition. I would humbly put my own scores into this category, one well populated with composers trying to break into the business, as well as music by Cole Coonce, the composer of additional underscore for *The Living End*. It is possible to have *both* cachet and effectiveness (for example, original music by a recognized artist), but this can be potentially very *expensive*. Consider Trent Reznor's score for *The Social Network* (David Fincher, 2010): Reznor was famous for fronting industrial-pop band Nine Inch Nails, and with co-composer Atticus Ross crafted a critically praised, Academy Award-winning original score for a film with an overall production budget of $40 million (Fritz 2010). Reznor's cachet and the quality of the score were both high, but it was not a low-budget job. These three angles, cachet, budget, and effectiveness, create a conceptual music supervision

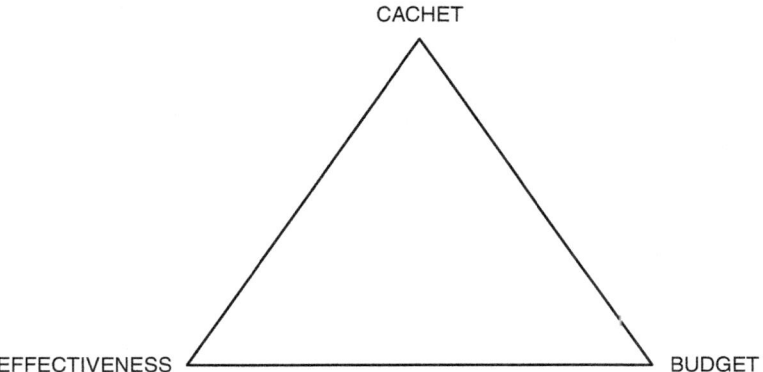

Figure 2.2   Cachet–effectiveness–budget triangle

triangle with realistic veracity. This conceptualization is especially apropos with the increased importance of the music supervisor, a professional dedicated to assessing filmmakers' musical requirements, finding suitable options, negotiating clearances and licenses, and placing pre-existing music in films (Smith 2001b). As music becomes increasingly commodified as a line item that is simply purchased or licensed, the cachet–budget–effectiveness triangle is an increasingly relevant paradigm for analyzing film music.

To consider this cachet–budget–effectiveness triangle, 'cachet' must be defined and clarified. A few academics, like David E. James and Melissa Anderson, have published articles examining cachet in independent or 'hipster' cinema. Their work examines qualities that target specific audiences situated within popular culture. Yet cachet transcends mere marketing; often 'hipster' audiences resist obvious marketing ploys. Anahid Kassabian introduces relevant, related ideas in discussing the 'compiled score,' one created from a pastiche of licensed, pre-existing tracks:

> Perceivers bring external associations with the songs into their engagements with the film [...] Compiled scores offer what I call *affiliating identifications* [...] these ties depend on histories forged outside the film scene. (Kassabian 2001: 3, emphasis in original)

Kassabian's notion of 'affiliating identifications' is a broad, basic appreciation of the connection between existing songs and a musically 'competent' audience. She acknowledges that more work needs to be done in this area: 'Throughout the literature on film music, there is very little work on identification processes. Yet music is one of the major tools Hollywood films use to track identifications' (Kassabian 2001: 13).

Filmmakers wishing to enhance a calculated reputation or build a particular audience use coded signs and signifiers to show that they are 'in the know' about audience subculture, and use these means to coordinate a presentation of their own hipness and cachet. This examination of cachet needs to be extended specifically to film music, which is often chosen because it is cheap and speaks to a target audience, even if it lacks narrative meaning or fails to be reactive to the motion picture.

This chapter operationally defines 'cachet' and 'effectiveness' and discusses their relevance to filmmaking and film music. The budget–cachet–effectiveness triangle is then applied to music from the New Queer Cinema, using Gregg Araki's *The Living End* as an example. I examine the selection of music from the queer industrial club scene, particularly vibrant in Los Angeles at the time; this music resonated with the film's creators and target audience. Such music contains many general signifiers of cachet without assisting narrative drive or reacting to picture. Frequently in a low-budget market, filmmakers opt for music that is inexpensive but has cachet; *The Living End* presents one significant example of this approach. I close with an examination of further problems and arguments as this triangle extends to independent cinema of today.

Cachet

'Cachet' indicates a quality of *membership* in, *knowledge* of, or significant *resonance* with a *target audience or subculture*. Cachet is purely that quality of association. I make a fine distinction between 'cachet' and 'hipness.' In a similar fashion, what can be considered 'hip' is also dependent upon target audience or subculture, but 'hipness' connotes an additional weight of *judgment*. For example, when 'Mods' and 'Rockers' were in cultural conflict in early 1960s Britain, a scooter and a smart suit indicated cultural cachet within the Mod community, but *not* among Rockers. Note that this statement avoids taking sides as to who is the *hipper community*. One might argue that Mods were hipper and more forward-looking; but each community had their own objects and signifiers that had or indicated cachet. Cultural cachet should be measured *by* the target audience. The importance of cachet, as a collection of *significant markers to a target audience*, is a representation of *inclusion*, a quotient of *audience associations*, whereas 'hipness' invokes a *judgment* of a subculture.

Without using either of these terms, Kassabian noted the use of songs in *Dirty Dancing* and *The Big Chill* 'to help audience members identify with their peer group as it is being represented on screen' (Kassabian 2001: 77). Clearly those songs had cachet for their intended audience; opinions would differ as to which musical style employed would be more 'hip.'

Scholars of cinema studies have long considered the notion of cachet or what is 'hip' in film, but have rarely discussed it directly. Popular film criticism contains frequent arguments or perspectives that take notions of cachet or hipness for granted, without directly hitting them on the head. Films are rarely reviewed solely on their merits alone; fascination and even obsession surrounds directors, actors, and various personalities, providing an indication of who is 'in' and who is 'out.'[3] There is a presumption that readership, whether of a journal, magazine, or blog, will share the perspective of a given author in regards to cachet or hipness. Thus, even if cachet informs much of film criticism, few authors have the meta-perspective to unpack its operation.

Here I present several instances where authors have endeavored to directly parse or consider the importance of cachet. I present these chronologically, even though there seems no theoretical progression in the understanding of cachet and its function. Cachet may be a slippery area, but one deserving further analysis.

Discussion of 'hipster cinema' dates to 1966 when Thomas Kent Alexander wrote an essay on 'San Francisco's Hipster Cinema,' published in 1967 (Alexander 1967: 70–74), that examines experimental filmmakers including iconic queer filmmaker Kenneth Anger. Anger's presence in Alexander's list reinforces a notion of queers in the arts having special cultural significance. Alexander's use of the word 'hipster' denotes the Beat generation, the experimental New American Cinema of the 1960s, and a secular humanism that was a reaction to a 'mechanized, depersonalized [...] society' (Alexander 1967: 70). Anger's presence here strengthens Alexander's countercultural posture. According to Alexander, 'Being aware and keeping cool are the essential qualities of being hip' (1967: 70). These qualities are vague and amorphous, but Alexander clearly connects his notion of hipness to queers and other outsider artists, not to the mainstream.

The academic publication record during the 1970s through the 1990s occasionally employs the word 'cachet' in passing, and the expression 'cultural cachet' appears periodically. There is little cultural analysis that directly addresses the topic until 2002, with Melissa Anderson's 'Candied Glam: The Cultural Cachet of Candy Darling.' The title is full of theoretical promise, but Anderson neglects to precisely define what she means by 'cachet,' instead presuming an implicit understanding of 'cachet' as a form of cultural and media literacy. Anderson discusses the 'knowing nod' to archetypal images and the 'underground' and 'self-made' star system of Andy Warhol (Anderson 2002: 60). The 'knowing nod' here is an indication of insider knowledge and coded signs to audients who are in-the-know. These signs include 'glamour that both lauds and smartly critiques the excesses' (Anderson 2002: 64) of Hollywood and tributes that 'delicately balance homage with irony' (Anderson 2002: 67). Revealingly, 'Candy masters the discourse of excess – an idiom spoken and recognized by the shrewd devotee' (Anderson 2002: 68). Anderson implies that cachet is a quality understood by an elite, educated audience. The 'knowing nod' and the 'shrewd devotee' are valuable concepts, elucidating the connection that cachet makes to an intended insider audience.

John Leland's 2004 book *Hip: A History* endeavors to unpack hipness but lacks academic rigor. Leland uses influence on popular culture as a guiding principle. 'In judging what is hip and what is not, I've sided with things that shaped or predicted whatever came next' (Leland 2004: 2). Consequently, Leland looks not to subcultures, but rather to how the American mainstream has been influenced and makes mass cultural valuations. 'Everybody knows what hip is. Or at least, everyone can name it when they see it. For something that is by definition subjective, hip is astoundingly uniform across the population' (Leland 2004: 4–5). Leland name-drops Thelonious Monk, Lou Reed, Andy Warhol, Jack Kerouac, Miles Davis, Bob Dylan, Kim Gordon, and other predictable but meaningless examples. Ultimately the book favors the adoption of black culture by whites, a true but safe narrative that limits the definition and discussion of hipness. 'Hip represents a dream of America. At its best, it imagines the racial fluidity of pop culture as the real America, the one we are yearning to become' (Leland 2004: 6). Leland indulges a clichéd confusion between hipness and ethnicity, tracing hipness to the adoption of African American culture by whites, and propagating a narrative that couches hipness in nationalist and racial terms. Leland's use of mainstream popular culture as a rear-view mirror to evaluate hipness contrasts starkly with Alexander's countercultural favoritism. David E. James adopts a more flexible approach.

James' 2009 article 'L.A.'s Hipster Cinema' acknowledges the meaning of 'hipster' is 'presently in flux.' James says it refers to 'consumers of indie music and film' whom he characterizes as largely working in 'the city's multiple culture and infotainment industries' (2009: 57–58). According to James, the term carries a 'derogatory implication of [...] appropriation of the accoutrements of various post-punk and hip-hop cultures combined with the refusal or avoidance of whatever real social contestation these might have entailed.' This nuanced working definition allows James to critique audiences as well as films, and to analyze irony, ambivalence, signs, and commodities.[4] While this definition is geographically specific and may fall out of date, its simultaneous connotation as a compliment and as an insult is quite brilliant. More work needs to be done analyzing cachet, its impact upon filmmaking, and producing a precise working definition. Nevertheless, there is enough foundation to bring the discussion of cachet into the world of film music and music supervision.

Cachet can be created through existing membership, insider knowledge, references, or allusions that are appreciated by a target audience. Indications of membership in a select group can give a director cachet;

a film by Gus Van Sant or Todd Haynes, who are openly gay, may have a built-in audience of gay men. Araki indicates in *The Living End*'s 2008 DVD director's commentary that the film was made for an audience of himself and his friends, and is therefore a film by a queer for queers (Araki 2008). Insider knowledge of what music is currently favored by a target audience builds cachet, whether or not a director is a member of a target audience. Some films may bear an entirely contrived cachet, based upon insider knowledge rather than a director's actual group membership. (*Fellini Satyricon*'s [1969] homosexual master–lover–slave triangle may be a classic queer film sequence that hits all the right marks even with a heterosexual director.)

Perception of cachet depends upon whom a director is trying to reach. In the early 1990s, the time period of *The Living End*, music that resonated with youthful angry urban queers would be different than, for example, music that resonated with youthful urban Sunset Strip metalheads. Cachet is highly specific to the target audience, but still a pervasive concern to business, marketing, and production. Music supervisors and filmmakers look for tracks with cachet, but those tracks will differ based upon the particular project.

Effectiveness

'Effectiveness' is another vital part of the cachet–budget–effectiveness triangle. Given that cachet relates to music's resonance with an informed *audience*, effectiveness relates to music's resonance with a *particular film itself*. Effectiveness is a subjective measure of reaction to picture or narrative cueing, or how music bears an *informed relationship to onscreen action and characters*.

Such a measure as 'effectiveness' has a long-established history in the analysis of film music. Composer (and erstwhile theorist) Aaron Copland listed ways that 'music serves the screen,' including establishing time and place, psychological refinements, and giving theatrical build-up and finality to scenes (Copland 1949). Claudia Gorbman, in her seven 'principles of composition, mixing and editing' (Gorbman 1987: 73) provides analytical tools for examining film music from the 'classical Hollywood' period. Gorbman's literary background and perspective give nearly all her principles a dramatic intent, such as narrative cueing or signifying the presence of emotion; these principles would fall into the definition of 'effectiveness' outlined above. Gorbman also identifies the principle of 'continuity,' as does Copland, that provides 'formal and rhythmic continuity,' particularly between shots and transitions.

This continuity principle falls outside my definition of 'effectiveness.' Gorbman's principle of 'unity' considers repetition and variation that will aid in 'the construction of formal and narrative unity' (Gorbman 1987: 73).

This type of formal unity is a concern for directors and music supervisors. Formal unity could encompass stylistic markings of genre (this is a horror film), but also thematic constructions that help identify the film's score as belonging *uniquely to that film* (this is *Night of the Lepus* [1972]). As repetition and variation occur on both small and large scales, from minimalist cell structure to overarching form, Gorbman's 'unity' principle is broad and musically vague. But on either the small or large scale, formal unity can be satisfied by any music that is not necessarily otherwise 'effective' by my definition. If a music supervisor places music that is all from the same narrow genre, say speed metal, into one film, picture cuts are bridged and generification of music easily establishes unity for the film, but that soundtrack may lack sufficient variety to be dramatically effective. My definition of 'effectiveness' gives more weight and value to music that reacts to onscreen narrative and dramatic elements of cinema, rather than to purely visual elements like cuts and transitions. *Any* type of music can bridge cuts and transitions; the purpose of music in visual transitions is *not* to follow the action, but to *smooth* it out over jump cuts. As long as a film has a stylistic musical direction, music that simply bridges visual transitions is easy to select, because any will suffice.

Anahid Kassabian notes that soundtracks establish 'affiliating identifications' 'by mobilizing popular musics to tap emotions and associations that audiences connect with the musics before they ever enter the movie theater' (2001: 85). This is certainly a valid justification for music in film, but it does not describe what I call effectiveness; in some ways it is closer to what I call cachet. It is valuable for an audience to identify with and feel affinity for a film, and indeed this can be achieved through music. 'Affiliating identifications' are about informed connections to preexisting audience sentiments, rather than dramatic efficacy within the unexpected world of the motion picture in question.

My definition of effectiveness may be flawed; much film score music, particularly that used for continuity and generification, is useful and idiomatic without being 'effective' by this definition. But acceptance of my definition, even for the sake of argument, will allow further analysis and insight into music supervision and music placement as indicated by the cachet–budget–effectiveness triangle.

Budget

The last component of this triangle is budget. Budget is a major concern in niche market cinema; many filmmakers have entered production simply because, among other things, it is cheaper than ever to do so. Digital video has enabled 'do it yourself' projects, often with questionable appropriation decisions. Music budgets now often fall below catering or craft services budgets. Consider independent narrative films like the *Eating Out* franchise (2004–2012), discussed later in this chapter. Such films may be shot over eighteen full days with cast and crew, easily bringing catering or craft services costs into thousands of dollars, yet composers can be offered nothing whatsoever.[5] Often music is not budgeted at all until production is complete; in many cases films are financed along the way, and there exist a number of grants and competitions for 'completion funds' (Frameline's Completion Grant, for example, on whose jury I served in 2008). In these situations, often no provision was made for a composer, and a filmmaker's music options become narrower, especially if there are festival or screening deadlines to be met. In these cases, licensing preexisting, prerecorded music becomes the simplest, most attractive option. While an inexperienced or upcoming composer is usually cheaper than licensed popular music, this route involves degrees of uncertainty and complications for a filmmaker. The filmmaker opting for a composer at this stage is forced into another collaboration, more meetings, more reviews, with unpredictable and unguaranteed results. Often the filmmaker's cleanest, simplest solution at this point, outside of using generic library music, is to choose from inexpensive musical tracks solicited through a music supervisor.

The triangle and the New Queer Cinema

These concerns, budget, cachet, and effectiveness, can be examined within the context of the New Queer Cinema. B. Ruby Rich wrote in *Sight and Sound* that '1992 has become a watershed year for independent gay and lesbian film and video' (Rich 1992: 30). Rich cites *Edward II* (Derek Jarman, 1991), *The Hours and Times* (Christopher Munch, 1991), *Swoon* (Tom Kalin, 1992), *The Living End* (1992), *Poison* (Todd Haynes, 1991), *Young Soul Rebels* (1991), and others as part of this wave, and certainly these films pushed the envelope of queer exposure, artistry, and independent thought. These films were made by both new filmmakers, like the young Gregg Araki, and by established filmmakers, such as Derek Jarman and Isaac Julien, who were fostered through a British cultural establishment concerned with maintaining artistic relevancy on the international stage.[6] Rich's article itself became an important critical and academic touchstone as an alert to a major shift in recognition granted to queer cinema by the mainstream. The name she coined, 'New Queer Cinema,' stuck, adopted by critics, audiences, and scholars in both the popular sphere and academia. Rich continued to write about queer film, and in 2013 Duke University Press published her monograph *New Queer Cinema: The Director's Cut*, containing twenty years of writing and reflection upon the genre.

Queerness itself has a potential for a special relationship with cachet. Because queers routinely form communities that are outside the mainstream culture, queerness readily creates heightened modes of cultural cachet. Queer people have long identified through different cultural institutions and appreciations; these are shifting associations but historical examples might include opera, musical theatre, Barbara Streisand, Billie Jean King, Madonna, and Judy Garland. To identify as queer, or to discover 'closeted' queers, has long been achieved through identification with objects that have cachet within queer culture. Consequently, the New Queer Cinema is an ideal subgenre with which to examine cachet.

Kassabian notes that *Desert Hearts* (Donna Deitch, 1985), a lesbian love story that predates the New Queer Cinema, uses song selection to both build and identify its potential audience:

> Those particular relationships between perceivers and songs help listeners identify with the lovers through our own memories of learning about our sexualities [...] By bringing memories, with their associated emotions, from audience members' unconsciousness and consciousness, it both particularizes Cay and Vivian's relationship and provides particularizable paths of entry for identification. And, since Patsy Cline – two of whose songs are used in the film – has a wide following in gay and lesbian communities, it manages to address two distinct audiences – heterosexual and lesbian – along different lines at the same time. (Kassabian 2001: 73)

Songs by Patsy Cline would be known by a general audience but would bear a particular cachet among lesbians in 1985. Cline's music holds another layer of associations and meaning for the in-the-know lesbian audience; this 'knowing nod' indicates to lesbians that the film is made especially for their enjoyment and benefit.

Production styles in the New Queer Cinema varied, as did their budgets and financing sources; the New Queer Cinema was more a result of zeitgeist or coincidence than a concerted campaign. Within the production and business contexts in which each of these films existed, low budget was the norm, and budget-conscious techniques such as guerrilla filming were common. Julien's *Young Soul Rebels* was well financed in comparison to Araki's *The Living End*, but for a film that BFI and Channel Four Films intended to compete internationally, it was made within tight financial constraints. These New Queer Cinema films were unified not by style, but by the way disparate gay and lesbian voices were newly noticed and heeded, and by the way their powerful, edgy content surmounted obstacles placed by restrictive budgets. None of these films had Hollywood stories or budgets, but they all managed to impact a wider culture. Some of these films used composers, and some used soundtracks comprised of licensed songs. As music is an integral part of cinema, it deserves study in this group of films. Furthermore, the budget and means of securing music is a relevant part of their history.

In her article on the 'New Queer Cinema,' Rich's only mention of music is in regard to Laurie Lynd's short film *R.S.V.P.* (1992). The film has very little dialogue; instead, a recording of iconic soprano Jessye Norman's rendition of the aria 'Le Spectre de la Rose' from Berlioz's *Les Nuits d'été* is broadcast across Canada, uniting various survivors of a man who died of AIDS. Norman has cachet as a 'diva' idolized by gay fans of opera; she is further imbued with outsider status by virtue of being an African American singer in the predominantly white world of opera. Although Norman's aria is central to the film, Lynd, according to Rich, did not ask for permission to use it until *after* the film was completed. Lynd had already made a film, *Together and Apart*, in 1988, so it is unlikely he would be ignorant of clearances. Therefore Lynd, perhaps only interested in festival screenings for *R.S.V.P.*, was happy to pay nothing and use what music he liked. (*R.S.V.P.* premiered at the Toronto Film Festival.) While Lynd gets all three, cachet, budget, and effectiveness, this exception proves the rule, since Lynd bypasses budgetary constraints by simply completing the film without music clearance.

Isaac Julien's *Young Soul Rebels* was one of the first feature films to deal with the intersection of race, sexuality, black people, and black culture in Britain. The film had a healthy budget of £1.2 million, financed through the British Film Institute and Film Four International with government subsidies (Julien and MacCabe 1991: 20). Executive producer Colin MacCabe recounts, 'Without subsidy, I say, we would never be making a film by a young black film-maker' (Julien and MacCabe 1991: 21).

While this may be true, Julien had nevertheless already directed the successful BFI film *Looking for Langston* (1989) (winner of the 1989 Teddy Award at the Berlinale), so the £1.2 million was not risked on an unproven director.

Young Soul Rebels is a period piece based around popular music, in particular disco and soul music from London nightclubs. Director Isaac Julien explains how music is central to the film's depiction of 1977, and how it is politicized within the film's setting of time and place.

> Now everybody knows about [...] 'punk,' which was at its height in 1977 [...] But there was another counter narrative, much disdained by the left; which was the growth of a black popular culture particular in terms of disco music – soul music. All the left had to say was that disco music was part of the capitalist music industry and that one should adopt the punk ethic of dismantling it. (Julien and MacCabe 1991: 1)

Julien further discusses the cultural significance of this marginalized soul music and how it was situated within British culture of the time. The music holds importance beyond being a mere soundtrack. Julien connects the music to the very themes of the movie.

> Because there were no real examples of the signifying practices of black British culture in the dominant media, the youth movement had to do it by connection with the soul music from America often through the medium of Pirate Radio. Of course, with Soul II Soul, we take all that for granted now, but in 1977 it was hard to get hold of this black American music. It was difficult to find icons, but the reinvention started around that music, opening up a space for a whole number of transgressions – both sexual and racial: these were the first clubs with black and white, straight and gay mixed in the audiences. That political and cultural element had never been figured in the dominant medias and I was determined to make people feel how exciting the moment was. (Julien and MacCabe 1991: 2)

This specific Pirate Radio soul music was necessary to tell the story Julien wanted to tell, and to delve into the 'transgressions' that fascinated him. MacCabe agrees, 'the soul clubs of 1977 must have been as crucial a space as Isaac Julien describes [...] and the film-maker and all the cast and crew must have realized that space for others' (Julien and MacCabe 1991: 13). But despite the *stated* importance Julien and MacCabe give to music, when it comes to MacCabe's discussion of theory as it relates to their film, music is surprisingly overlooked.

In a section of the published production diaries discussing auteurism and elements outside the script, Colin MacCabe neglects to mention music. I find it striking that this 'digression,' a lesson on history and theory, forgets music, which otherwise seems so important to the filmmakers. MacCabe itemizes a sample list of example elements beyond the script: 'The Cahiers critics were concerned to challenge the prevailing dominance of the script in French movies by stressing those elements – shot sequence, lighting, performance – which made up the specific elements of the experience of film' (Julien and MacCabe 1991: 47). Likewise, there is little discussion of the role or importance of the composer; indeed, at one point in the production, Isaac Julien seems to prioritize the film's composer beneath the film's hairdresser:

> [Executive Producers Ben Gibson and Colin MacCabe] obviously gave Nadine [Marsh-Edwards, producer] a hard time today in relation to the music – Colin pushing for [composer] Simon Turner and me pushing for Courtney Pine. I wasn't at that meeting, but still at least things are getting done. But my main worry is the hairdresser: who's going to be cutting the actors' hair – we've got to get a good black hairdresser. The hair cuts the black soul boys had in 1977 are very particular. (Julien and MacCabe 1991: 25–26)

Julien's suggestion that the hairdresser is more important than the composer may in fact be related to timing; when a motion picture goes into production, finding a hairdresser is a more immediate concern than finding a composer, who is not necessarily needed until post-production. Yet there is something telling in the way Julien recounts this anecdote. Music is given high importance when Julien describes the film and its impetus; but that importance only refers to the *cachet-laden historical music of the 1977 time period and culture*, not to newly composed original music. What is important to this film is not music per se, but rather the *cultural cachet* behind selected tracks.

These particular tracks have important cultural resonance to a specific community whose stories and experiences are the centerpiece of the film. That cultural *cachet* is the filmmakers' desired object, *not* music itself as an absolutist abstraction.[7] The film's healthy budget gave it a privileged position that enabled the acquisition of the desired period popular music. The film has music that is both effective and full of cachet, but it was not acquired cheaply. Three music supervisors, Bonnie

Greenberg, Ian P. Hierons, and Jill Meyers are given prominent credits in the film. Music clearances are credited to Media MusiConsultants. There are nineteen songs licensed in the film, including tracks by prominent artists Parliament, Funkadelic, Sylvester, War, and X-Ray Spex. While *Young Soul Rebels* is perhaps low budget by Hollywood standards, the budget nevertheless adequately covered the exact music the filmmakers wanted. The result is music that is effective, full of the appropriate cachet, but not cheap.

In contrast to the well-financed *Young Soul Rebels*, Gregg Araki's *The Living End* was made for a humble $20,000 (Duralde 2008). This film makes for fascinating study with respect to the budget–cachet–effectiveness triangle analysis, especially when its budget is contextualized by other independent films of the same period. *Reservoir Dogs* (Quentin Tarantino, 1992) was made for $1.2 million, even less than *Young Soul Rebels*. While *Reservoir Dogs* is certainly not New Queer Cinema, it is a benchmark for successful art-house cinema of the time. Other New Queer Cinema films had significantly smaller budgets than *Reservoir Dogs* that nevertheless exceeded that of *The Living End* by five to ten times. Todd Haynes' *Poison* had a $250,000 budget, and an original score by James Bennett (Vachon 2006: 41, 46). Tom Kalin's *Swoon* had a budget of over $125,000, and also had an original score by James Bennett (Vachon 2006: 56–57). Gregg Araki's completion of *The Living End* for the comparatively paltry sum of $20,000 must be considered a remarkable achievement in low-cost feature filmmaking. This was achieved through cost-cutting measures such as 'guerrilla' filming (filming without location permits), borrowed equipment, donated labor, and a minimal crew.

Despite a minuscule budget, Araki crafted a remarkable and controversial film that provoked a strong audience response to the suggestion that since gay men with AIDS were abandoned by society and doomed to early deaths, they were also in a privileged position to challenge, attack, and rebel against society. By way of context, in the early 1990s there was no cure and little effective treatment for HIV or AIDS, and little governmental political will or resources to change that. It was a time of great queer anger and activism, exemplified in groups such as ACT UP and Queer Nation who were especially active in urban centers such as Los Angeles. Araki's vision raised moral and ethical questions that were pertinent to the lives of gay men. It was very easy for audiences at the time to extrapolate the larger implications of the film.

In terms of genre, *The Living End* is a buddy movie, outsider film, and road movie all rolled into one. Luke is the strange outsider who arrives unexpectedly and changes everyone's life. He and Jon are young HIV-positive men who become buddies and lovers. They go on a petty crime spree and on the lam for murdering gay bashers and a cop. Their road trip from Los Angeles to San Francisco and back is enabled by a stolen credit card. The film is an argument against passivity with far-reaching implications for gay men, suggesting that if one's days are numbered, one is free to do whatever is pleasurable or necessary for survival. This argument was extremely powerful among gay men who had little help or sympathy from the existing political and social structures of the time.

Araki's edgy, low budget feature typifies the cachet–budget–effectiveness triangle in its musical soundtrack, where budget and cachet are prioritized over effectiveness. The music is nearly all preexisting tracks that resonate with an informed audience. These tracks were acquired cheaply. According to the film's producer, Strand Releasing executive Marcus Hu, the music licensing 'was primarily done gratis or with token amounts' (Hu 2012).

But these tracks often fail to serve onscreen action. In two aspects, bridging transitions and representing subculture, the tracks work well. In moments of real high drama, they fail or are not used at all. The tracks successfully connect successive scenes and smooth choppy picture edits, fulfilling Copland and Gorbman's continuity function, helping to pull the viewer through the film. The tracks also represent queer urban subculture, helping the intended audience to identify with characters, and to situate the film outside mainstream cinema and inside queer culture. These tracks furthermore situate the film outside an older, dated, gay 'clone' culture; they characterize the film's anti-heroes as young and radical even within the larger gay community. In regard to unity, continuity, and audience identification, the tracks work well. However, in scenes where there is action, a fight, a gun is drawn, a conflict unfolds onscreen, the static tracks are unable to accent hit points or follow the overall shape of the scene. In these scenes, the music fails to support the drama, or is simply left out. In these narratological aspects, the music is ineffective.

The soundtrack features music by KMFDM, Coil, Drance, Babyland, Psychic TV, Chris and Cosey, Biohazard, and other music from the underground queer industrial scene. The music is a compilation of tracks predominantly by artists on Chicago-based industrial label Wax Trax! or bands based in Araki's Los Angeles locale. The composer credited on the film, Cole Coonce, was in the Wax Trax! band Braindead Soundmachine based out of Los Angeles. The film's screen credits include the line, 'Benevolent music gods: Matt Adell and Jim Nash at

Wax Trax!' Jim Nash (1948–1995) was the founder of Wax Trax! and Matt Adell was a staff worker at the label, known for its American domestic releases of industrial music (Reed 2013: 233–51).

Additionally, the film makes visual or spoken references to Joy Division, Revolting Cocks, Nitzer Ebb, Echo and the Bunnymen, and the Smiths. These popular bands had gay followings, and references to these bands serve as signs or cultural markers to the target audience. These acts would have been far too expensive to license, so they appear in the film either visually or through dialogue. Araki uses music as coded markers for his audience; the junction of music and cachet emphasizes character associations and positions the film inside urban queer culture.

The industrial music placed in the film has been carefully chosen. Araki himself knew this music from queer industrial nightclubs popular in Los Angeles at the time. He considered this a personal movie not made for a wide audience (Araki 2008). He self-identifies as being part of 'gay culture' and 'post-punk industrial subculture,' as well as having worked in the late 1980s as a music critic at the *LA Weekly* (Araki 2008). Araki easily falls into the 'L.A. hipster' identity outlined by both Thomas Kent Alexander and David E. James, and, given his own credible background, Araki is perfectly positioned to identify appropriate tracks for his queer niche market.

The connection between dance music, and music generally, to subculture and marginalized subcultures has been widely noted. 'Evolving dance cultures [have] provided a new generation of mostly young people with a focus for the construction of their own particular forms of identity and community' (Luckman 1998: 45). 'Music is one of the more powerful vehicles for expressing marginality culturally, to the extent that musical characteristics have come to define certain cultures' (Fikentscher 2000: 8). Others, including Sarah Thornton and Fiona Buckland, have studied the importance of club music to queer culture. 'As the objects of repetitive hearing in clubs, these tracks became the vehicles for a vast range of private and social associations and for individual and social memory' (Buckland 2002: 75). Music represents identity for many in the queer community; it is natural that club music would be an integral part of Araki's film's world.

Industrial club music, while identifiable as a cultural artifact, has certain musical features. It tends to be 4/4, beat-heavy, and to make use of pronounced distortion in vocals and sonic textures. In *The Living End*, most of the music falls within 126 to 132 bpm, a reasonably allegro tempo. Industrial music connects to synthesizer-driven, experimental new wave through such bands as Cabaret Voltaire, early Human League, Ministry, and Skinny Puppy; going back further, this electronic new wave connects to earlier 1970s electronic disco, notably through Georgio Moroder, Telex, Sparks, and Mi-Sex. Industrial club music favors electronics, drum machines, and synthesizers, but also various percussive or sustaining noise elements; these can be of acoustic or electronic origin, including anything from power tools to tapes of found sound. If there are guitars, for example in KMFDM's 'Go To Hell,' they tend to be heavily distorted and compressed, as vocals frequently are. Stephen Mallinder of Cabaret Voltaire, an iconic Sheffield industrial group, describes the genre:

> We made music that was often sonically brutal, we challenged ideas of authority and control, we toyed with moody and often taboo imagery, we were simultaneously intellectual and anti-intellectual, we thought ourselves iconoclastic [...] The recording studio became the most valuable writing tool; tape machines, effected voices, 'treated' instruments, tape loops, and drum machines. Song structures and linear arrangements were abandoned [...] The music was intended to be primal, visceral, and provocative. (Mallinder 2013: ix, xi)

Another important aspect of the industrial dance music chosen by Araki is its connection to the gay scene and gay activism around issues of AIDS, a major thematic concern of *The Living End.*

Drance, a Los Angeles band co-founded by Robert Woods and John Munt, has two songs in the soundtrack. Robert Woods died of complications from AIDS in 1995. Drance performed at Club Fuck! and other venues that catered to a queer, 'modern primitive,' industrial clientele, often involved in activism. Drance was well connected to the gay scene, the industrial scene, the activist community, and to Araki personally. Keyboardist and songwriter John Munt recalls:

> Drance was based in the Silver Lake area of L.A., and was part of a group of other bands at the time based in Silver Lake and nearby areas: Extra Fancy, Ethyl Meatplow, Glen Meadmore, Babyland [...] Drance was connected to the queer scene in L.A. in that we were a completely 'out' gay band, we played at benefit shows for ACT UP and Queer Nation, and many of our shows were performed at gay bars/venues. We played at clubs like Sinematic, Club Fuck!, and Ground Zero that were quite industrial-music heavy. (Munt 2013)

Michael Matson, who took production stills and publicity shots for *The Living End*, dated Gregg Araki and moved in the same circle as Drance. Matson recalls the Silver Lake community:

Robert [Woods] rented a one-bedroom apartment in a fourplex building in Silver Lake [...] Fuck! was held in the space that was originally the Black Cat, which had been turned into a gay Latino club called Basco's at the time and was located just a few blocks from Robert's apartment. Silver Lake's gay bar scene was primarily leather and S&M themed. The aesthetic of these clubs appealed to the ACT UP and Queer Nation types more than the West Hollywood scene [...] Silver Lake was a mix of working class Latinos, young activist and artistic gays, straight underground music and culture aficionados. And quite a few of its residents were participants of the Modern Primitive movement. Next door to Robert's apartment was Being Alive, which was a non-profit organization assisting people with AIDS and HIV. (Matson 2013)

Matson explains the history and connections between Gregg Araki, Drance's Robert Woods, industrial music, the Silver Lake nightclub, Club Fuck!, and Miguel Beristain, one of that club's founders.

Gregg was a regular patron of an 'alternative' club Robert Woods was a DJ at in Long Beach in 1990. Gregg would go and dance all night to the primarily industrial music Robert played (Nitzer Ebb, Front 242, Cabaret Voltaire, Chris & Cosey, Nine Inch Nails, Scraping Foetus, Ministry, Skinny Puppy, etc.) mixed with L.A. Punk, '70s rock, and always Depeche Mode (Robert's favorite band) [...] Gregg was living on the lower west side of L.A., and Robert was in town all the time hanging with the people who would go on to create Fuck!, so he would often drop me off or pick me up from Gregg's apartment. Gregg came with me to a party at the Fontenoy apartment building in Hollywood where Miguel Beristain lived. These parties were the precursor to Fuck!. Gregg would come to Drance shows. (Matson 2013)

The Living End strikes a radical, activist tone in its message against complacency and government conservatism, and Drance likewise had connections to the activist community in Los Angeles.

We played at least a handful of benefit shows for ACT UP and Queer Nation. Robert Woods and many of Drance's inner circle were very involved in these activist groups. (Munt 2013)

Munt further explains how these politics were incorporated lyrically into Drance's music.

Drance, especially Robert Woods, was very sexual and pushed for shock value in performances – this seemed to go along with the rebellious and hard-partying, sexual, performance artist nature of that time. Also, Robert had HIV/AIDS and wrote songs about sexual taboos. Many of the lyrics were about sex, and the stigma of 'safe sex' at the time, concepts of sex, HIV, and push-back against the government and society's view of HIV. (Munt 2013)

The aggregation of this activist stance, social connections between Araki and Woods, the cachet and audience affinities already in place within the industrial genre, all amplify the inclusion of Drance's music in *The Living End*. Given the personal connections, there might have been an opportunity for Drance to customize music specifically for the film. However, this did not happen. Band members did not work with Araki to modify, remix, or rewrite their tracks for greater effectiveness. 'There was no scoring to picture by Drance, and [the tracks] probably were edited for the film by Gregg, his editor, or whoever laid the music into the film' (Munt 2013). The preexisting tracks were used as an off-the-shelf commodity that could be cheaply and easily accessed. Munt recalls, 'I don't believe Drance was paid anything for the music usage' (Munt 2013). Matson summarizes the band's business strategy:

Drance did not have any management or a manager [...] Robert and Brandy both dealt with legal issues, as best that I can recall. Both filed legal documents, such as ASCAP [writer and publishing registration forms], but they never retained a lawyer. Drance was not a money-making venture. We were all middle class kids from the suburbs who became involved in Los Angeles' vibrant punk scene of the late 1970s and early '80s. All we wanted were creative lives with integrity. You could do that in Los Angeles back then. Rents were cheap and there always seemed to be plenty of work that you could live off of. (Matson 2013)

While Araki had local friends and compatriots who could help supply music, he also used music by acts of international stature. Coil, an English duo on the Wax Trax! label, is another act appropriately chosen for the film's soundtrack. The band Coil was 'one of the first to be based around a gay male couple' (Larkin 2006), and their music explores lyrical themes including 'religion, sexual freedom, and alchemy' and includes a '17 minute eulogy to "male sexual energy"' (Larkin 2006). Their songs include 'The Anal Staircase' and 'Penetralia.' 'with lyrics based almost entirely upon the duo's Satanic homosexual practices' (Hayes 2006: 9). These particular songs are not used in the film, but they help to contextualize Coil's popularity in queer industrial nightclubs and the band's inclusion in the film's soundtrack. Even if Coil's unique history is unknown to a target audience member, the musical style and its nightclub associations are clear and recognizable.

For creating social associations and lasting social memory, Araki's music choices were solid. According to Alonso Duralde's 2008 *Advocate* review of the DVD reissue of *The Living End*, the 'dark and driving post-punk soundtrack [...] has never sounded better' (Duralde 2008). This music is in fact now quite dated and sounds exactly the same as it did in 1992; Duralde really means to say that the music is still recognized for lasting social associations and memory. It defines a period and a subculture. Araki says:

Music has always been a really big influence on me [...] It's really super inspired by a lot of the post punk music I was listening to at the time. In fact the whole attitude of the film is very industrial music, very this kind of angry kind of post-punk kind of sound to it. Also there's certain lines of dialogue in the film that are directly quoted from lyrics from songs. [...] That whole period I was very, I am still very much influenced by my CD collection. (Araki 2008)

Even if the music is dated and ineffective in its response to onscreen action, it still carries cachet, implicit and explicit meanings, and significance for the filmmaker and audience. The cachet and significance are adequate for the music to support the film, even if narratological effectiveness is wanting. For Araki, in this film, it is less important that the music underline narrative action than it is for music to define and authenticate the film for the audience. Araki discusses how musical influence manifests itself even to the level of the script, with overt lyrical references.

This line that Luke says [...] 'it's living inside me,' that's actually also from a Jesus and Mary Chain song, I think off *Psychocandy*.[8] I was very, very influenced by a sort of British, post-punk music and also industrial music when I was making this film and also *Totally Fucked Up*. (Araki 2008)

Araki uses music to establish characterizations and provide direction to actors. Preexisting musical tracks with the proper cachet and subcultural associations are ideal for this purpose, functioning as a sort of temp music to inform actors in the same way temp music might inform a composer.

Craig [Gilmore, who plays Jon ...] was talking about how I made him a cassette tape of a bunch of British bands of that time, and gave him lyric sheets. I was talking about how that music was so important to his character. And I remember also when we did *The Doom Generation* I did the same thing for [actor] Jon Schaech. I remember he really wanted to listen to music for his character. So I made him a cassette tape back in the days when people made mix tapes. (Araki 2008)

Araki explains his characters to an insider audience through music. As a result, his audience identifies with them; the cachet of the music builds audience identifications, understandings, and affinities with the characters, as well as, by extension, the film overall. In this way, the cachet of the chosen music serves to create identity both for the characters in the film and for the audience itself. Even if the music is narratologically ineffective, it still holds power in characterization and audience identification.

This considered and deliberate use of music does not necessarily mean that it will help the film dramatically, however. While insider music helps build audience sympathies and identification with characters, its dramaturgical effectiveness is another matter. While *The Living End* excels in using music to target its audience, the placement of music is often fudged. It often appears as a wallpaper backdrop for dialogue and action, and its relation to onscreen narrative is tangential.

As for 'spotting' – the selective positioning of music within film – *The Living End* employs music in a consistent fashion, frequently diegetically, often ostensibly or explicitly tied to automobiles or car stereos. It is mostly used as a 'bed' that does not react to onscreen action. In some cases, it covers or obscures dialogue. In some dramatic scenes, music is either unsuccessful in making a relevant contribution, or it is not used at all.

In an early scene in a nighttime parking lot, three fag-bashers wielding baseball bats attempt to attack Luke, who shoots them in return (DVD, Chapter 3, 0:14:30). There is no music, just creepy sound effects: the buzz of the parking lot lights, the metallic clang of the bats. While some theorists have correctly argued for a liminal space between music and effects, whereby the identity or function of either is blurred, there is a clear distinction within the production process of *The Living End*. These sound effects were recorded or laid in by the filmmakers, whilst the music was licensed; those preexisting tracks occupy a distinct space within the soundtrack. A theoretical approach whereby sound effects and music are interpreted as sharing the same sonic or ontological space may be tempting, but is not evidenced by the production process used in *The Living End*. In this scene, a conventional approach using music would have added tension to the scene *before* we see the actual threat. This approach has been called a 'sound advance'; it pulls us forward across a visual cut into the next scene (Buhler et al. 2010: 18). Underscore used in this manner would have been highly effective in this instance. Instead, in a similar fashion, we hear offscreen dialogue, 'Prepare to swallow your teeth, faggot,' *before* we see the three bashers. This dialogue, spoken before the picture cut to the actual threat, offers the same benefit that a musical 'sound advance' would, drawing us forward into the scene following the visual edit.

As the bashers advance on Luke, music could have easily heightened the tension. Luke draws his pistol and replies, 'Guess again, fucking three stooges.' This dramatic turn could have been emphasized by a responsive, dramatic underscore. The bashers freeze momentarily as we see, from Luke's point of view, Luke's pistol vacillating between the three assailants, whom Luke then shoots, one of whom while fleeing. This dramatic scene would not have worked with an accompanying bed of nightclub music, so music is left out. The audio track is simply dialogue and effects, with no music to underscore or emphasize the full narrative importance of the scene. Music begins later as a kind of eerie diegesis in Jon's passing car, which Luke flags down in fleeing the scene. Here the music seems a strange, disassociative calm, Jon's world, ambivalent, grooving on down the road as simple background noise.

Araki relies further on the device of tying music to car radios. After Luke kills a cop, he and Jon drive to San Francisco. In one of many driving scenes, music appears diegetically, and, as happens on a number of occasions, is referenced specifically *in dialogue* (DVD, Chapter 5,

0:35:50). Luke, driving as Jon is trying to rest, complains of the music, 'Man that stuff is putting me to sleep.' He changes the cassette tape, selecting a louder, more aggressive track. Jon responds passively and sarcastically, 'Thanks for the nice relaxing nap music,' making the music part of the narrative. The interchange highlights the self-centered, thoughtless aspect of Luke's character, as well as defining him as the more aggressive, dominant 'alpha' male in the relationship. But in order for this licensed source music to have narrative importance, it is explicitly mentioned in dialogue. This music is effective narratologically by being discussed and used as a tool of characterization.

The film has awkward balances of music, dialogue, and effects. In a montage of a spending spree fueled by a stolen gold card (Figure 2.3), music gives the film a push forward, even as it covers some unessential dialogue (DVD, Chapter 4, 0:25:10). This music, initially seemingly non-diegetic, carries over into the following scene, a confrontation with a homophobe, where the source appears to be revealed as Luke's portable 'boom box.' Here the music obscures important dialogue, but does not significantly add tension to the situation. In this instance, music fails to support the dramatic intent of the confrontation scene. The music has cachet and helps to bridge the visual cuts, but has little effectiveness beyond that. When Luke attacks the homophobe (offscreen and slightly reflected in storefront windows) the music is momentarily pumped louder, adding a little bit of chaos, but also obscuring sound effects that would otherwise more clearly inform the viewer of an altercation. Here the soundtrack fails to support the dramatic narrative; an original score composed to picture could have handled this situation more effectively. Changes in volume and chaos could have been written into the music; space for dialogue could have been planned in advance; original music could have been tailored to emphasize the arc of the scene from threat to altercation to escape. As it is, changing volume in the final sound mix attempts to mimic what could have been easily executed with original music.

Changing the *volume* of music, in an effort to compensate for lack of musical *reaction*, occurs elsewhere in the film's audio track. When Luke shoots an uncooperative ATM, music is again tied diegetically to the getaway car (DVD, Chapter 9, 1:08:47). Music begins after Luke's gunshots, under a ringing alarm and a prominent sound effect of tires screeching. The music bridges a brief cut to black, and then a cut to the car interior. The music continues through the dialogue, and turns off with the car engine. During this sequence, several 'rides' are made to the volume level of the music. While an original underscore would

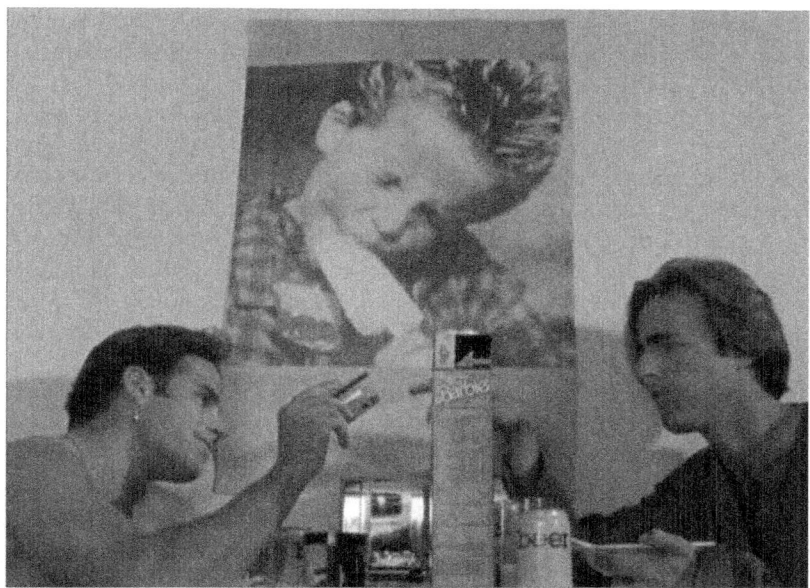

Figure 2.3 *The Living End*. Gold card, Smiths poster, Barbie cereal, and Ralphs Grocery generic beer

likely have had such changes musically composed as part of the cue, in this case there is an attempt to fix the static quality of the track by 'riding' its amplitude in the mix. This is a common technique in the application of source music, but it is not as effective as an original score composed to picture. The sound mixer knows what is happening onscreen and tries to compensate for that; the songwriter of the licensed track does not. This disconnection, which usually starts out in sync but gets progressively worse, has not gone unnoticed by audiences or academics.

> Pop song cues match visual tracks quite easily at their entrances, but very rarely do they continue to match tightly. While such sequences could, for example, use music-video-style rhythmic visual editing, or could structure a sequence precisely to follow musical structure or lyrics, such breaks with continuity editing are rarely permitted. Because continuity editing is so inviolable, pop soundtracks have an aleatory quality – the songs have only a very loose fit with the visuals. (Kassabian 2001: 80)

This 'loose fit' with visual and narrative elements is, I argue, both evidence of and symptomatic of lack of effectiveness on the part of the music.[9]

Carey and Hannan note that 'Although the use of previously recorded popular songs does not allow for precise synchronization with already-edited film, the reverse process of shooting and cutting the film to the music can be just as effective' (Carey and Hannan 2003: 169). There are successful examples of this technique, but it is especially difficult to achieve in action sequences or sequences with many sharp dramatic turns. It is possible that *The Living End* was edited to music, my criticisms notwithstanding, but this would not be apparent simply because the music is so static in intensity and dynamics.

In the film's final scene, Luke has tied up his boyfriend on the beach and rapes him while holding a pistol in his own mouth (Figure 2.4), with the clear and presumably real intention of killing himself during his last moment of sexual gratification (DVD, Chapter 11, 1:18:00). The scene plays out with no music and only minimal dialogue. It contains no nudity but is nevertheless graphic. Licensed music from songs would

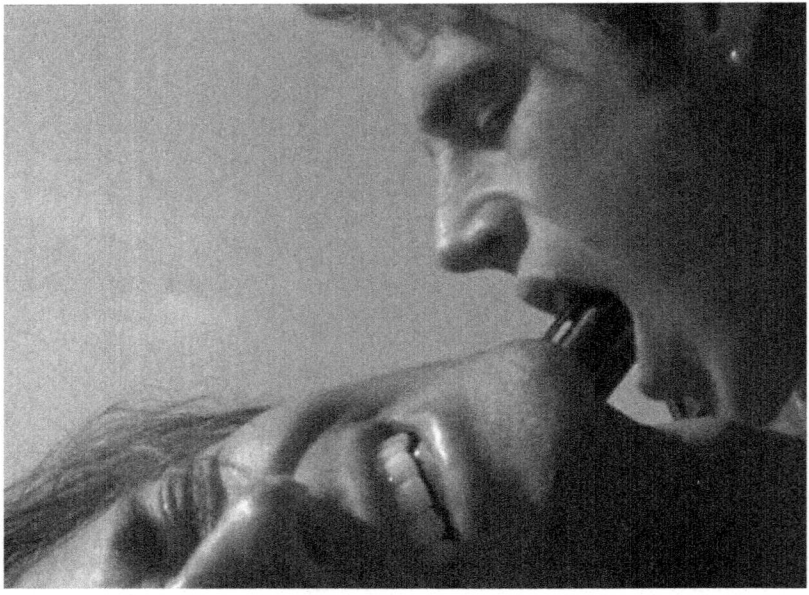

Figure 2.4   The Living End. Rape sequence

have destroyed this cinematic moment, and so music is left out alto-gether. The industrial music which otherwise so successfully character-izes *The Living End* would have been far too distracting to support this dramatic ending.

It might be argued that music in *The Living End* was not used in dra-matic scenes in order to maintain realism and diegesis, giving the film a heightened reality of the kind later espoused by the Dogme 95 move-ment. However, this does not seem to be a consistent goal of a film that also includes humorous interruptions for whimsical prop jokes (the squeaky toy in the shape of a butt, 00:09:50 DVD) and gratuitous walk-ons (a man in a shopping cart pulled across the visual field from his collar by a leash, 00:10:20 DVD). In opting to use only industrial club music, the filmmakers removed the option to have an effective dramatic underscore. They simply left music out because it was an expedient choice: given the budget and stylistic musical approach, no licensed songs could possibly have satisfied the dramatic topography delineated by the narrative. The only viable solution was to omit music from the greatest dramatic moments of the film.

It might also be argued that the sourced club music is effective in set-ting appropriate tone, making sage lyrical references, and acting as suit-able mood music, all of which might constitute preferable approaches to mickey-mousing dramatic scenes. But such an argument subjectively privileging source music over mickey-mousing rejects the traditional dramatic possibilities and responsibilities of musical underscore. Music in cinema today frequently accomplishes less and less as it becomes a highly repetitive wallpaper, but this is hardly cause for celebration. If music does not 'know' what is going on onscreen, merely being appro-priate in tone and mood does not make it effective, but only a static backdrop that matches the other décor of the film.

Araki's film illustrates a situation where cachet is favored over effectiveness as a result of budgetary constraints, and this production scenario continues today in queer cinema and other niche markets. This is highly problematic artistically and for the advancement of new composers. Audiences less and less expect to hear reactive, informed music, and filmmakers feel less and less compelled to hire and pay composers for their services. Two examples of recent practices will serve to illustrate this.

Q. Allan Brocka is a successful film and television writer and director in the queer niche market. His work includes the *Eating Out* franchise, *Boy Culture*, and the *Rick and Steve* animated series for Logo television. In 2011, Brocka posted on Facebook (Figures 2.5 and 2.6) soliciting music

Q. Allan Brocka
Singers/Bands – looking for pop, alt rock, dance and R&B tracks for our soundtrack – no pay but great exposure to boost your itunes sales!
14 hours ago · 💬 7 👍 7 · Like · Comment

Figure 2.5   Soliciting music

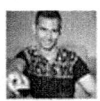

Q. Allan Brocka
It's not too late to have your music featured in Eating Out 4 & 5. No fees but great exposure. Email eocrew@gmail.com for further info.
May 3 at 4:34pm · Like · Comment

Figure 2.6   Soliciting music

for *Eating Out 4* and *5*: 'Singers/Bands – looking for pop, alt rock, dance and R&B tracks for our soundtrack – no pay but great exposure to boost your itunes sales!' (Brocka 2011a), and three months later, 'It's not too late to have your music featured in Eating Out 4 & 5. No fees but great exposure' (Brocka 2011b).

Brocka is not the only prominent queer filmmaker to look for free music. Canadian filmmaker Bruce LaBruce revealed that DVD reissues of his earliest films from the early 1990s were hampered by the fact that he had used music at the time without securing clearances (LaBruce 2011). LaBruce soon learned to get music clearances for his films ahead of time, but still routinely prioritized budget and cachet over effectiveness. By the mid-1990s this became LaBruce's standard practice. In 1993, I produced the album *Hot Horny & Born Again* for Los Angeles performance artist and musician Glen Meadmore, who had a part in Bruce LaBruce's 1996 film *Hustler White*. For the film, we allowed Bruce to use three tracks from the album in *Hustler White* without charge. Handsome Boy, a Canadian label distributed by BMG, offered to release a soundtrack CD. They offered, in exchange for a 'perpetual worldwide license,' no advance, a 1 percent royalty rate for two songs, and the stipulation that 'the method of payment, calculation of royalties, royalty base and all other pertinent information [...] shall be set forth in a more formal agreement to be executed at a later date' (Eastwood, 1996). These terms were not favorable to the artists, and their offer was rejected by all the musicians involved. We didn't mind Bruce using the tracks because we loved his work, but the BMG connection seemed suspicious.

In 2010, I supplied another track for Bruce's *L.A. Zombie* (2010). This was a track I already had lying around, and Bruce was not particular. I offered to score to picture, but his preference was to use finished, existing tracks at the lowest possible cost. This enabled him to cut in music to his liking at low cost without direct involvement from a composer. Composers can be seen as outside interference by directors, who otherwise consider music an off-the-shelf item. This simplifies things for the director but also reduces the dramatic possibilities of the musical soundtrack.

Filmmakers with low budgets routinely opt for music that has cachet but does not enhance their film dramatically. Music 'blind' to onscreen events will not be effective in relation to visual narrative. If the narrative contains many turns and hit points, licensed *dramatic* music will be difficult to synchronize, so directors will favor licensed music that is relatively static and prolongs an appropriate mood. It is expedient to favor repetitious music or 'mood music' over more dramatic music that could create difficulties in editing and synchronization. Music Araki chose for *The Living End* is appreciated years later for defining a precise moment in the queer community, rather than for its dramatic flair.

My notion of effectiveness accepts rather than rejects the concept of spectatorship. The audience are indeed viewers, and calling them 'listeners' or 'perceivers' is dogmatic but elides the presence of the visual. My notion of cachet allows for audience identification, affiliations, and various intertexts. Cachet signifies objects and histories *external* to the film, whilst effectiveness signifies or represents relationships to objects or narratives *within* the film. My triangle sets these two concerns, effectiveness and cachet, in opposition or in balance, depending upon budgetary constraints.

This music supervision triangle easily extends beyond New Queer Cinema to other niche market cinema. But there are consequences to favoring club music or other preexisting tracks, beyond reducing the effectiveness of the soundtrack. Filmmakers risk their films becoming dated if they rely solely on music that speaks to a niche audience at a particular point in time. As tastes change, source music can become quaint or retro. Films without an effective score can suffer from less dramatic impact overall, not just in particular scenes. A soundtrack of licensed music can also be predictable, robbing a film of its individuality, or giving it the musical diversity of an infomercial. Nevertheless, notions of cachet still drive directorial decisions regarding music selection, supervision, placement, and licensing.

3
Brokeback Mountain Music

Debate and perspectives

Ang Lee's *Brokeback Mountain* (2005) has generated a storm of critical response, from scholars and writers including B. Ruby Rich, Dave Cullen, D. A. Miller, William Handley, Ara Osterweil, Eric Patterson, Daniel Mendelsohn, and many others. The film has garnered defenders, detractors, apologists, and proponents, who have unpacked everything from script, production design, and cinematography to marketing and advertising. Several books are devoted entirely to the film.[1]

Academic readings reveal problematic biases in the film and narrative; consider *Film Quarterly*'s special issue on *Brokeback Mountain*.[2] From a progressive standpoint, *Brokeback Mountain* is not queer film; it fails to buck convention, other than refuting the invisibility of homosexuals. Its perspectives, audience payoffs, inspiration, and morbid conclusion fail to fulfill the queerness of the scenario. Ara Osterweil notes, 'tragedy need not necessarily have been the outcome. There are alternative, less generically conservative modes of affect available, especially considering that *Brokeback Mountain* is set during the peak of Underground Cinema' (2007: 38–39). Vito Russo, author of *The Celluloid Closet*, would have included *Brokeback* in his 'Necrology' catalogue of homophobic films in which gay characters must die (1981: 261–62).

On its surface, *Brokeback Mountain* appears to be a gay-positive film. Certainly, from a Hollywood perspective, *Brokeback Mountain* is unusual in its choice of subject matter. Two gay men serve as protagonists in what is structurally a cross between 'buddy' film and melodrama. However, closer readings of the film reveal a stereotyped, heteronormative vehicle. D. A. Miller notes:

Far from bringing its public together in compassion or tolerance, as some have suggested, the film diligently solicits, in all their fractiousness, the main divisions of American opinion [...] under one aspect or another, it lends support to virtually all the conflicting positions, attitudes, and judgments that make it so thrillingly – and bankably – contentious. (2007: 50–51)

This does not deny the film's influence. Numerous authors, including Patterson, Cullen, and Handley praise the film. Cullen's *Ultimate Brokeback Forum* website has collected numerous stories from audience members deeply touched by the film, some claiming the film has changed their lives. But by 2007, Rich, who was at first enthusiastic, recognizes: 'sophisticated gay men in urban enclaves complain of conservatism and retrogression, a soppy package wrapped around an out-of-date stereotype' (Rich 2007: 48).

One aspect of *Brokeback Mountain* that has not been sufficiently examined is music. While many scholars have studied music in Western film, including Kathryn Kalinak, Neil Lerner, and Peter Stanfield, musical analysis has not been carefully applied to *Brokeback Mountain*. I posit that musical tropes of Gustavo Santaolalla's score reveal an unprogressive perspective that portrays Ennis as an antisocial character, emphasizes a fixation on stasis and death, and perpetuates stereotypes of loneliness and tragedy.

I begin with a look at the film's generic context, then hone in on the underlying story, the screenplay adaptation, and D. A. Miller's notion of 'craft' or production value, and their relation to the score. I then focus on music: the use of improvisation, minimalism,[3] repetitive structures, Western tropes, the use of diegetic music and singing, as well as descriptions of the score as 'elegiac' by composer and director. As a coda to this analysis, I look at how the Hollywood establishment and popular press have cast Argentinian composer Santaolalla as an outsider, effectively 'queering' the composer through astonishing racial profiling. These circumstances add a complexity to his participation in the film, recalling musicologist Susan McClary's indictment of women composers who fail to challenge the status quo in their own scores (1991: 19).

Western genre context

Brokeback Mountain is ostensibly a Western, but also fits neatly into the genre of classic Hollywood melodrama (Kitses 2007: 26–27). The Western aspect might be superficial, but the film's marketing, plot, and situations depend upon its Western context. D. A. Miller argues that the Western tableaux function as window-dressing to seduce audience sentiments (2007: 50–52); Santaolalla's guitar-heavy score contributes to this seduction.

Popular film genres establish audience expectations and aid in the marketing of studio product. These genres are presented through the exploitation of conventions that audiences readily recognize. In the Hollywood Western, these conventions typically include depictions of cowboys, settlers, horses, prairie, as well as stereotypes of masculinity and femininity, and various musical markers like folksong.[4] Particular narratives and themes are also associated with the Western: the tale of the outsider or outlaw, the taming of the wilderness, and stories of personal freedom, independence, and self-determination.[5] Many of these depictions and themes are exploited in *Brokeback Mountain*.

Film critic and cultural theorist B. Ruby Rich initially credited *Brokeback Mountain*'s (heterosexual) creative team with having 'queered' the Western.

> With utter audacity, renowned director Ang Lee, aided and abetted by legendary novelist-screenwriters Larry McMurtry and Diana Ossana and master storyteller Annie Proulx, have taken on the most sacred of all American genres, the western, and queered it. (Rich 2005)

That is a bold claim, as queerness came already built-in to the Western genre, a point that has been argued by scholars and critics including Richard Dyer, Vito Russo, Carl Freedman, and others.[6] Rich herself noted:

> Critics [...] have already begun to build on the obvious, informing readers that westerns were already gay; there has already been a rush of wanton nomination as genre favorites are reconsidered. (Rich 2005)

But Rich saw *Brokeback Mountain* as surpassing homoerotic subtexts that had already existed in the Western.

> *Brokeback Mountain* goes much further, for it turns the text and subtext inside out and reads the history of the west back through an uncompromisingly queer lens. Not only does the film queer its cowboys, but it virtually queers the Wyoming landscape as a space of homosexual desire and fulfillment, a playground of sexuality freed

from judgment, an Eden poised to restore prelapsarian innocence to a sexuality long sullied by social shame. (Rich 2005)

A playground of sexuality? Hardly. *Brokeback Mountain* was made with a deliberate ignorance of the joyful homoerotic possibilities of the Western genre, featured in other films such as Andy Warhol's *Lonesome Cowboys* or Madonna's 'Don't Tell Me' video.[7] Even though Westerns fostered an image of rugged, manly, American machismo, they were also home to homos, both in terms of innuendo and casting. Consider the innuendo as Montgomery Clift and John Ireland compare guns in *Red River* (1948); consider the casting of homosexual actors, particularly Rock Hudson (in *Gun Fury* [1953], *Horizons West* [1952], *The Lawless Breed* [1953], and others), Tab Hunter, Anthony Perkins, and William Haines. Even the televised 2006 Academy Awards ceremony presented a tongue-in-cheek montage of Western movie highlights in the romanticized style of queer 'slash' fan videos that mash up visual images to create or magnify homosexual and homoerotic moments.

Despite such recent attention, queer content is not the imagination of today's scholars, nor a creation of 1970s feminist critics, but was perceived as early as the silent film era. Kathryn Kalinak discovered period reviews that observed the dominance of the chemistry between men in *The Iron Horse* (1924), John Ford's idealized tale of the construction of the transcontinental railway. This silent Western's protagonist, Davy Brandon, a surveyor and railway proponent played by George O'Brien, befriends and bonds with an Irish laborer, Dinny, played by Jack O'Brien.

While *The Iron Horse* clearly privileges the heterosexual couple, it cannot quite contain the eroticism circulating around the men in the film. The passion of Davy and Dinny's reunion at the joining of the rails (Davy, bare-chested, embraces Dinny, and for one brief moment it seems as if the two will passionately kiss) surpasses anything transpiring between Davy and Miriam. Even reviewers in the 1920s noted something unconvincing. (Kalinak 2007: 39)

One of the conventions of the Western is a rugged ultra-masculinity so strong and pure, through its rejection of all things feminine, that it ultimately *preferences homosocial behavior and norms above opportunities for active heterosexuality*. Such extreme images of masculinity may have appealed to preadolescent boys in the audience who were still not developmentally ready to relate to their female counterparts. According to critical theorist and scholar Carl Freedman, 'In many instances, the truth of American macho turns out to be an aversion to women, shading into a fear of feminine sexuality, and a concomitant emotional commitment to the "male bonding" of masculine friendship' (2007: 18). As macho as the Western genre may be, it fosters a masculinity so extreme it leads to the creation of homoerotic or homosocial environments. As Freedman describes it:

> Active heterosexuality can never be fully masculine [...] To act on heterosexual desire necessarily removes a man from the sphere of pure masculinity, shackling him to the feminine. For a man to want and to actively seek a woman is to confess that masculinity is incomplete, and he thereby places himself [...] under womanly power. (2007: 19)

Freedman parses presentation and image of masculinity in Western film, carefully analyzing that icon of masculinity, John Wayne. During the height of his career, Wayne's characters were infused with an ultra-masculinity that created an ironic sexual and social identity. The constructed masculinity of John Wayne's roles and cinematic persona exemplify 'post-heterosexuality,' a hypothetical stage of male development beyond sexuality with women.

> The typical John Wayne character carries no significant suggestion of same-sex eroticism, but is not sexually involved with a woman either. He is a man with a heterosexual *past*, who has outgrown that phase of existence and so is free to glory in his unalloyed masculinity without being suspected of the least abnormality. (Freedman 2007: 19)

Post-heterosexuality shows that mainstream studio Westerns created characters and spaces that fell outside of normative heterosexuality. John Wayne is not merely post-heterosexual, but he is allowed to be so with *impunity*. This impunity contrasts starkly to the harsh consequences for non-normative sexuality in *Brokeback Mountain*. Freedman's calling heterosexuality a 'phase of existence' is a humorous twist on the old bromide that homosexual 'tendencies' in adolescent males were only a 'phase.' In many John Wayne films, heterosexuality is a phase that younger, weaker males must pass through before they can attain 'post-heterosexual' masculine strength that can withstand feminine wiles. While Wayne's characters lack significant homoerotic development, the rejection of heterosexuality in itself suggests a queer space in these Westerns. They often revel in creating exclusively male spaces similar to those presented in *Brokeback*.

While *Brokeback* adheres to melodramatic structure and pathos, it is the Western genre that influences the score. The obvious, symphonic scoring style frequently associated with classic Hollywood melodrama is eschewed in favor of smaller, sparse, restrained, guitar textures and improvisations. While many classic Hollywood Westerns are known for their symphonic scores,[8] *Brokeback* is better considered a 'postmodernist western.'[9] Santaolalla's score neatly evokes Western conventions while satisfying the expectations of a contemporary audience.

Script, pre-production, and music

In relating *Brokeback*'s script to its music, I wish to emphasize three points. First, the script to *Brokeback Mountain* is fiction; it is pure fantasy, based upon a short story by Annie Proulx, first published in 1997 in the *New Yorker*. Secondly, the music adopts only the viewpoint of the script itself; it does not offer any external commentary, humor, irony, or meta-perspective. It does not wink at the camera or advance its own agenda. Thirdly, the music was composed largely during pre-production from the script itself, not to a rough cut, using conventional Western tropes.

While *Brokeback Mountain* producer and Focus Features executive James Schamus has credits in the New Queer Cinema,[10] the film is nevertheless a pure fiction constructed by a heterosexual writer, a heterosexual director, and two heterosexual screenwriters. While there is nothing inherently wrong with heterosexuals, in this situation a group of them has attempted to tell a story of gay men, someone else's story. It proves impossible for them to surmount an inculcated heterosexist ideology. D. A. Miller unpacks Proulx's 'Homosexual' narrative:

> For to designate the Homosexual here is at once to begin elaborating fantasies of his being harmed: 'a gay is being beaten.' First, the woman envisions the damage that may have been inflicted on him in childhood, then [...] she foresees the danger he runs in adulthood. (2007: 53)

Miller exposes the thematic message of the film as an uncontested vision of gay lives as necessarily tragic. This message is never contested by Lee or Santaolalla, who defer to Proulx's short story as the basis to which everything should be faithful, as opposed to an accurate or unbiased portrayal of gay lives.

'If you read the original short story and you read the [*Brokeback Mountain*] script, you'll see that nothing was lost from the original story,' Santaolalla said. 'You end up totally connecting and feeling for those people.' (Aguila 2006)

Here 'those people' ostensibly refers to the characters in the original short story. Santaolalla fails to mention the inherent difficulties in Proulx's original work.[11] Death and homophobia originate here, in the fictional narrative, and this is never questioned. While the story is poignant, it makes a questionable basis for a feature-length film. It is problematic to pin blame on Proulx, who seems to realize the dilemma: 'Urban critics dubbed it a tale of two gay cowboys. No. It is a story of destructive rural homophobia' (Proulx et al. 2005: 130). However, Proulx wrote this statement *after* the story was already made into a film, so it would be quite easy for this to be an a posteriori position informed by criticism from the queer community. It also begs the question, why does anyone need a story of destructive homophobia? Don't we have enough of that already?

Even before filming began, literary, cultural, *and* musical tropes were already established. Santaolalla began composing soon after getting the script.

Within two weeks [...] he had written ten pieces [...] a collection of free-floating themes and soundscapes [...] Explains Lee: '[...] With Gustavo, what's really unique, the music is basically done beforehand. So I was hearing it as I was doing location scouting, so I kind of built the movie on those pieces of music.' (Gurza 2006)

Delivering music as early as location scouting is unusual, but Santaolalla used a conventional style and instrumentation that neatly fit the story's Western tropes. The film's action unfolds so slowly that long tracks in improvisational form can easily accompany the moving image. These tracks helped Lee visualize the film and guide the actors, further cementing the conventional tropes at play. The score avoids the over-wrought, romantic, symphonic musical clichés of the Hollywood melodrama, but manages to fit the film's melodramatic tropes as well.

Ang Lee [...] told Mr. Santaolalla he was seeking a sound that was 'sparse and yearning,' sent him a script, and two weeks later received a CD [… of] new compositions intended for *Brokeback Mountain*. 'Usually you don't talk about the music until after the first cut,' Mr. Lee said, 'but with Gustavo, I had music for seven scenes while we were still in preproduction, in fact before we had even scouted for locations […] And when the major actors were rehearsing I shared the music with them, to set a tone for what we were doing.' (Rohter 2008)

Music delivered during pre-production helped push the actors into desired terse and tragic interpretations of their roles. If indeed the music is 'laconic' and 'elegiac' as Ang Lee has described it, and was used to set a tone for the acting, then it proves itself as the director's model for the film's intentionally stiff, unhappy performances. Yet despite claims that Santaolalla's score was largely delivered during pre-production, not all the music was composed in advance. Much of it may have been conformed to picture and tailored to director notes.[12] Says Santaolalla:

In the case of *Brokeback Mountain*, Ang Lee knew exactly what he wanted. He has tremendous vision on how to tell a story, and this applies to music. He would direct me like he was directing an actor. It was remarkable working with him. (Santaolalla in Aguila 2006)

Lee and Santaolalla did share a vision for the film as a Western and as a tragic story culminating in death. Proulx's original short story, mediated through Larry McMurtry and Diana Ossana's screenplay, drove the initial musical conception, and those musical tropes were adopted without questioning the heteronormative ideology of the narrative.

Craft and music

Miller argues that it is the production value or 'craft' of *Brokeback Mountain* that makes the film appealing, and that this craft obscures the lack of gay advocacy. 'In a word, the craft of *Brokeback Mountain* is the Closet of the Closet' (2007: 52). Miller argues that audiences are hoodwinked into liking the film because it is *well-made*; a gay man's likely response to the film is to 'forfeit his reputation for taste and mistake a middling piece of Hollywood product for a major work of art' (2007: 50).

Miller discussed the cinematography and stunning Western tableaux as examples of production value. The film was nominated for the Academy Award for Best Achievement in Cinematography. Rich noted the significant use of A-list talent, a point that seems, to Rich, to merit the film special consideration.

[T]here has never been a film by a brand-name director, packed with A-list Hollywood stars at the peak of their careers, that has taken an established conventional genre by the horns and wrestled it into a tale of homosexual love emotionally positioned to ensnare a general audience. (Rich 2005)

Rich's appraisal, predicated by the involvement of Hollywood stars, supports Miller's argument that the film was judged differently than other films because of production value. But 'A-list' talent does not assure a major work of art, and may simply distract from an honest valuation of the film. Consider *Philadelphia* (1993), starring Tom Hanks and Denzel Washington, which used 'A-list' talent in a gay context or narrative; initially considered groundbreaking, *Philadelphia* has not maintained influence or importance.

Just as the Western tableaux function as window-dressing to seduce audience sentiments, Santaolalla's guitar-heavy score contributes to this seduction as part of a net of high production value intended to ensnare a wide audience. The score is a clean, beautiful recording using contemporary studio techniques. It is lush, not a campfire strum. The score won the 2006 Academy Award for Best Original Score, as well as the Golden Globe for Best Original Song; the score was also nominated for BAFTA Best Film Music and Golden Globes Best Original Score awards. These awards and nominations affirm its superior production value and, arguably, its political viability among peers and jurists. The score inspired a rash of other acoustic guitar copycat film scores,[13] a further indication of its mainstream 'craft.' Like cinematography and other aspects of craft described by Miller, the music may be hypnotically beautiful, but it does not advocate for queer empowerment and falls closer to 'Hollywood product' than 'major work of art.' It draws people into the film and creates a subsequent illusion of advocacy.

In this chapter, I wish to focus on Gustavo Santaolalla's original score, rather than the licensed, off-the-shelf source music used in the film. This source music (Tammy Wynette, Allman Brothers, Merle Haggard, Willie Nelson, to name a few) benefited from a healthy music licensing budget and would align with Miller's argument on 'craft.' Andrew Holleran notes the music's placement:

The editing and the score follow a single pattern throughout, alternating the magnificence of the mountain scenery (guitar and orchestra) with the squalor of the men's domestic life (the whine of the country-western songs). (2006: 14)

The placement of country western songs to indoor, domestic settings is a straightforward strategy. Holleran notes the soundtrack 'alternates between the pastoral beauty of Gustavo Santaolalla's theme on the guitar – so spare, so haunting – and the raucous, messy world of the bars' (2006: 15). It is this pastoral beauty and the extensive use of guitar that I wish to further interrogate.

Improvisation

The preponderance of the score is wistful improvisation on acoustic guitar. The extensive use of improvisation could suggest tropes of independence and freedom, as well as position the score in a less generically conservative, more independent or art-house space. Yet Santaolalla's improvisation is what guitarist and author Derek Bailey terms 'idiomatic' improvisation (1992: xi–xii). While it uses a certain degree of musical freedom to generate the music, it conforms to an existing mode of guitar performance, a style of playing and chord voicings that are both idiomatic to the instrument and familiar to listeners. Just as *Brokeback* can be read as an ostensibly 'gay' film but leans more to heteronormative upon closer inspection, the use of improvisation in the score *seems* progressive yet adheres to conservative musical modalities.

As discussed above, Santaolalla improvised extended tracks to create impressionistic pieces for Ang Lee during pre-production. Santaolalla recounts bringing his guitar to an early meeting with Lee (Rath 2005). Presumably, Santaolalla may have demonstrated ideas or improvised on the spot for the director. Lee may have encouraged an improvisatory approach; likely, the director would have been familiar with an earlier art-house Western that used a similar improvisatory approach.

Dead Man (1995), directed by Jim Jarmusch, uses a Neil Young score that is highly improvised. Claudia Gorbman describes the process and the result in *Music and the Western: Notes from the Frontier*.

Jarmusch invited Neil Young to watch the film and improvise to it, essentially responding to the film as he went [...] The score features primarily the lone guitar, the minor-modal tonalities and melodic lines that can be heard in any number of westerns, reaching for the heroic quality of man-meets-landscape – but this western music is electrified, fragmented, its pedigree weakened, attenuated, and in the process exaggerated. (2012: 206–7)

Neil Young's electrified grunting and scratching guitar textures are more adventurous than Santaolalla's pretty plucking. Still, while Santaolalla's improvisatory guitar style could be a 'post-modernist'[14] reaction to actual symphonic Western scores of the Hollywood studio period, the resultant lines and tonalities can be heard in any number of Westerns; this merely indicates how idiomatic the improvisation is. Like Neil Young, Santaolalla is a skilled, tasteful guitarist, but both adhere within established idioms for the guitar as instrument and musical conventions or expectations of the Western.

Use of this improvisational style is an attempt to make the score sound edgy and experimental, while still maintaining its Western coding. Ang Lee intentionally references a different kind of arena by using improvised music, a non-mainstream, avant-garde, art-house cinema. This is intended to add to the credibility of the film, and to position it comfortably for a liberal audience; as Miller suggests, seducing the audience through craft. At the same time this improvisatory feel suggests freedom, the score, without a harmonic or melodic goal or direction, indicates there's nowhere to go, and endless time to get there. Melodies are fragmented, and the fragments rhythmically augmented; harmonic goals are elided or left unresolved. The music negotiates the liminal space between musical development and simply undirected, meandering guitar noodling. Likewise, Jack and Ennis stagnate and meander in life and relationship.

Minimalism, repetition, and Western tropes

Gustavo Santaolalla employs conventional minimalism, repetitive patterns, and standard Western tropes in *Brokeback Mountain*'s wispy, solitary guitar score, emphasizing the rugged Wyoming terrain and the loneliness, sadness, and isolation of Jack and Ennis. Understated simplicity and the predominant use of acoustic guitar mark the score as Western and give it an earthy quality. Joshua Clover and Christopher Nealon describe the score as 'Santaolalla's tragic, organic, pluck' (2007: 65). Tragic subtext in *Brokeback Mountain* is articulated through slow tempos; the 'pluck' is the guitar, and the 'organic' quality is the simple open chords and folksy, plagal progressions.[15] The persistent loneliness of solo guitar is bogged down in lugubrious tempos indicative of lasting depression or insurmountable stasis.

Musicologist Mariana Whitmer describes the conventional use of music in the traditional Hollywood Western, noting its typical functions and deployment within the genre.

> Music [...] defines characters, aurally distinguishing the good guys from the villains; it can control the pacing of the action, and enhance the tension that accompanies confrontations. Music can also lower the threshold of disbelief for a narrative that is chronologically distant from our own experiences, as is the case in Westerns. In addition, music can establish a mood or atmosphere for the particular setting in which the cowboys often find themselves, from wide-open prairie to high mountain range and from dusty town to raucous saloon [...] In Westerns music was particularly necessary for distinguishing the time period and geographic location. (2012: 80)

Brokeback's score does all this. It reflects the film's slow pacing, establishes mood and atmosphere, and reinforces time and geography. If music indeed lowers the threshold of disbelief, I would argue it helps a skeptical audience accept the existence of homosexual cowboys. In these ways, Santaolalla's score functions like a typical Western score, rather than a Hollywood melodrama score that would romanticize and exaggerate internal emotions.

The guitar is a reliable if clichéd Hollywood marker of the American West.[16] The sound is familiar to audiences, and was an easy marker to employ in *Brokeback*. Andrew Holleran noted, 'this is just another middlebrow tearjerker based on the usual stereotype: love that doesn't work out, done with gay men, guitars, and horses' (2006: 14). This sounds like the 'elevator pitch' for the film! Now, who would you get to do these guitars?

Prior to *Brokeback*, Santaolalla had already established a style and instrumental palette that neatly fit Lee's story's Western and melodramatic tropes. Santaolalla describes his musical style for an earlier film, Walter Salles' *Motorcycle Diaries* (2004), as

> 'minimalist, heartfelt and full of space and air' instead of a lushly orchestrated score. 'It's a deliberate choice,' he said. 'I am a fervent supporter of the idea that you don't have to have wall-to-wall music in good films.' (Santaolalla in Rohter 2008)

Minimal and spacious music reflects the open expanse of the cowboy West, the large skies and sweeping vistas so frequently presented in

Westerns. This is a common musical trope that has persisted for decades, widely attributed to the influence of Aaron Copland; Neil Lerner has catalogued a number of sources that credit Copland with shaping this sound and influencing later film composers (Lerner 2001: 479–81). As observed by Lerner, 'recognizable strains of Copland's musical personality are regularly put into the employ of visual narratives. [For example,] The pastoral codes of *Appalachian Spring*, the "Western" codes of *Rodeo*, and the U.S. patriotic codes of the *Fanfare for the Common* Man' (Lerner 2001: 479). Santaolalla's incorporation of this minimalist, spacious Western trope into his film music is highly conventional. The 'heartfelt' qualities Santaolalla indicates fit the melodramatic mood and create an underlying tension to small events.

Santaolalla's playing is poignant and sometime modally ambiguous, suggesting open interpretations, an ambiguity that Miller has noted inhabits the film overall. Slow tempos reflect the slow pace of the movie. The score does establish mood and atmosphere, and reinforces time and geography. It marks the existence of homosexual cowboys not as comedy but as tragedy, as noted by Clover and Nealon.

Elegy and dead space

Interviews with Gustavo Santaolalla and Ang Lee confirm that both men shared a mutual musical vision for the film as far back as pre-production, before shooting had begun.

> As the two men talked, they discovered they shared a similar musical vision for the film. Having read the script, Santaolalla had imagined open landscapes, the spare sound of two guitars, and most important, a silence pregnant with unspoken feelings. (Gurza 2006)

Santaolalla says of the emptiness of the score:

> Silence is something that I love in music, and here I could stretch that even more. In other words, the space you are defining between two notes [...] That is not dead space. That is active space. (Santaolalla in Gurza 2006)

Santaolalla's overt denial of 'dead space' raises three salient points. First, it acknowledges that listeners do perceive this music as static and ponderously slow. Santaolalla's notion that the spaces between his notes contain an 'active' energy is highly personal and contestable. The music simply does not contain enough harmonic tension to create a strong pulling sensation from the standpoint of music theory.[17] Harmonic motion is tediously slow, and vertical structures are relatively simple and consonant.

Second, Santaolalla's word choice of 'dead space' suggests a relation of the score's overall aesthetic to the symbolism of death. Death and stasis are central themes to the film, and to the music as well. The narrative meanings and interpretations of the film spring from the ultimate finality of Jack Twist's death that serves as both a climax (or anti-climax) and a fulfillment of prophecy foreshadowed by Ennis' flashback to a gay-bashing that also serves to justify his paranoid homophobia.

Thirdly, if the space between notes is 'active,' that would suggest that the emptiness of the narrative, with its long silences and lingering shots of beautiful Western tableaux, *also* contains some kind of unstated activity. This activity can only be, at best, an emotional subtext. While it is possible that the audience is highly moved by the film and needs the empty spaces to recuperate, that would only validate Miller's argument that they have been seduced by craft, rather than actual queer friendly filmmaking.

Ang Lee also describes Santaolalla's music in terms relating to death, notably referring to the music as an elegy.

> 'The notes are laconic,' Lee says. 'They are lucid, yearning, and most of all elegiac. That's something you cannot talk about, only feel. Like the mythical West is dead. And he really captured that.' (Lee in Gurza 2006)

It seems unlikely that the death in the film is the 'mythical West;' if anything, Lee works hard to propagate dated Western stereotypes in order to situate the film as a Western genre picture. Rather, I posit that the death in the film is that of Jack Twist. Any elegy would be for Twist and, by extension, his unrequited love for Ennis. Lee's comment seems like a smoke screen, an attempt to deflect attention away from the truth of the film.

Peter Grimes

Brokeback Mountain's opening music bears an uncanny resemblance to Benjamin Britten's first *Sea Interlude* from *Peter Grimes*, with a repetitious, descending semitone motive (Figures 3.1 and 3.2). This similarity is not likely intentional; rather it is a fascinating parallel gesture worthy of

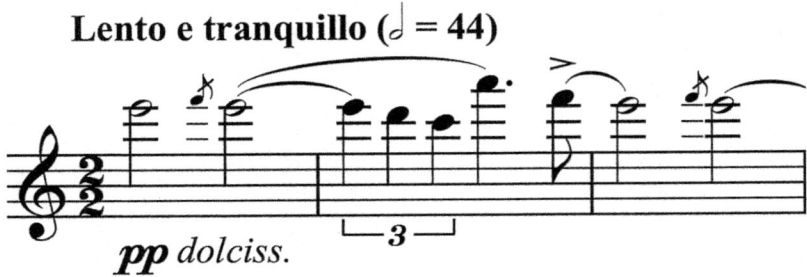

Figure 3.1   Britten *Sea Interlude* I from *Peter Grimes*, mm 1–3

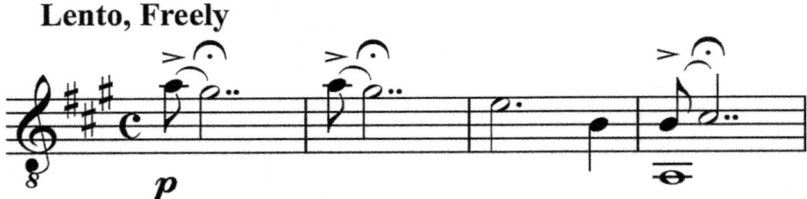

Figure 3.2   *Brokeback Mountain* Opening, mm 1–4. Transcribed by the author

mention, given the tortured nature of the men in both works. Andrew Porter, quoted in Philip Brett's *Benjamin Britten: Peter Grimes* (Cambridge Opera Handbook), says, 'Grimes's inner struggle [...] is against a homosexuality that neither he nor, for that matter, his creator is consciously aware of' (1983: 195). Both excerpts feature a simple, improvisatory feel, relying on repetition to create a feeling of hesitation. Much of film music is based not upon radical ingenuity, but upon the deployment of existing dramatic musical tropes, and this semitone motive, at a slow tempo, with an otherwise wandering melodic contour, seems to imply a restrictive angst present in both works.

Song and diegetic music

The construction of masculinity in the Western is complicated by diegetic music, notably the use of singing. Although singing is a significant part of many Westerns, societal norms dictate that it must be used judiciously in order not to threaten masculinity. Kathryn Kalinak correlates music and masculinity in the iconic Westerns of director John Ford.

> Music traditionally has been associated with the feminine in Anglo culture, causing gender trouble for men who have performed it. And yet, Ford's cowboys sing and his cavalry troops dance without compromising their manliness [...] In a sense, Ford would colonize music for the sound western, making it safe for his male western protagonists to sing. (2007: 46–47)

Kalinak raises an interesting paradox; however, I am not convinced that male singing, in the Western or otherwise, is a 'feminine' activity. It is a preposterous notion that the *act* or *behavior* of singing can be given a gender or promoted as a gender stereotype: both men and women are capable of making music and singing, and have always done so.

Kalinak's paradox can be explained by an examination of performance technique. Ford's cowboys, as well as the significant singing cowboys such as Gene Autry, Tex Ridder, and Roy Rogers, were by and large baritones who did not sing particularly *well*. Their voices were neither operatic nor suitable for Broadway musicals. Their vocals are often gravelly, have poor intonation, or verge on Sprechstimme. When they sing, the message is clear that they are not the sissies of calculated, flamboyant musical theatre. Their singing is not a compromise of masculinity, but typically a *reinforcement* of it, by nature of the quality of voice and the style of performance. While singing cowboys may have been included or designed to appeal to a broad, family audience, as argued by Peter Stanfield (2002: 4), the voice is one that sounds like it belongs to a typical heteronormative male. This is carried forward in the singing styles employed in *Brokeback Mountain*.

Kalinak argues that in the John Ford Western tradition, good guys participate in music, and bad guys or antisocial characters either fail to participate in or disrupt music-making. There has been debate as to who is the 'aggressor' in *Brokeback*'s homosexual relationship, and how well Jack and Ennis fit into broader straight society around them.[18] One way to gauge their socialization is to follow their participation in music, following Kalinak's model, including singing, dancing, and playing of instruments.

Jack Twist plays harmonica at their campsite, which annoys Ennis, who makes occasional disparaging comments about it. Jack Twist whistles and sings along to a diegetic 'King of the Road' while driving his truck. His singing is masculine and his rendition is a rough approximation of the actual melody, in keeping with my description of acceptable Western performance technique. Jack's goodness is emphasized by his willing and easy participation in music.

Jack also sings an a cappella ersatz 'Pentecostal hymn' (Proulx et al. 2005: 17). This is Jack's most significant musical performance in the film.

> I know I shall meet you on the final day
> Water Walking Jesus, take me away
>
> (Proulx et al. 2005: 17)

This hymn is an original composition by Proulx, screenwriter Larry McMurtry's son James McMurtry, and songwriter Stephen Brown (Proulx et al. 2005: 149). Although it is performed in a joking manner (Figure 3.3), the lyrics cast Jack as one who is redeemed in death, foreshadowing his grisly demise at the end of the film.

Ennis has a markedly different relationship to music. He dances with women in bars twice in the film, but does so only awkwardly. In one instance, the script calls for him to sing. In a flashback to 1963, Ennis embraces Jack. Ennis follows these scripted lines of dialogue: 'Come on now, you're sleepin' on your feet like a horse. My mama used to say that to me when I was little ... and sing to me.' The script then instructs: 'ENNIS sings low, a childhood song, from some long-ago memory'

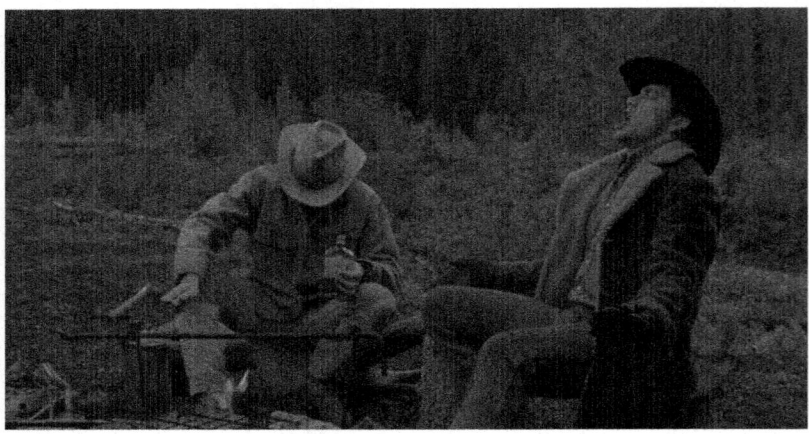

Figure 3.3   Jack Twist sings 'Water Walking Jesus'

(Proulx et al. 2005: 84). However, the line 'and sing to me' is barely intelligible. Then, Ennis does *not* appear to actually sing, and if he does, it is completely covered by the underscore. This effectively negates Ennis' singing specified in the script, or makes it at best some kind of private event, possibly tinged with regression to childhood or to embarrassment.

In fact, Ennis openly professes disdain for singing. His daughter, Alma Jr., implores him, 'Daddy, the church picnic's next weekend. Will you be back from fishin' by next weekend? Can't you take us, Daddy, please?' Ennis replies: 'All right, long as I don't have to sing' (Proulx et al. 2005: 58). This connects singing, church, and family obligations as things that Ennis would rather not endure.

Applying Kalinak's analytical model of music participation to *Brokeback Mountain* emphasizes antisocial aspects of Ennis Del Mar's character. His aversion to music reflects other antisocial behaviors, such as fighting, refusing to attend church, and declining Jack's invitations to build a ranch life together. By contrast, Jack seems the more humane, more loving, and more sincere of the two men. Participation in music depicts Ennis as an outcast, aloof and disconnected, and Jack as a good guy, who is more innocently drawn to Ennis.

The circular ending

The score in the film's ending scene follows a conventional form: conclusion and subsequent transition to credit roll. The audience sees Ennis alone in his trailer with Jack's old shirt. In this final scene, Santaolalla's adlib guitar tune at last settles and solidifies into a rigid, cantabile theme with the addition of supporting strings for emphasis (Figure 3.4).

Like Ennis' trailer interior, the melodic contour of this ending theme exists in a tight, confined space. The strings give a false impression of soaring; the musical intervals stay very close within a narrow range. Its greatest leap is a third, otherwise the tune moves diatonically by step, keeping within the overall range of a tritone. Furthermore, the theme begins and ends both melodically and harmonically in the same place,

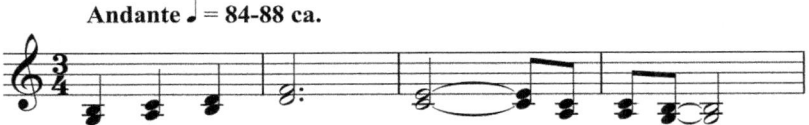

Figure 3.4   *Brokeback Mountain* end theme. Transcribed by the author

so the ends and beginnings blur together. This tight melodic space symbolically suggests entrapment or being stuck. Other notable features are the mixolydian modality and a distinctive snap-rhythm in the fourth bar, which lends a bit of folksy Americana flair.

Ennis' eyes water as he revisits Jack's old shirt and a photograph of the mountain where they met. The music's repetitious, conventional, four-bar phrases vary only slightly, obsessively circling continuously even as the film goes into credits. The music cycles on, a final declaration of the film's compulsive, pessimistic message: it is what it is, and is incapable of changing. The music resolves back to where it starts, the low point of the tune, in the same way that Ennis, who began the film as a lonely, single man, ends the film as a lonely, single man, whose one stab at true love was a doomed failure.

Just as Miller argues that the film 'lends support' to 'conflicting positions,' this ending is likewise open to multiple interpretations. Ennis has agreed to attend his daughter's wedding; this can be seen to represent his reintegration into life as a decent family man, or as a final mockery of his own failures in love and relationships. The music reinforces a sense of 'timelessness': the Ennis of 1984 is older but not much different from the Ennis of 1963. And musically there is certainly no modulation to victory; the score is beautiful but as musty, worn, and static as Jack's old shirt.

Race and music

There is a further complication in considering the *Brokeback* score, and that is a strain of racially inflected criticism leveled at Argentine composer Santaolalla. This criticism is relevant because, in many respects, as an outsider and unconventional personage in the Hollywood entertainment industry, there is something 'other' about Santaolalla himself. This criticism has appeared in published commentary and profiles, adding context to popular perception of the score. It has been reported that Santaolalla 'doesn't read musical notation' (Barrera 2005), a charge often leveled, accurately or not, at many popular Hollywood composers such as Hans Zimmer and Danny Elfman (Wright 2006: 1032–33). This dismissive claim seeks to marginalize composers by attacking their foundational musical skill and expertise. Some commentary on Santaolalla goes beyond attacking his talents, and reveals startling biases in comments having little or nothing to do with his music.

The *New York Times* ran a brief commentary by Santaolalla himself about how he was checked at airport security for bringing his large, metal, British Academy of Film and Television Arts Award for *The Motorcycle Diaries* score as a carry-on item (Santaolalla 2005). While the *Times* piece does not address racial profiling, it raises questions about editorial selection. If the *New York Times* has the opportunity to run a piece by a prominent, award-winning composer, why is the topic a light, fluffy story about going through security? While it is a charming anecdote, it does not say much about Santaolalla or his music, and reduces him in stature to a guy carrying a suspicious metal object. The mistaken-identity joke (is he a security threat or an honoree?) is the driving force behind the piece; Santaolalla is saved by a manager who recognizes the BAFTA award, but it is the *award* that is recognized, not Santaolalla.

The Oscar nominee profile of Santaolalla in the *Los Angeles Times* begins, 'The affable fellow washing dishes by hand at the sink is not somebody's South American houseboy' (Gurza 2006). While ostensibly this article paints a portrait of the composer as a casual guy who does his own dishes and has 'no manager and no full-time publicist,' the obvious implication is that he is not from the establishment, and would be mistaken for a Latino houseboy.

Santaolalla's ethnic, racial, and national identities are relevant here because of the irony that a marginalized composer would create music that propagates the marginalization of gay men. Rather than recognizing and challenging *Brokeback*'s stereotyping, Santaolalla's music furthers it. Musicologist Susan McClary aptly describes this situation, writing of women composers: 'they are fully capable of deploying the entire range of the semiotic code they have inherited [... but] they still face the problem of how to participate without unwittingly reproducing the ideologies that inform various levels of [...] discourses' (1991: 19). McClary suggests that women composers ought to examine the premises of established conventions, so as to create new meanings, rather than prolong existing stereotypes. Santaolalla's music fulfills existing heteronormative ideological expectations for *Brokeback Mountain*. Even so, he is still castigated as an outsider, a 'South American houseboy' type who cannot read music, who would suspiciously bring a metal object onto an international flight.

Conclusion

I do not think that there was any *conscious* intention on behalf of the filmmakers to make a dated, homophobic movie. However, music exposes choices that belie common prejudices and stereotypes. The pristine recording matches the beautiful cinematography and scenic vistas, all of which is a glossy veneer of craft. With the score consistently sad, tragic, and lonely, *Brokeback Mountain* remains open to any *unhappy* interpretation, reinforcing Miller's position that the film lends support to every fractious opinion about homosexuality, but most of all, that there is no happiness for queers. Miller says 'erotic disappointment may well be the only genuine homosexual response to *Brokeback Mountain*' (2007: 50). Likewise, the music is sad, perhaps even sensual, but never sexy.[19]

One could argue that the music supports a reading of the film as tragic tale of homophobia meant to appeal to a broad audience and encourage empathy and understanding. But I believe that in an *unintended* way, the innocence and simplicity of the musical score also reflect the naïveté of the creative team in the manufacture of an unintentionally backwards, biased film. The filmmakers had plenty of opportunities, and perhaps even an obligation, to subvert, expand, or push the genre in a more radical way. They failed to do so.

In a manner of poetic justice, this failure is being rectified by a community of gay men who reinterpret *Brokeback Mountain* through fan fiction. By doing so, they are turning *Brokeback* into an accidental, but *innately homosexual*, camp classic; like *Star Trek* 'slash' fan fiction that romanticizes and eroticizes an imagined requited relationship between Kirk and Spock, the fans are able to turn Jack and Ennis from tragic homosexuals into *actual* queers, 'queering' the 'gay' movie. Oddly enough, this has not sat well with Annie Proulx, who is not amused.

> I wish I'd never written the story. It's just been the cause of hassle and problems and irritation since the film came out. Before the film it was all right. [...] [U]nfortunately the audience that 'Brokeback' reached most strongly have powerful fantasy lives. And one of the reasons we keep the gates locked here is that a lot of men have decided that the story should have had a happy ending. They can't bear the way it ends – they just can't stand it. So they rewrite the story, including all kinds of boyfriends and new lovers and so forth after Jack is killed. And it just drives me wild. [...] I can't tell you how many of these things have been sent to me as though they're expecting me to say, Oh great, if only I'd had the sense to write it that way. And they all begin the same way – I'm not gay, but ... The implication is that because they're men they understand much better than I how these people would have behaved. And maybe they do. But that's not the story I wrote. Those are not their characters. The characters belong to me by law. (Proulx in Cox 2009)

Poor Annie Proulx, suffering the indignity that her story has taken on a life of its own, subsequently subjected to notes, fixes, corrections, and script doctoring by hoards of gay men! But this is the way of popular culture; the original artifact has been optioned, adapted, and, given its popular success, fallen into the public space of fan culture. Like a Kleenex, whose registered trademark has become genericized, it has become a product in which anyone who so desires can blow their nose as they please.

There is another complication with stories like *Brokeback Mountain*, and that is an audience attraction to tales of misfortune and woe. Heather Love's *Feeling Backward: Loss and the Politics of Queer History* describes a phenomenon whereby queer people relish a retrograde sob story; much of queer literature (Radclyffe Hall's *The Well of Loneliness* or James Baldwin's *Giovanni's Room*) indulges a desire for tragedy or self-pity. So, why not allow queers to indulge themselves in one more tragic tale? After all, *Brokeback*'s tragic failure implies the beautiful possibility that *could have been*; it allows the thwarted love to be perfect, rather than the more likely scenario that, for example, Jack and Ennis would buy that ranch together, start diddling one of the ranch hands, struggle with a gradually souring open relationship, and go through a bitter divorce after seven years, arguing over the rodeo belt buckles. In light of Love's ideas on loss and queerness, Santaolalla's score seems perfectly fitting for the story of rural homophobia and the failed love of Jack and Ennis, camp icons waiting to be resurrected and healed through the magic of fan fiction.

Ang Lee, despite employing music that uses extensive improvisation, was ultimately less concerned with underground cinema than with conventional genre tropes. The music in *Brokeback Mountain* reveals a conservative perspective that allows the male couple little joy, happiness, or fulfillment in their sexuality, relationship, or life. While the music is beautiful and part of the high production value of the film, it represents stasis, meandering, and solitude. As reappraisals and debate over *Brokeback Mountain* continue, musical analysis will be a necessary part of the discourse.

Part II
Fighting the Patriarchy: Dykes, Misogyny, and Gender Fear

4
A Tale of Two Walters: Genre and Gender Outsiders

This chapter contrasts the histories of two transgender film composers, one English and one American, who each began life as 'Walter' and who each finalized male-to-female gender transition through surgery in the difficult time period of the early 1970s. These composers overcame marginalization and other obstacles to have a significant impact in mainstream media.

Angela Morley (1924–2009) was born Walter ('Wally') Stott in Leeds, England. Morley built a reputation as a skilled composer of 'light music' or 'easy listening' and worked as a conductor and arranger on many albums for Philips Records, including Scott Walker's seminal solo albums. In 1970, Morley underwent what was then called a 'sex rectifying operation' (Gaughan 2009). Morley moved to the United States following her surgery to begin a new phase of her life and career. Morley assisted John Williams in orchestrating *Star Wars* (1977), *Superman* (1978), and *The Empire Strikes Back* (1980). Morley composed original scores for *Watership Down* (1978)[1] and for the television series *Dallas*, *Dynasty*, and *Falcon Crest* in the 1980s and 1990s. She won three Primetime Emmy awards and was nominated for two Academy Awards, for *The Little Prince* (1974) and *The Slipper and The Rose: The Story of Cinderella* (1976).

Wendy Carlos (b. 1939) was born Walter Carlos in Pawtucket, Rhode Island. Carlos built a career as a proponent of the Moog synthesizer, having a hit series of themed albums beginning with *Switched-On Bach* (1968), the first classical recording to reach 'Platinum' sales in the United States (Pinch and Trocco 2002: 131–32). Rachel Elkind, Carlos' 'silent partner' (Carlos 2001), produced Carlos' albums and the two shared a creative partnership from 1967 to 1980. Carlos underwent 'sex change' surgery in 1972, following 'hormone treatments' that began in

1968 (*New York Magazine* 1979: 65; Bell 1979; Pinch and Trocco 2002: 137). Carlos, still credited as 'Walter,' composed and arranged the score to Stanley Kubrick's dystopian *A Clockwork Orange* (1971) adapted from Anthony Burgess' novel. Credited finally as 'Wendy,' Carlos composed music for *The Shining* (1980)[2] and *TRON* (1982). Carlos has been outspoken yet reclusive, suspicious of media attention in light of how the popular press handled her transition.

Both Morley and Carlos faced various societal and business pressures. Carlos' record label persisted in releasing her albums as 'Walter' even after she transitioned; Morley, who had worked extensively as a conductor, feared session musicians would mock her on the podium (Leigh 2009). Their musical successes, likewise, were on the periphery of critical respectability. Morley's background in arranging 'light music' for orchestra would serve her well in Hollywood, but this genre was not considered 'serious' music. Likewise, Carlos' interpretations of Bach on synthesizer were marketed and largely regarded as gimmicky pop music.[3] Both Carlos and Morley were able to transition into Hollywood and cinematic success with their biggest projects, *A Clockwork Orange* and *Watership Down* respectively. Both these films were dystopian fantasies: one very adult, one dark but intended for children, but each notable for distinctive and memorable music. The strict time of Carlos' electronics reflects the control of Kubrick's dystopian world, while the Debussy and jazz inflections of Morley's score add to the whimsy of the animated rabbit adventure.

Carlos and Morley both flourished in genres that were marginalized or liminally placed between masculine and feminine musical stereotypes. Carlos' electronic music synthesized representations of acoustic and imaginary instruments and relied upon extensive multitracking and tape splicing, forms of audio surgery and augmentation; its live performance relied upon the reproductive technology of tape machines, since the Moog on its own was not capable of what Carlos had done with it. Morley was a master of orchestration and 'light music,' or 'easy listening,' an art form that demanded extensive classical training but garnered little artistic respect or reputation. Carlos and Morley negotiated their genders, careers, and music in ways that reflect their displacement from heteronormative expectations and status quo rationales.

This chapter uses 'Walter,' 'Wendy,' 'Wally,' and 'Angela' to best historicize personal and projected identities at their appropriate times. Where an overarching, long-term nomenclature is needed, 'Wendy' and 'Angela' are preferred.

Walter and academia

Walter attended Brown University 1958–62, studying music but majoring in physics. Walter attended Columbia University 1962–65, earning a master's degree in music composition, studying with Otto Luening and Vladimir Ussachevsky, early pioneers of tape and electronic music, and co-founders of the Columbia-Princeton Electronic Music Center in 1958.

The Columbia-Princeton Electronic Music Center was home to the 'RCA Mark II Sound Synthesizer,' designed by RCA electrical engineers Harry F. Olson and Herbert Belar and manufactured by the Radio Corporation of America at their Sarnoff Lab in Princeton, New Jersey (Patterson 2011). The RCA machine, installed in 1959 in one of the Center's studios at Columbia in Prentis Hall on 125th Street, was built into rows of tall equipment racks and large enough to dominate the lab. It was the centerpiece of the Center. Access to the instrument 'was mostly limited to a handful of senior staff members as primary users, especially Milton Babbitt' (Gluck 2007: 20).

Although Carlos' training in physics and work at Columbia with pioneers of electronic and tape music would seem an ideal academic foundation for her future, it was complicated by greater issues within the academy, in particular an anti-tonal sentiment that Nadine Hubbs argues stemmed from a heteronormative reaction to the success of midcentury modernist homosexual composers. During Carlos' time at university, serialism and atonality were *the* required systems of compositional study and practice. These requirements stood in opposition to the freedoms that electronic music otherwise promised. Carlos shows distaste for orthodoxy, dogma, and pretensions in music and academia.

> That was one of the darkest periods for serious music. A lot of composers with good instincts were crushed for a long time under what was effectively, if not deliberately, a repressive time. [...] I'm still angry to think about it today. [...] Everyone I'd encounter seemed to champion ugly music, the uglier the better. (Carlos in Oteri 2007: 3)

Hubbs argues that the atonal, serial style was promoted by the academy in reaction to a perceived circle of Parisian-educated, New York gay modernist composers, represented by Virgil Thompson, Aaron Copland, David Diamond, Ned Rorem, Leonard Bernstein, Marc Blitzstein, and others, whose successes stoked bitterness and jealousy in outsiders. 'Whispered rumors and theories of a homosexual syndicate had swirled around Copland and other gay artists for decades' (Hubbs 2004: 158). But the academy's backlash was real and well documented: Diamond and Rorem listed faculty and students dismissed from Eastman in the 1930s and 1940s for being gay (Hubbs 2004: 156). Things did not improve during the postwar period, as 'the nerve center for American art music shifted from the concert hall, ballet, and opera house to the university. [...] From its beginnings atonal and dissonant music had been associated with exclusivity and elitism, as well as heteronormative masculinity, not only by audiences, but also by its creators' (Hubbs 2004: 162).

Academic justification for serial music and atonality relied upon notions of science, mathematics, progress, and technology; a lineage to Schoenberg, Webern, Berg, and the Second Viennese School of chamber music; the importance to a peer-review, academic paradigm of writing music which was somehow 'new';[4] a positioning of serial composition as 'emblematic of artistic freedom' in contrast to Soviet and Stalinist enforcement of dated tonal styles (Hubbs 2004: 169); and a growing preference for postwar globalism over 'national' musical styles. Of these arguments, the one that manifested itself most evidently in academic music was an implementation of mathematical formulae to determine pitches, durations, and dynamics, and thereby construct compositions. These 'serial operations' supplanted traditional, aesthetic rules of 'functional harmony' that had been the bedrock for tonal composition.

But Carlos knew better. Carlos sensed fakery, and knew that the new music wasn't truly about an obsessive interest in mathematics, science, or progress. There may have been justifications for new academic compositional styles, but Carlos was not buying it.

> Having had a background in physics and mathematics, I saw that a lot of it was pretty inane number-play, simple combinations and permutations. I had seen far more impressive theories in the math department and wasn't about to be taken in by silliness, even if it seemed to be weighty material to many other musicians and composers. It wasn't so easy to keep a straight face or to endure the endless talk – hyperventilating over such forgettable, unlovable writing. And one last thing – nearly everyone sounded so similar, much less variety than non-serial music. This bothers me greatly, as it suggests that the technique itself tends to mask an individual's personality. Nearly no one speaks about that. (Carlos in Oteri 2007: 3)

Carlos' criticism of serial operations and their resultant obfuscation of a composer's individual identity is a subjective argument. Many twentieth-century specialists can easily distinguish between Schoenberg and Webern or between Foss and Xenakis, even if an unindoctrinated listener cannot. Furthermore, a similar argument might be made about tonal music: can an unschooled, casual listener distinguish between Mozart and Haydn or Brahms and Beethoven? What Carlos saw was *restriction*: the academy endeavored to rope composition students into learning a certain provided style or musical language. Let us accept Carlos' observation as she saw it from her perspective as a young, gifted music student within the Ivy League: the compositional systems being taught tended to 'mask' composers' personalities, as it prevented them from writing other types of music. To Carlos, this was imposed conformism. It was not artistry or freedom; it was oppression, majority rule masquerading as the avant-garde. As a result of this masquerade, Carlos said:

> I was never into the avant-garde. That kept me out of peer groups of students who saw eye-to-eye on the type of music that ought to be written. But they all got into serial mathematics and 12-tone rows. Having a math background, I thought it was all gibberish. I didn't go for that type of non-rhythmic, non-melodic, non-harmonic music. It seemed more concerned with what we don't do than what we do. I think university music is probably still caught in that trap. (Darter and Armbruster 1984: 122–23)

Hubbs might argue that the oppression Carlos felt at school was not merely the imposition of a *musical* approach, but symptomatic of heteronormative masculinity trying to reclaim American art music from midcentury modernist queers. Carlos came to the same conclusion in her own allegorical terms, and described how this oppression, this reassertion of masculine supremacy, was insinuated into the academic environment:

> [The academy] turned their backs on an awful lot of the best parts of music and taught us to purge them from our music, too. First sign of a lapse, they sneered – polite, informal sneers. It wasn't a conspiracy, nothing that sinister, planned or organized. But the effect was the same. It's not unlike how prejudice operates – racism, sexism: with an obliviousness and perpetual denial that anything 'unreasonable' is in effect; 'who, me?'! It's seldom conscious – but subtle, over time, signaled by exclusion and casual presumptuous [sic]. (Carlos in Oteri 2007: 3)

Carlos' description of how prejudice operates is right on the money, and, coming from a transwoman, well informed. Carlos' quote emphasizes how academic or musical prejudice connects to other prejudices like racism and sexism; this collusion of prejudices is clear to those subjected to them by the academy. Consider that the academy is not only a learning environment, but also a work and social environment through which professional networks are built and extended. Academic musical dictates can be seen as part of a larger, institutionalized system of heteronormative masculine oppression.[5] Carlos' argument compels us to consider that the lack of variance and personal expression *in the music itself* is evidence of a system of oppression. The proof is in the pudding, so to speak.[6]

Ussachevsky, director of the electronic music studio and supportive of Carlos' work, allowed Carlos use of the equipment after midnight, in a compact unknown to noisy and intrusive janitors (Ramey 1972). From 8 p.m. to 4 a.m. nightly, Carlos would create sounds from tape recorders, mixers, and other electronic equipment available (Reed 1985).

Carlos graduated in 1965; her work at the Columbia-Princeton Electronic Music Center facilitated her first two commercially released recordings, featured on a compilation LP with fellow students Ilhan Mimaroglu, Andres Lewin-Richter, and Tzvi Avni. *Electronic Music* (1965) on Turnabout Records concludes with 'Variations for Flute and Electronic Sound' and 'Dialogues for Piano and Two Loudspeakers' by Walter Carlos on side B. 'All the music was produced with the technical resources of the Columbia-Princeton Electronic Music Center' (Klein 1965). The *New York Times* gave the album an overall favorable review, but found Carlos' pieces 'the least imaginative.' 'He has followed a prevalent and bad example of combining so-called natural sounds with electronic ones. [...] These aural montages simply don't work. The ear soars in free flight with the electronic sounds only to be pulled to the ground by the crude, limited sounds of the instruments' (Klein 1965). If combining electronic and 'natural' sounds was 'prevalent' in 1965, I would surmise the reviewer was already familiar with the burgeoning field of electronic music.

After graduation, Carlos, encouraged by Ussachevsky, took a job as a tape editor and recording engineer at Gotham Recording Studios in midtown Manhattan. Carlos would work there for three years. This gave her cutting-edge technical skills and facilitated the purchase of her own equipment. Carlos struck up a friendship with inventor and electrical engineer Robert Moog; Carlos bought her first Moog synthesizer in 1966, and Bob installed it personally. With this Moog, Carlos helped companies with music and sound effects for TV commercials (Ramey 1972; Reed 1985). Carlos would press Bob Moog for improvements to the device.

In 1967, Nonesuch Records released Morton Subotnick's *Silver Apples of the Moon*, recorded in 1966 and performed entirely on two Buchla 100 synthesizers (Subotnick 2012). This set the stage, commercially and conceptually, for Carlos' *Switched-On Bach*, performed entirely on a Moog Modular System, one year later.

In the fall of 1967, Carlos made an appointment with the Benjamin Foundation, founded by Dr. Harry Benjamin, author of *The Transsexual Phenomenon* (1966). By early 1968, Carlos was taking estrogen, progesterone, and pituitary hormone treatments (Bell 1979). *Switched-On Bach* would be released in the fall of 1968, contemporaneously with Terry Riley's *In C*, also on Columbia Records (Pinch and Trocco 2002: 131). In May 1969, Carlos began living permanently as a woman. 'After that, I made only a few appearances as a male for the sake of my business, such as a concert with the St. Louis Symphony. Otherwise. I would have made none at all' (Carlos in Bell 1979).

Surgeries and the medical establishment

Carlos and Morley both underwent surgeries, Morley in 1970 and Carlos in 1972, to finalize their gender transitions in a physical, *bodily* way. It is important to contextualize their transitions with the time period, as political and sociological circumstances would impact how Carlos and Morley would negotiate the continuations of their already-established careers and interactions with the press.

The medical establishment at the time was characterized by a 'rise of university-based sex change programs during the late 1960s and early 1970s [...] These years, between the mid-1960s and the late 1970s, represent what could be called the "Big Science" period of transgender history' (Stryker 2008: 93). The 'male-to-female genital conversion operation' (Stryker 2008: 94) had been performed in Europe since the 1940s (Stryker 2008: 47), and although the zeitgeist of the atomic age encouraged scientists to expand, exploit, and perfect what was possible, political and social consciousness lagged behind. Even as social movements such as feminism, flower power, and sexual liberation expanded, transgender people were still widely excluded or misunderstood.

1973 represented a low point in U.S. transgender political history. Trans people, when they transitioned from one gender to another,

still routinely faced loss of family and friends, housing and employment discrimination, high levels of social stigma, and greater risks
for experiencing violence. (Stryker 2008: 101)

The conservatism of multinational record labels and film studios was to
be expected. But it would be not only businessmen and executives who
would become obstacles; otherwise 'progressive' and feminist communities themselves would be unwelcoming.

Progressive political movements, rather than critiquing the medical
system that told transgender people they were sick, instead insisted
that transgender people were politically regressive dupes of the patriarchal gender system who, at best, deserved to have their conscious-
nesses raised. (Stryker 2008: 101)

Morley would move permanently to the United States in 1980. 'Wally
Stott' had records and credits of his own, but was not a known com-
modity in the public eye in the United States. 'Wally' would not follow
Angela around in the United States, except in some professional circles.

Transphobia and the record business

In 1967, Carlos met and developed a close partnership with Rachel
Elkind. Elkind, like Carlos, had worked at a recording studio in New
York City, but also knew the record business. Elkind had been secretary
to Goddard Lieberson, president of Columbia Records, who in 1964 was
also elected president of the Record Industry Association of America.
Lieberson was credited with introducing the LP format to the public
(Hess 1977). It would be difficult to imagine a better industry connection. Elkind advised Carlos and helped her shape an album of interpretations of Bach on the Moog synthesizer. Elkind was savvy, and knew
better than to bring their proposition to Lieberson herself.

Elkind knew the music business was 'very much a man's world,'
so she persuaded Ettore Stratta in Columbia's Artists and Repertoire
department to submit a proposal for her (Pinch and Trocco 2002: 141).
Columbia paid Elkind and Carlos $1000 for the finished master record-
ing, to be released as *Switched-On Bach* in the fall of 1968.[7] Carlos and
Elkind took the deal, 'although it was clear to both of them that the
record company had no real interest in them personally' (Pinch and
Trocco 2002: 142). The album of electronic Bach renditions was a fit
with Columbia's marketing scheme and a response to Jac Holzman's

newly developed Nonesuch label. Nonesuch had released pioneering electronic albums such as *Silver Apples of the Moon* (1967) and Beaver and Krause's *Nonesuch Guide to Electronic Music* (1968).[8] Those albums were selling, and Columbia was ready to move in on the territory.

At this time, Carlos was already on hormone treatments, begun in early 1968; she would start living full time as a woman in May 1969. Elkind told Pinch and Trocco, 'It was really after I had made the deal with Columbia that she [Wendy] told me about this problem [of gender identity], which is why the album really was done the way it was with "Trans-Electronic"' (Pinch and Trocco 2002: 146). The front cover and spine of the original LP read, 'Trans-Electronic Music Productions, Inc. Presents Switched-On Bach.' The acronym, TEMPI, is a musical term, the plural of 'tempo' or speed. Only the rear cover credits 'Electronic Realizations and Performances by Walter Carlos with the assistance of Benjamin Folkman.' It seems that it was only after the ink was dry on the contract with Columbia Records that Carlos discussed her gender with Elkind.[9] Elkind suggests that inventing and highlighting the credit 'Trans-Electronic' was both a means of downplaying Carlos' name and making a subtle reference to her 'transexuality.'[10]

Although Carlos would be, understandably, frustrated by her public image as a man, it was Carlos herself, with the help and encouragement of Elkind, who hid her identity from Columbia Records, keeping it a secret to protect her career. *Playboy* interviewer Arthur Bell pointedly asked Carlos in 1979, 'Did Columbia Records catch on?' Carlos replied: 'I doubt it, though some people there obviously did. [...] Eccentric genius was the term they used as an explanation. What they really meant was, "Hey, there's something strange here."' Bell pressed: 'But you never blew your cover?' Carlos: 'It was close.'

Carlos was forced to cross-dress *as a man* in publicity appearances including the *Today* show with Hugh Downs in February 1969, *The Mike Douglas Show* (with co-host George Carlin) on 6 October 1969, and *The Dick Cavett Show* on ABC on 28 January 1970 (with actor Peter Ustinov). Already on hormones, Carlos wore dark stick-on mutton chop sideburns and makeup to simulate male facial hair growth. The close call was at the *Today* show on NBC. *Switched-On Bach* was still the best-selling classical album, with *The Well-Tempered Synthesizer* (1969) following in its wake. There was a 'brouhaha' backstage as people argued about Carlos' true gender (Bell 1979).

Carlos' discretion interfered with her private life. Intrigued by her groundbreaking electronic music, artists including Stevie Wonder, George Harrison, and Keith Emerson wanted to meet Carlos. But 'all visitors were told by Rachel Elkind – Carlos' producer, collaborator and housemate – that Walter was away. "I would listen to them from upstairs," says Carlos. "I accepted the sentence, but it was bizarre to have life opening up on the one hand and to be locked away on the other"' (Reed 1985). When Stanley Kubrick engaged 'Walter' to compose the score for *A Clockwork Orange* (1971), Wendy would dress in men's clothing for their meetings. Carlos later told an interviewer, 'I could tell he felt something was strange, but he didn't know what' (Reed 1985).

Even if the deception was unpleasant for Wendy, she kept recording albums, and Columbia kept releasing them, all under the name 'Walter': *Sonic Seasonings* (1972), *Walter Carlos' Clockwork Orange* (1972), *Switched-On Bach II* (1973), *By Request* (1975), and *Bach: Brandenburg Concertos Nos. 3, 4 & 5* (1975).

Things had to change. A mutual friend, Elly Stone, a singer and actress known for interpretations of Jacques Brel songs, connected Wendy Carlos with journalist Arthur Bell, who seemed a safe and logical choice to get the scoop. Bell was a columnist for the *Village Voice*, 'a homosexual rights activist,' and 'one of twelve founding members of the Gay Activists' Alliance, a homosexual rights group based in New York' (*New York Times* 1984).[11] Bell wrote two books, *Dancing the Gay Lib Blues* (1971), and *Kings Don't Mean a Thing: The John Knight Murder Case* (1978) about the 1975 murder of wealthy homosexual newspaper heir John Knight III. Bell, a mutual friend, gay man, and legitimate journalist, would have seemed a patient and sympathetic ear. Carlos slowly opened up for Arthur Bell, who interviewed her between December 1978 and January 1979. Transcription of the taped interviews yielded *800 pages* of unedited text.

Playboy magazine published Bell's interview in May 1979, prioritizing the explicit. Carlos must have felt violated and distraught. While Bell escapes Carlos' personal website's 'Cruel List,' '*Playboy* Magazine Editors' are awarded three 'black leaves,' indicating 'arrogant selfish prig, with a genuine sadistic streak' (Carlos 2014). But the cat was finally out of the bag. Carlos granted an interview as Wendy in December 1979 to Dominic Milano for *Keyboard* magazine, published with photographs. The article simply treats her as a musician and does not go into the matters of gender, sexuality, and surgery that the *Playboy* article did. Carlos' work on *The Shining* (1980) and *TRON* (1982) were credited to Wendy. Walter was finally gone.

In 1980, Rachel Elkind married an astrophysicist and moved to Europe. About the same time, Wendy met Annemarie Franklin, who would become her new collaborator.

Angela Morley

Angela Morley was born Walter Stott on 10 March 1924 in Leeds, Yorkshire, England. His father was a watchmaker who sold watches, clocks, jewelry, and silver plate. Walter had piano lessons at age eight, which ended when his father fell ill and died unexpectedly of angina three months later at the age of 39. One year later, Walter's mother sold the shop and the family went to live with her parents at Swinton, near Rotherham, Yorkshire. At age ten, Walter took up violin but his 'prank-ster' grandfather smeared butter or grease on the bow so it would no longer play (Morley 1999, 2008).

Walter began his career playing clarinet, alto saxophone, and accor-dion in 'juvenile' bands that toured England playing in ballrooms. On tour, bands would cram three players into a double bed; in one case, a room with three beds held nine musicians. With the advent of the Second World War, Walter was in demand as an undrafted teenager who could sight-read music. Walter also worked as a projectionist in a cinema, but made mistakes, repeating reels or getting them out of order. At age twenty in 1944, Walter joined the Geraldo Orchestra, play-ing several radio programs a week for the BBC and contributing to the arrangements.

In 1953, Philips Records, founded by the Dutch electronics company, expanded and opened an office in London. Stott was made musical director, arranging and conducting for British artists and occasionally for American ones including Rosemary Clooney and Mel Tormé. Stott continued to work in radio, composing and conducting for the wildly successful BBC radio comedy show, *The Goon Show*. Philips touted Stott as 'one of the best-known and most successful arranger-conductors working in London today' and noted that 'he has composed music for many films' (Philips 1958: 8). In 1958, Wally Stott and His Orchestra recorded 'As I Love You,' written by Jay Livingston and Ray Evan, for Welsh singer Shirley Bassey. It rose to Number One in the UK Singles Chart in January 1959.

'Wally Stott and His Orchestra' and 'The Wally Stott Chorale' would record their own albums as well, many in the genre of 'light music' fueled by the success of the long playing record (LP) and a demand for postwar home entertainment (Keightley 2008). Stott's recordings included instrumental versions of Gershwin, Irving Berlin, Christmas music, American show tunes, and the like. Some of these recordings found their way on to RCA Reader's Digest box sets, such as *Background Moods* (1965) and *Magical World of Melody* (1963).

Wally married Beryl Stott, a singer, choral arranger, and leader of the Beryl Stott Singers (varyingly credited as the 'Beryl Stott Chorus' and the 'Beryl Stott Group'). Wally and Beryl had a son, Bryan, and a daughter, Helen.[12] Beryl Stott killed herself in October 1967, 'a devastating event for the family, Wally in particular' (Parker 2015). Wally met Christina Parker, also a singer, on recording sessions in London. Parker recalls:

> I was freelancing so took part in a large choir on Norman Luboff and Wally Stott LPs. Also Wally was music director at Philips Studios, so I was quite often on sessions there with Wally conducting his own arrangements for orchestra and choir, backing soloists like Harry Secombe or John Hanson (Parker 2015).

Wally married Christine on 1 June 1970. In addition to work and the new marriage, there was something else going on. According to Max Geldray, harmonica player in *The Goon Show*, Morley had 'a lifelong mental struggle with gender identity, a fact that, for all those years, he had kept sealed tightly inside himself' (Gaughan 2009). Recalls Parker, 'I think Wally had taken hormones before we met, intermittently' (Parker 2015).

Christine would stay with Morley through thick and thin. 'Angela and I stayed together because we had a great relationship: both musicians and linguists and both from Yorkshire, and we saw no good reason to divorce' (Parker 2015). Morley credited Christine with helping to resolve her gender identity: 'It was only because of her love and support that I then was able to deal with the trauma, and begin to think about crossing over that terrifying gender border' (Morley in Gaughan 2009). Max Geldray called their relationship 'an extraordinary story of two people's love and devotion [...] which has gone far beyond the barriers of what most of us have faced in our lives' (Geldray in Gaughan 2009).

Details of Beryl's death and Wally's surgery were reported inconsistently and incorrectly by several sources.[13] According to Parker,

> The transition surgery took place in June 1970 in Casablanca. Most people thought it was 1972 as that's when Angela 'came out'. We didn't want it in the newspapers so Angela lived in the shadows taking only work that didn't involve going to studios. (Parker 2015)

Stott took the name Morley, her mother's maiden name. She continued to work as an arranger for BBC Radio 2, arranging standards, continuing her work in 'light music.' She declined to participate in *The Last Goon Show of All*, simulcast on radio and television in October 1972, 'because she had not yet gone public about her sex change' (Gaughan 2009).

As described by Stryker, this was a particularly difficult period for transgender people, even if the surgical and medical treatments were advanced. Stott had been well known as a conductor, but Morley was initially prepared to give this up, fearing mockery.

> Musicians can be coarse and blunt, and rather than be a figure of ridicule, Morley told [Philips Records producer Johnny] Franz that she would no longer be conducting. Franz persuaded her to continue and, largely because of her superb musicianship, she was accepted. (Leigh 2009)

Max Geldray recalled, 'It didn't take me very long to find out that, in all the ways that mattered, the person I found now was still the person I had known' (Geldray in Gaughan 2009). All the same, Morley moved increasingly into arranging and film scoring through her established connections, the most important of whom was orchestrator and arranger Herbert W. Spencer (1905–1992), a Hollywood veteran who had begun working on films in the 1930s.

In 1955, Spencer was in London supervising the recording of the musical film *Gentlemen Marry Brunettes* (1955) starring Jane Russell and Jeanne Crain. Spencer needed help with the arrangements, and Stott was a known quantity, so Spencer called him up.

> Herbie asked me if I would come to his apartment and work on one of the numbers for the film. And so I went along there. I discovered [composer Robert] Bob Farnon was already there and the three of us wrote one arrangement by passing pages. I wrote all the band stuff, Bob Farnon seemed to write all the backing vocal stuff, and Herbie wrote all the orchestral stuff. We were each in a separate room. Herbie had the only piano. So we did that, and we were friends from then on until the day Herbie died. That friendship meant a great deal to me. (Morley 1999: 25:15)

Spencer got Morley work on Norman Jewison's film production of *Jesus Christ Superstar* (1973), with music by Andrew Lloyd Webber. Again, Morley found that it was 'always a joy to be doing anything with Herbie' (Morley 1999: 36:30). They worked together again in 1974 on the musical *Good Companions*, with music by André Previn.

Importantly, Spencer was the principal orchestrator for film composer John Williams, and this connection led to more work. Parker recalls:

> We had met John Williams in Hollywood and attended his recording sessions at Denham Studios when he was working there; he was a good friend. I sang on some of his film tracks, too, and so did Helen [Angela's daughter]. It was an honor [for Morley] to be asked to orchestrate for him, and he was always most appreciative. He did ask Angela directly, and she also did a good many arrangements for the Boston Pops. (Parker 2015)

Spencer enlisted Morley to help with *Star Wars* (1977). She would continue to work with Williams and other orchestrators on *The Empire Strikes Back* (1980), *E.T.* (1982), *Hook* (1991), *Schindler's List* (1993), *Home Alone* (1990), and *Home Alone 2: Lost in New York* (1992).[14]

Morley composed the score for the animated feature film *Watership Down* (1978) in London. Emmys and Oscar nominations for other projects notwithstanding, this film is widely considered her finest work among fans and soundtrack collectors. Like Scott Walker's solo albums, it features lush orchestral arrangements and a highly evolved sense of style. The writing is dramatic and capably evokes romantic and jazz styles, a culmination of technique and years of experience. The success of *Watership Down*, as well as their John Williams connection, encouraged Angela and Christine, who had been on visits to southern California (Morley 1999). Christine recalls, '*Watership Down* had done well in UK and we hoped it would help get Angela started in the USA. We had several good friends there and loved the climate. [...] We had become disenchanted with British politics and the climate!' (Parker 2015). Morley recalled that in the late 1970s 'England was going through a bad patch, strikes' (Morley 1999).

Angela and Christine moved to Los Angeles in 1979. Morley's first work composing in the United States was three episodes of *Wonder Woman* in 1979, and the TV movie *Friendships, Secrets and Lies* (1979). Angela and Christine rented a place until they sold their English house, then bought a house in the Los Angeles area's San Fernando Valley. They received their green cards by May 1980 (Parker 2015). Upon relocating, 'the work Angela got was largely for TV, like *Wonder Woman*, *Dallas*, *Dynasty*, and a few TV films' (Parker 2015). According to Parker, 'We never met Wendy Carlos, to my knowledge' (Parker 2015).

Film scholar and author Ed Sikov interviewed Angela Morley in conjunction with research for a biography of Peter Sellers, star of *The Goon*

Show. Morley was clearly at peace with her journey, and not overly worried about how she was presented.

> When I spoke with Angela Morley, I asked her how she wished to be identified in this book, and she replied, 'It's a judgment you'll have to make and I'll have to accept.' My judgment is to attribute her quotes to Wally Stott, since he was the person with whom Peter Sellers worked on *The Goon Show*, and to thank Angela Morley for them in the acknowledgements. (Sikov 2002: 78–79)

Christine Parker remained married to Morley until Morley's death. Angela Morley died on 14 January 2009 in Scottsdale, Arizona. It was 50 years to the week since she hit Number One in the UK with Shirley Bassey (BBC 2011).

Carlos and privacy

Central to Wendy Carlos' management and direction of her own career have been issues of privacy and marginalization. Carlos wishes to be taken seriously as a composer; her website has illustrated how she has felt as odds with academia, the music business, the press, and those who sensationalize her past and her gender identity.

> People and publications [...] have betrayed a cruel indifference to anyone's interests but their own. They have tried to turn me into a cliché, to treat me as an object for potential scorn, ridicule, or even physical violence by bigots (no joke in these dangerous times of beatings and deaths at the hands of the intolerant). At best, they have arrogantly used me and abused me to grind their own prurient axes, to profit by and justify their own agendas. (Carlos 2014)

Carlos has isolated herself from discourse on 'queering the pitch' and from cultural inquiry around sexuality and gender identity within musicology, even as such discourse has been legitimized by scholars such as McClary and Hubbs. Although Carlos could be portrayed as a heroic example of queerness and overcoming heteronormativity in music, Carlos' website makes clear this line of inquiry is unwelcome and offensive to her.

> Of all the composers who were and are secretly or openly gay, you won't find that bit of information about them in any of the general

music websites or books on musicians and composers. The reason is trivial: it's irrelevant. Why announce that Bernstein had blue eyes, or that Virgil Thompson stood only five feet four inches tall? What has that to do with music? [...] I'm the sole exception, picked on in ways the writers would protest loudly, if similar 'reporting' appeared about *their* personal histories. Shame. (Carlos 2000, emphasis in original)

Recent scholarship on composers including Thompson, Copland, and Tchaikovsky *has* addressed homosexuality; scholars including Hubbs and McClary have argued the relevance of sexuality in musicology. Carlos' life experiences and struggles are informed by the times in which she lived and fought her battles; she maintains a strong defense of her public persona and private life. Carlos holds the importance of her *music* paramount, and is skeptical of any interest in private matters, gender transition included. It is problematic to claim Carlos as, for example, a 'gender queer' electronic 'riot grrl,' even if it is easy to argue a direct connection to such artists today. Carlos has lived and identifies, simply, as a woman, and how she got there is a distraction from her work as a composer and musician; this is how she might see it. Arthur Bell's article and interview in *Playboy* might offend Carlos, but it preserves information that will be important to scholars interested in the new musicology.

The conundrum of Carlos' determination to remain private, and her argument against the relevance of sexuality, digs up an unexpected critical test of McClary and Hubbs' position that we must consider sexuality within musicology. In Wendy Carlos we have a transgender person, woman-identified, a 'transwoman' if you will, who might argue that her gender and sexuality are *not* part of the equation as a composer and musician, as far as she is concerned, outside of the prejudices to which she has been subjected. Carlos' objections may not impugn McClary and Hubbs' logic, but their politics are certainly called in for questioning.

While it's impossible to call Carlos 'closeted,' Carlos is very clear that she sees her work as independent of identity and sexual politics. If a trans or queer composer says that these aspects of their life are not relevant to music, should that point be taken or are they in denial? Are there indications of where and how music might reveal the impact or influence of a transgender life story?

Synthesizer as transgender object

Authors Pinch and Trocco proposed a casual association or 'resonance' between audio synthesis and gender transformation. I suspect Carlos does not agree with this theory: Pinch and Trocco, like the editors of *Playboy*, also get three black leaves for cruelty on Wendy's personal website, which calls them 'Coulter & Limbaugh wannabees' (Carlos 2014). Their argument is intriguing, problematic, and only briefly explored.

> The question arises as to whether Wendy's metamorphosis, which occurred just around the time she was developing as a synthesist, had anything to do with the Moog, and with synthesis itself. Perhaps there was something about this most unusual instrument that resonated with the most unusual transformation its star performer was about to undertake. (Pinch and Trocco 2002: 137)

This 'question' implies possible interpretations of 'instrument' and 'equipment'; such correlations on their own do not necessarily imply any particular gender or sexuality. Furthermore, the Columbia-Princeton Electronic Music Center was fairly male-dominated; synthesizers might stereotype masculinities as much as they suggest transition. Even so, the focus on synthesis as 'transformative' is worthy of unpacking. But there are more salient considerations relevant to Carlos' connection to the Moog.

Synthesizers facilitated private and introverted personalities, like Wendy's, to create music. With synthesizers and tape machines, you don't have to glad-hand, network, schmooze, or organize a group of players; things can be done in your own time, in your own way. Commands can be issued and programs executed without offending anyone; scheduling problems are eliminated as long as the power is on. It is a case of technology exploiting the difficulties of working with real people.

At the time, it was rare to make an album without a recording contract. Wendy and Rachel were able to record *Switched-On Bach* on their own equipment in their own studio before signing a contract with Columbia Records. The Moog, as well as Carlos' recording knowledge, made this possible.

Pinch and Trocco stumble upon realizing they have implied that synthesizers, as 'technology,' might be gendered or carry masculine markers, falling into the cliché of prescribing which 'toys' (or instruments) are for boys and which are for girls.

> The question of gender and the synthesizer is a tricky one. Certainly electrical music technologies have traditionally been used for building masculine identities – the boys and their latest toys. But different sorts of masculinity can be involved in how men interact with

technologies, and several women [...] notably Suzanne Ciani and Linda Fisher, have developed intense personal relationships with their synthesizers. (Pinch and Trocco 2002: 138)

The musician's relationship with equipment is not necessarily about masculinity or gender; it can also be about other things, such as control issues or introversion. Pop star synthesist Gary Numan (of 'Cars' fame) has said that he prefers working with machines because he is introverted, has Asperger's syndrome, and found it easier to deal with synthesizers than people: 'I'm completely tied to [technology]. That's the way my brain works. I've got Asperger's syndrome and I'm not a very good people person, so I've always been more comfortable around machinery' (Perry 2011; see also Reynolds and Press 1995: 105). Likewise, it may have been easier for Carlos, as a transwoman undergoing her transformation, to work in her own studio with electronic gear than to entertain other, more extroverted or publicly visible projects.

A more favorable way to theorize the synthesizer as a 'transgender' object is to consider it a tool that can remove or defy binary categorizations. For the sake of argument, let us imagine a high woodwind, perhaps a flute or an oboe. Ignoring other possible high winds for a moment (piccolo, clarinet), the instrument in the player's hands is one or the other, a flute or an oboe. With a synthesizer, we might have a dial that can select or modify waveforms throughout an infinite continuum. With traditional instruments, the instrument we hold is the instrument we have. But the Moog, its recognizable electronic sound aside, can supply a range of sounds that lie outside of simple binary categorizations. It would be possible to create a sound that is neither flute nor oboe, but imitates qualities of both, or lies somewhere between the two; the Moog itself might even encourage the user to experiment with such liminal sounds. The Moog can thusly be seen as a movement away from the rigid categorizations of traditional instrumentation. Judith Butler argues, 'When the constructed status of gender is theorized as radically independent of sex, gender itself becomes a free-floating artifice' (Butler 2006: 9). With the Moog synthesizer, we don't have a flute or an oboe; we have a 'free-floating artifice' that can artificially imitate or assume qualities of either instrument, or merge them with entirely imaginary instruments or new sounds. To frame Pinch and Trocco's argument in these terms makes it far more plausible.

Another complication in Pinch and Trocco's analogy involves the correlation of performative aspects of the synthesizer to performative aspects of gender, as described by Judith Butler.

If, as Judith Butler argues, gender identities have to be performed, a key prop in the performance of these synthesists is the machine with which they spent most of their waking hours interacting – the synthesizer. What we want to suggest with Wendy and her synthesizer is that it may have helped provide a means whereby she could escape the gender identity society had given her. Part of her new identity became bound up with the machine. The transformative power of the synthesizer may have allowed her not only to conjure up a new musical meaning but also helped her find herself as a newly gendered person. [...] Wendy, we suggest, may have used it to help her transcend her former body and former gender identity. (Pinch and Trocco 2002: 138)

If this were the case, how ironic it is that live performance on synthesizer was problematic for Carlos! While gender identity must be performed, synthesizer performance could not be a simple substitution or sublimation of such performance. Carlos' live performance on the Moog was difficult for three reasons: her music involved the use of multitracking and tape edits which could not be performed in real time; the Moog required extensive set up and patching just to make basic sounds; and she was uncomfortable in live situations, a discomfort that can be attributed to likely causes including introversion, reclusion, and stress around concealing her gender identity. When Carlos was engaged to play, it would be with the reinforcement of an accompanying group such as the St. Louis Symphony, or as a 'demonstration' of the Moog instrument, as on *The Dick Cavett Show*.

Pinch and Trocco's arguments are fanciful and perhaps relevant to Carlos, but are not evidenced by a rush of transgender people into synthesis because it reflects their identities or experience. (A better correlation might be the number of heterosexual cisgender males in prog rock who wore capes to play synthesizer onstage!) Other musical genres have proven equally alluring or expedient to transgender musicians: the documentary film *Riot Acts: Flaunting Gender Deviance in Music Performance* (2010, dir. Madsen Minax, USA) interviews a wide swath of transgender musicians who align with folk, indie rock, and riot grrl genres and traditions. But, by the same token, Carlos would not likely wish to be included in a 'trans-fabulous rockumentary' of 'transgender and gender variant musicians.'

I have devoted space to Pinch and Trocco's arguments not because I agree, but because I respect such attempts to relate music and, by extension of Wendy's repertoire, film music to gender, sexuality, and queerness. This book encourages such thinking, and the publication record bears out that, despite Carlos' objections, this is an area of established interest and relevance. There are no easy answers, and plenty of existing stereotypes; composer and memoirist Ned Rorem notably categorized the whole orchestra and other musicians by gender, religion, and sexuality ('Male organists, all gay') (Rorem 1994: 346). Rorem's humorous stereotyping connects to Pinch and Trocco's psycho-theoretical idea of the synthesizer as a transgender instrument: amusing and superficial, yet oddly thought provoking. (Why would all male organists be gay?) Such conjecture can be a starting point for serious discourse and research.

Clearly, not all transgender musicians are drawn to the synthesizer, even though it made a huge impact on film scoring, both in terms of broadening the palette of available sounds and in the preparation of demos. Angela Morley spoke about the synthesizer, not in support, but bemoaning its influence.

> Another big change has been the coming of synthesizers. Producers long, and understandably, frustrated by their inability to look into what the composer was up to and having to wait until the scoring session to find out what the music was going to sound like, discovered that the composer could make a synthesizer demo and play it with the picture. Today, composers are given far less time to write their scores than has been the practice in the past, and to be distracted by the constant requirement to make demos of everything must be a giant headache. (Morley 2008)

The idea that the synthesizer might represent an embodiment of transgender liberation or of performative aspects of gender did not cross Morley's mind. And while Carlos was using synthesizers to make film scores, Morley adhered to more traditional sounds. But Morley was likewise subject to Rorem-like gender stereotyping resultant from her work in 'light music,' which, although informed by rich orchestral traditions, was subject to its own set of prejudices.

Transformation of Debussy from Faun to Seagull

Morley's depth and experience as an arranger and orchestrator in popular and light music gave her a skill set that facilitated a rising career in film and television. After surgery in 1970, Morley lay low, spending eighteen months quietly studying clarinet chamber music at Watford

School of Music (Musiker and Musiker 1998: 253). She returned to work as an orchestrator on *Jesus Christ Superstar* (1973), working with her old friend Herbert Spencer. She was soon nominated for an Academy Award for 'Best Music, Scoring Original Song Score and/or Adaptation' for *The Little Prince* (1974). A second nomination followed for 'Best Music, Original Song Score and Its Adaptation or Best Adaptation Score' for *The Slipper and the Rose* (1976).

Morley displays her strengths in swing, classical, and romantic period styles in full force in her original score for *Watership Down* (1978), Martin Rosen's adaptation of Richard Adams' popular novel. The rabbit adventure combined elements of magical realism, fantasy, and children's genres at a time when Tolkien's *Lord of The Rings* was a college campus favorite; the film stars John Hurt as Hazel, Richard Briers as Fiver, and Zero Mostel as Kehaar. While the animated movie was seemingly directed at children, it is dark and graphic with violent scenes.[15]

Watership Down's rabbits help Kehaar, a grounded seagull, recover from his injuries. In return, Kehaar helps the rabbits against their enemies, becoming their reconnaissance and airpower. Kehaar has a dedicated theme, fully realized when he takes his first flight after his recovery (Figure 4.1). For this theme, Morley takes a fragment of the opening flute motive of Debussy's 'Prélude à l'après midi d'un faune' (Figure 4.2), and spins it into a majestic, soaring, romantic swing waltz, an amalgamation of her work in French romantic style orchestral scoring and big band swing. Alto sax takes the tune; the surrounding orchestration has a rich, symphonic, romantic, classical Hollywood sound,

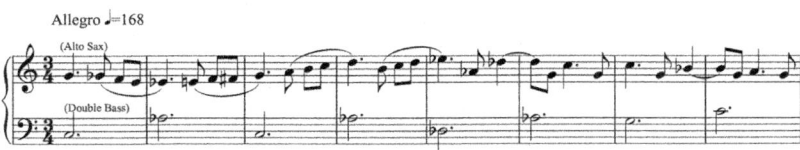

Figure 4.1 Angela Morley, 'Kehaar's Theme.' *Watership Down* (1978). Transcribed by the author

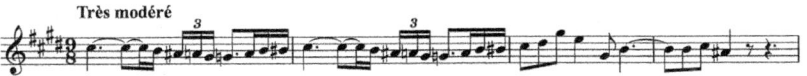

Figure 4.2 Claude Debussy, 'Prélude à l'après midi d'un faune' (1894) (flute)

not unlike the orchestrations Morley did for John Williams. In addition to this mastery of style and technique, the opening I–bVI progression is fresh and contemporary; the 'borrowed' bVI chord had been used in earlier psych rock but would become prominently featured in the 'new wave' popular music of the time.[16]

One of the foundations of musical composition is development through transformation, or how a theme may be altered and modified by techniques including fragmentation, augmentation, reharmonization, and other means. Morley appropriates the Debussy motive's chromaticism and melodic contour, but gives it a rhythmic regularity. Subsequent sections of the theme use polyrhythms; in bars 5–8, the rhythm of the sax becomes a 2/4 figure even as the orchestra stays in 3/4. In subsequent bars the sax goes into 6/8 against the orchestra's 3/4. These are not overly complex polyrhythms, but idiomatic for jazz and swing. Morley ably develops musical ideas originating in the Debussy motive and creates a new composition with her own musical signature.

A faun is half-human, half-goat, a mythological forest creature, one who might even inhabit the verdant world of the animated rabbits, if that world were not so strongly rooted in the vérité of the British Social Realism cinema movement. Morley's adaptation takes Debussy's faun and tosses him in the air to become the seagull Kehaar: the swaying waltz and swirling accompaniment figurations evoke soaring flight, floating and swaying on an optimistic wind.

Morley's handling of 'Kehaar's Theme' and its orchestral accompaniment shows a technique well honed not just from film work, but from years of working in 'light music' where romantic accompaniments and swing tunes were frequently employed. While not an 'easy listening' version of Debussy, 'Kehaar's Theme' nevertheless suggests how one might conceive of such a thing and execute it with finesse.

While a close reading of 'Kehaar's Theme' shows connections to both Debussy and to Morley's 'light music' past, scholars might be more inclined to privilege the lineage to Debussy. 'Easy listening' and 'light music' have long suffered negative connotations, and have been derided in academia and popular culture. Although Morley is one of the best examples of connections between 'light music' and film scoring, a list that includes composers Henry Mancini, Lee Holdridge, and Stu Phillips,[17] academia (and film score fan communities) still ignore or downplay light music and its ties to film scoring. There are a handful of reasons for this prejudice: easy listening has been dismissed as feminine, racist, inauthentic, and banal.

Light music is seen as inherently gendered, and is subject to the same misogyny that other art forms, like quilting for example, have suffered. Although marketed and sold to a wide audience, light music's associative terms 'soft, smooth, soothing, romantic, easy, gentle' are associated with 'femininity' in 'Western ideology' (Keightley 2008: 315). Often light music cover versions of popular music were seen as weaker, diluted, and softened; hard electric guitars replaced by soft, mellow strings. This type of re-instrumentation reflected existing gender stereotypes: easy listening LPs turned 'masculine' bands like The Rolling Stones, The Doors, The Beatles, Elvis, The Beach Boys, and many others into something mother might enjoy on the family hi-fi. Even much of the artwork and many album covers incorporated line drawings, curlycues, and other visual signifiers of femininity.[18] While 'men and women equally enjoyed easy listening' (Keightley 2008: 327) and 'music itself does not have a gender' (Keightley 2008: 327), easy listening is nevertheless often denigrated or derided based upon misogynist perceptions.

In its marketing, repertoire, and execution, light music is seen as racist. Josh Kun (2005) describes easy listening as failing to incorporate voices and sounds of immigrants and African Americans in its canon. Even if swing tunes that evolved from jazz are incorporated into the light music canon, they are highly denatured and whitewashed, distant from the original expressiveness of the appropriated idiom. Light music's inclusion of bossa nova stylings, 'Tijuana' sounds, and 'exotica' albums arguably did not help either, being more appropriation than informed ethnomusicology, and largely complicit in establishing the 'cocktail' subgenre.[19]

Light music is seen as inauthentic; its albums do not feature original versions.[20] They are facsimiles or approximations made with a frequent blandness that results from trying to market to the widest possible audience. Consequently, light music is seen as purely commercial. Its goal was to maximize sales, and so it did. While *Billboard*'s singles chart, the Hot 100, 'was the noisy, public face of popular music, the album charts told a quieter story about where the real money lay' (Keightley 2008: 323). A complication in light of this broad audience was that light music was also seen as bourgeois, with its glossy album covers and deluxe box sets, a reflection of prosperity and consumption.

Much light music was sold through record clubs, like RCA's Reader's Digest series that included Wally Stott's music, and this contributed to light music's image as banal. Light music is associated with the 'middlebrow' movement in popular culture; there were also 'semiclassical' easy listening albums, with arrangements of popular classical tunes.

The use of the word 'easy' in 'easy listening' also implied simplistic or dumbed-down, as well as associations with relaxation and bourgeois consumer products like 'Easy Off' cleanser and 'Nice and Easy hair color' (Keightley 2008: 312–13).

In light of the importance of Angela Morley and others, easy listening needs to be reconsidered and reevaluated, especially by film music scholars. Light music is historically, commercially, and culturally significant for a variety of reasons. Considering composers who were involved in the production of *both* light music *and* film scores, we find a group of important figures whose work overlaps multiple genres, including film-scoring, easy listening, and concert music. Angela Morley's sheet music for her own 'classical' pieces, 'Liaison,' 'Rêverie,' 'Valse Bleue,' and 'Harlequin,' is published by Novello & Co. Lee Holdridge's *Concierto para Mendez* (2006) has been performed by the Los Angeles Opera and Boston Lyric Opera. Working in light music required a high level of musicianship and attracted people who were capable and creative musicians.

Easy listening and film scoring underwent similar production processes in their creation. Both easy listening and film scoring involved strict deadlines, orchestras, musicians' and technicians' unions, studio notes and interference, and big business. There was cross-pollination between film scoring and easy listening; Lee Holdridge commented on how the successes of his arrangements of Neil Diamond songs opened doors for him at Universal Pictures (Dubowsky 2014). There is a similarity in easy listening and film scoring in that practitioners see both as legitimate; Holdridge did not see his work in 'orchestral pop' arranging as any less legitimate than his film scoring work (Dubowsky 2014).

There is a strong similarity in orchestration style used for film scoring and for light music. Orchestration in both employs a knowledge and adoption of classical techniques. Both film scoring and easy listening feature heavier reliance on strings than on brass or winds (Keightley 2008: 325); in both, this serves to make the music less obtrusive when so desired. Compositionally, both film scoring and easy listening are marked by the subjugation of traditional musical 'development' to the demands of commercial and structural form. These similarities show how both film scoring and easy listening are simultaneously derivative of and push away from traditional Western concert music.

Even as 'Kehaar's Theme' adopts swing-style chords, polyrhythms, and an alto sax lead, the orchestration leans heavier on the strings. The lush sound owes much to intricate countermelodies, ornamental details, and symphonic flourishes, aligning it closely with a romantic 'classical' Hollywood style, similar to Morley's work with John Williams. 'Kehaar's

Theme' is a fine example of the junction of Morley's strengths in classical music, swing, jazz, light music, concert music, and film scoring.

Much of the *Watership Down* score is imbued with a weight and darkness that cannot be attributed to easy listening; the action cues are as heavy as anything Morley orchestrated for *Star Wars*. Other cues, such as the plaintive alto flute of 'Violet's Gone' or the harp and flute combination of 'Venturing Forth' are quite delicate and lovely. Pinch and Trocco might indulge an argument, paralleling their ideas on Carlos and her Moog, that Morley's musical hybridity reflects her own gender transition. I do not believe such conjecture is reasonable, but it is a logical extension of that line of inquiry. Ultimately, music is human expression, and composers of high caliber, whether transgender or cisgender, are quite capable of exploiting its full range. However, what needs to be emphasized is that there is a frequent marginalization of transmen and transwomen in the arts and music, as well as the marginalization of certain art forms and musical genres, often due to underlying misogyny or other cultural biases.

Conclusion

Wendy Carlos and Angela Morley both achieved commercial and professional successes in marginalized musical forms, Moog records and 'light music,' respectively. In each case, these backgrounds informed their work in film scoring, creating opportunities, directly or indirectly, and adding to their musical expertise. As transgender women, Carlos and Morley both suffered marginalization in their personal and professional lives. Carlos, sensitized by how she was treated in academia and later by publications such as *Playboy*, reacted by continuing an already reclusive life and letting people know her feelings through her website. Morley conducted less and moved to the United States, effectively beginning a new life behind the scenes in composing for television. While this allowed her to leave Wally Stott behind, she did not hide from her past, and allowed that she would accept how journalists saw or described her.

There have been suggestions that Morley's and Carlos' music could be representative of their lives or transgender experiences. Pinch and Trocco posited the Moog as a transgender instrument; Keightley described how 'light music' was associated with the 'feminine.' Carlos may have liked electronic music because it indulged her introversion or explored liminal spaces between sounds, or simply because it was new, exciting, and resonated with her technical background, rather than anything to do with gender. Morley may have worked in 'light music' because there were opportunities and a demand for it, rather than anything to do with the 'feminine' qualities of 'easy listening.'

The purpose of this chapter, in looking at Carlos and Morley together, is twofold. First, while Carlos and Morley had different paths and different musics, the common theme in their journeys, aside from film scoring itself, was the transphobic marginalization they suffered. This marginalization affected their career paths and personal lives. Both were talented, groundbreaking composers with unique voices who found ways to cope with and surmount obstacles that lay in their way.

Secondly, in putting this book together, I wanted to establish some visibility and history of transgender film composers. While Carlos has been quite clear that she wishes to be known simply as a composer, and private matters are no one's business but her own, I believe that this view is a natural reaction from anyone who lived through the period of transgender oppression and discrimination described by historian Susan Stryker. More recently, successful directors like Lana Wachowski have come out as transgender; Wachowski continued to make public appearances and discuss her transition to the press (Abramovitch 2012; Brooks 2012; Hemon 2012; Nathan 2012). Nevertheless, transfolk still experience discrimination, marginalization, and violence today.

Carlos, Morley, and their personal histories illustrate that there is no single, clear path in life, music, art, career, or gender. They may have both began life as 'Walter,' but each forged her own way; the similarities stop there for these genre and gender outsiders.

5
Mainstreaming and Rebelling

Introduction

The early 1990s were a fertile period for queer film. Period examples of films with lesbian representation came as a breath of fresh air to male-dominated independent and mainstream cinema. At both ends of the commercial spectrum, women were breaking stereotypes and creating new gender role models. In particular, two films stood out among their relative peers: MGM's box office hit *Thelma & Louise* (1991) and the smaller independent art-house film *Go Fish* (1994).

Thelma & Louise was widely hailed as a feminist film, its morbid ending notwithstanding. Many, including B. Ruby Rich, praised Ridley Scott's film starring Susan Sarandon, Geena Davis, and Harvey Keitel (Rich 2003). A major studio project with a respectable $16.5 million budget, the edgy result managed to be groundbreaking and controversial. *Go Fish* also tackles lesbian and feminist issues, albeit far more directly as an independent film can. The film breaks the fourth wall with sequences of commentary, debate, and free verse. Low budget, high concept, personal and original, director Rose Troche presents a drama that feels remarkably realistic, honest, and truthful.

Both these films are regarded as watershed moments of 1990s cinema, even with huge budget and production disparities This disparity extends logically to music budget and production. *Thelma & Louise* had Hollywood heavyweight composer Hans Zimmer, who had already scored two Best Picture Academy Award recipients, *Rain Man* (1988) and *Driving Miss Daisy* (1989), as well as ample budget for music supervision and the placement of licensed music. On the other side of the financial spectrum, *Go Fish* features music by three little-known composers, Scott Aldrich, Brendan Dolan, and Jennifer Sharpe. The use of music is another powerful filter through which to compare these two important films. This chapter considers the use of big-budget and low-budget music, the context of the commercial environment, and weighs their impact upon thematic and narratological messages.

Only a few years later, contemporary culture finally lauds cinematic portrayals of transgender protagonists in *Boys Don't Cry* (1999, two Oscar nominations; one win for Hilary Swank) and *Transamerica* (2005, two nominations). Country legend Dolly Parton was nominated for best original song for *Transamerica*'s 'Travelin' Thru.' In these films, music supports an advocacy stance carefully negotiated for mainstream audiences. Parton, although not transgender herself, is situated within a peculiar cultural debate on surgical body modification. Her breasts have received homage and commentary on a level rivaling any kind of serious transgender discussion in the United States.[1] It is important *not* to equate cosmetic surgery with transgender surgeries; however, Dolly Parton's proud and upbeat persona, musical and feminist background (*Nine To Five* [1980]), self-made image, and cottage industry (Dollywood theme park in Pigeon Forge, TN) make her a fascinating choice as artist and advocate for *Transamerica*. Likewise, *Boys Don't Cry*, produced by influential impresario Christine Vachon and Killer Films, brings a transgender protagonist and story to a broad audience. Music is carefully used to guide audience sentiment and perspective.

As these films simultaneously rebel against and court the attention of the mainstream, so does the music. In *Thelma & Louise* and *Transamerica*, conventional means of placing and employing music are used to further a queer narrative. Unconventional use of sound and music may be more suited to outsider art-house films, like *Go Fish*, that are independently financed and do not answer to the commercial constraints of a major studio. As feminism, gender diversity, and sexual identities become culturally mainstreamed, queerness can become marketed and banal. While gently spoon-feeding alternative sexuality and gender identity to a general audience, familiar cinematic techniques are used to engage the viewer. In the time period within the purview of this chapter, queer film marketed to mainstream audiences adopted techniques of mainstream cinema, including how popular songs were used, following an established model of the compilation score seen in films like *American Graffiti* (1973) and *Easy Rider* (1969).

Thelma & Louise: overview

At the time of its release, much critical discourse about *Thelma & Louise* revolved around perceptions and analyses of 'feminism' embedded in the film, the ways this feminism challenged expectations of established 'buddy movie' and 'road movie' genres and conventions, and the way this feminism, to some, even hinted at lesbianism. Extensive discussion of the film's feminist stance can be found in Greenberg et al. (1991–1992: 20, 22, 30), Hart (1994: 433), Sturken (2000: 9–12), and Slocum (2007: 137–8). Lesbian overtones were noticed, analyzed, or debated by Dowell et al. (1991: 29), Greenberg et al. (1991–1992: 20), Hart (1994: 440–2), Cook (2002: 182–3), Rich (2003), Slocum (2007: 123, 137), and Sturtevant (2007: 44). With two decades of hindsight, the film's feminism seems celebratory but unremarkably obvious, and the lesbianism, perhaps wishful thinking; nevertheless, the film is at once traditional, formulaic, and groundbreaking.

Dowell et al. contextualized the postulated lesbianism within existing Hollywood cinema of the same genre.

> The formula *Thelma & Louise* follows is the buddy romance-adventure, and it hews to the line faithfully enough to include even the flirtation with same-sex love that observers have noted in such movies as *Butch Cassidy and the Sundance Kid*. (Dowell et al. 1991: 29)

Thelma and Louise, while engaging in heterosexual relations, including Thelma's raucous sexual awakening with a young, smooth Brad Pitt, providing the real eye-candy in the film, seem to flirt deliciously with lesbianism because their buddy relationship is privileged above their relations with men. The two women share a kiss before driving off the cliff together, and while this kiss could exist comfortably within normative American society, here it carries additional weight because of the closeness of the relationship that has already been established. Hart and others suggest that their real transgression is not the kiss or even their violent acts, but their mutual rejection of men and patriarchy.

> Thelma and Louise are not criminals because they shoot a rapist, rob a store, or blow up a truck. They are criminals because they are together, seeking escape from the masculine circuit of desire. (Hart 1994: 445)

These atypical transgressions make the film a savvy reinterpretation of the road movie. Thelma and Louise break gender molds by becoming the center of the action, while it is the men who are the ones chasing after them or sitting on the sidelines.

> Just as historically a gender division of roles led women to depend on men for survival, women in films have also depended on men's control of the narrative. This identification of gender with the active/passive dichotomy became a stock feature in classical films where men portrayed dynamic characters in constant evolution, while women remained static spectators of male action-makers. (Eraso 2001: 63)

Thelma & Louise, in flipping this dichotomy, thematically centralizes agency and empowerment. Two rather ordinary, nearly stereotyped 'southern' women from Arkansas unexpectedly seize control and rebel against misogynist, heteronormative strictures of their quotidian existences. *Thelma & Louise* to a large extent unintentionally presaged the homo-activist road movie *The Living End* (1992) discussed extensively in Chapter 2. Although *The Living End*, with its open homosexuality, HIV, and AIDS, is a sociologically edgier film, it can be argued that *Thelma & Louise* goes further, with greater onscreen destruction, overt attacks on heteronormative society, and the grandiose double suicide at the end.

Thelma & Louise: existing critical discourse and use of song

In addition to the work cited above, whole books are devoted to *Thelma & Louise*, including a scholarly anthology, *Thelma & Louise Live!*, and Marita Sturken's monograph in the BFI Modern Classics series. Many of these academic studies do not address music, and even when they do, they privilege text-based analysis of songs, a rudimentary entry point from which to critique music in cinema. Analysis of song text is indeed helpful, and, by its very nature, open to lay people without musical training. One can hardly claim expertise in music just by virtue of understanding the lyrics, yet film scholars cannot simply ignore the audio track either. This dilemma has led to complications and insecurities within published scholarship, as the analysis of text within music, when present, becomes so heavily weighted.

This book, by overlapping the disciplines of musicology, cinema studies, and queer studies, does not intend to belittle or demean existing work, but rather to tie together various approaches and fill in gaps in scholarship. And indeed, prominent scholars of music and sound for cinema have addressed *Thelma & Louise*, including Claudia Gorbman (2007), Michel Chion (1995: 172–75), and Anahid Kassabian

(2001: 79–85). Jim Healey (1995) published an article specifically about the film's songs.

Gorbman's analysis correlates music and gender, for example which songs feature female performers (2007: 80), and argues that the film traces Thelma and Louise's 'acceptance and embrace of gender transgression, their pleasure in taking phallic power. At every turn, music's presence helps define the process' (2007: 81). Gorbman notes that '[Ray] Charles' presence gives cachet to the film for its thirty-something white middle-class viewership' (2007: 69), addressing issues of marketing and audience affinities addressed in Chapter 2. Kassabian likewise notes how the *Thelma & Louise* soundtrack works by 'mobilizing popular musics to tap emotions and associations that audiences connect with the musics before they ever enter the movie theater' (2001: 85).

Gorbman, in conversation with music supervisor Kathy Nelson, found that director 'Ridley Scott was thinking about specific songs for *Thelma & Louise* even before the film's actors were cast, and he clearly constructed a number of scenes around recorded songs' (2007: 70). Gorbman posits that *Thelma & Louise* features 'uncannily close synching of the songs and their lyrics with the scenes they accompany' (2007: 65), arguing that 'the songs invite a more active reading than orchestral underscoring: they define action, setting, and character, they engage references, parallelism, and metaphors, and sometimes they elaborate complex structures of point of view' (2007: 65). The songs' 'more active reading than orchestral underscoring' might indicate a weakness of Hans Zimmer's score as well, as Kassabian notes, 'Entire portions of the score sound as if they could belong in any film with a synth-pop soundtrack; for instance, the main title rhythm is a rock drum machine standard' (2001: 83). While Hans Zimmer remains popular among film score fan communities and has won numerous high-profile awards, his score for *Thelma & Louise* is marred by tinny, synthesized sounds and repetitious, generic country, blues, and rock gestures that push it away from grandeur and towards the dated 'synth-pop' described by Kassabian.

For my purposes, use of song shows how films like *Thelma & Louise*, *Boys Don't Cry*, and *Transamerica* court the mainstream yet foster sexual, gender, and social transgression at the same time. Although these films rebel against patriarchal heteronormativity, push queer concerns into the mainstream, and push the mainstream towards identification with queer concerns, they rely on traditional, conservative implementation of comfortable, familiar music to do so. As queerness interacts with mainstream cinema, its avant-garde artistry or aesthetic, exemplified by Warhol, Anger, and Smith for example, may be diluted; or its experimental aesthetic may be carefully negotiated, as it is in *Boys Don't Cry*, or carefully preserved, as it is in *Go Fish*.

Thelma & Louise and *Transamerica* deploy, as musical strategy, a similar use of the 'compilation score' whereby popular songs offer commentary or narrative explication through *lyrics*, whilst dramatic underscore is kept minimal and noninvasive. The popular songs' musical styles are used to establish characterizations or take advantage of audience affinities, but it is their lyrical content that is most resonant with the motion picture. Strictly musical features such as tempo and modality are often secondary concerns to messages embedded in the lyrics.[2]

The practice of deploying popular songs predominantly for their lyrical content, or audience knowledge of that content, dates back to the 'silent' period, as Rick Altman discusses in 'Cinema and Popular Song: The Lost Tradition' (2001). An obvious example of this is the repetitious use of 'Dixie' in D. W. Griffith's *Birth of a Nation* (1915), which aggressively signposts the notion of white, southern heroism promoted by the troublesome film.[3] Many people know this technique from its extensive use in cartoons; Carl Stalling, a musical director for Walt Disney, Ub Iwerks, and Warner Bros., relied heavily on this technique, as described by Daniel Goldmark in *Tunes for 'Toons* (2005: 10–43). From the 1930s through the 1950s many Stalling cartoons are a string of musical references.

This technique found a home in road movies and coming-of-age films, cinematic touchstones of youth, rebellion, and popular culture; strong examples of lyrically weighted compilation scores can be found in *The Graduate* (1967), *Easy Rider* (1969), *Harold & Maude* (1971), and *American Graffiti* (1973). As popular song fueled youth culture during this era, so it drives these films. *Harold & Maude's* songs emphasize 'freedom,' and the film boasts a spectacular vehicular suicide ending remarkably similar to *Thelma & Louise*, even if it is a fake-out. *American Graffiti's* songs correlate closely to the film's narrative, as described by Jeff Smith (1998). *Thelma & Louise, Transamerica, Boys Don't Cry*, and *Go Fish* all contain elements of the coming-of-age story; the first three also can be read as road movies. Idiomatic editing techniques, youth culture references, montages, flashbacks, car radios, and evocative situations offer many opportunities where songs can provide functionality beyond setting mood and bridging cuts.

As accompaniments to montages or as atmospheric underscore, compilation scores served all of the classical score's paradigmatic functions, but they tended towards those that maximized rock and roll's special sense of sociocultural specificity. For a new generation cf filmmakers who had grown up on early rock music, the idiom served as a handy and evocative signifier of specific times and places. Moreover, by alluding to particular titles, lyrics, or performers, filmmakers created a kind of two-tiered system of musical communication that augmented and enhanced a larger pattern of allusions to literature, art, popular culture, and cinema. Like this larger system, the patterns of musical allusions could be interwoven with the text's larger configurations of character, theme, and authorial expression. (Smith 1998: 184–85)

In *Thelma & Louise, Transamerica,* and *Boys Don't Cry,* the system is less 'two-tiered,' creating separate information for knowledgeable initiates, than it is a system to draw in a *wider* mainstream audience. This is crucial because the filmmakers endeavored to sell the story to a wide, non-queer audience, and the compilation score helps them do just that. Other factors described by Smith, such as service to the classical score's paradigmatic functions, apply to *Thelma & Louise, Transamerica,* and *Boys Don't Cry.*

Smith notes there are additional, economic conditions that favor compilation scores. The expense of recording a time-consuming orchestral score can be extravagant compared to licensing popular music that can sometimes create 'back end' royalty income for studios that own their own music publishing concerns. These financial incentives and factors

include the resurgence of film and music cross-marketing campaigns, the boom in soundtrack album sales, and the emergence of music supervisors as significant parts of the production practice. Taken together, all of these factors helped to create an environment in which popular musical allusions would flourish as a specific scoring technique. (Smith 2001a: 410–11)

Songs can also be deployed as puns or in an ironic manner, Smith notes.[4] This is not a concern in the films I am examining, which are more consistently ardent and sincere. Smith notes that intelligibility can be a factor in song placement; if a song is well known, lyrics can be inaudible; if lyrics are essential, that will affect its placement in the audio track.

A spectator's attention is mostly directed toward the film's narrative and not toward the decipherment of often unintelligible rock lyrics. However, if the song is already well-known, then the matter of song lyrics becomes more a question of recognition than cognition. (Smith 2001a: 418)

Michel Chion parses the use of songs in *Thelma & Louise*, describing the 'on air' phenomenon (1995: 172–75), a convention I noted in Chapter 2 employed throughout *The Living End*, whereby songs are tied diegetically to car radios. This allows an imitation of reality while transmitting a message embedded in song lyrics.

> Quite a few recent films, notably road-movies or travel films, play with a tapestry of songs heard on-the-air, with varying degrees of presence, intelligibility of words, montages of landscape traversed with song, producing what would seem to be happy coincidences whilst listening to music in the car. The cinema only imitates this game of fortuitous conjunctions, assuming an independent and autonomous existence of action and music or song, so as to organize them equally and give them a precise dramatic and emotional meaning, but making it appear as though it were occurring naturally. (Chion 1995: 174–75; my translation)

Chion notices that, in *Thelma & Louise*, a song will travel through parallel action in different locations, making ambiguous its point of acoustic origin, even as it imitates diegesis. Chion cites the use of Glenn Frey's 'Part of Me, Part of You' that bridges hotel room, swimming pool, and phone call to Jimmy's location back home. Healey, furthermore, notes a shifting meaning in this song, which lyrically 'takes an important twist as the action on the screen changes' (1995: 112). The way such songs are used in *Thelma & Louise*, as knowing commentary sonically situated to suggest diegesis, places them within the 'fantastical gap' proposed by Robynn Stilwell (2007). The gap is a liminal space situated between fully diegetic music, here exemplified by Charlie Sexton's onscreen vocal performance in a bar, and unambiguously non-diegetic music, audible without any logical onscreen source, here exemplified by Hans Zimmer's original score comprised of synths, guitar, drum machine, and orchestra.[5] The 'fantastical gap' concept has usually been applied to *underscore*, but Stilwell's construct fits well in films with compilation scores, because these songs are often 'scource' music, acting simultaneously as underscore, as text-based commentary, and as off-the-shelf licensed source music, with an ambiguous onscreen source.

When the boundary between diegetic and nondiegetic is traversed, it does always *mean*. It is also hardly ever a single moment – one moment we're in the diegetic realm and in the blink of an eye, like walking through Alice's mirror, we are in the nondiegetic looking-glass world. (Stilwell 2007: 186)

The 'fantastical gap' is exploited in *Thelma & Louise* so that songs both convey meaning and beg to appear naturally, making their effect as verbal commentary somewhat subtle. The songs and the 'gap' suggest a space between fiction, reality, and possibility: a place where the story blossoms as vicarious existence, freedom, and rebellion that we all desire. Hence, this metadiegetic gap is another way the film broadens its appeal to a wider audience.

> The trajectory between diegetic music and nondiegetic music that might more precisely be called metadiegetic is not an uncommon trope in modern movies, and is often used as a way of drawing the audience into the subjectivity of a character. (Stilwell 2007: 194)

The metadiegetic songs not only pull us into the time and location of the film's setting, but also represent Thelma and Louise's ambitions and internal compasses, and build our affinities with their characters. In spite of the powerful impact of this trope, the songs seemed to go largely unnoticed or taken for granted by the popular press, as Healey notes:

> Few articles mentioned one aspect of the film which contributed immensely to Thelma and Louise's odyssey: the 18 songs heard throughout the film. When the soundtrack was mentioned, the songs were usually handled in one sweeping sentence. [...] Without the 18 songs, many of which the viewer does not even consciously perceive, *Thelma & Louise* would be a less-than-complete cinematic experience. The songs are the fuel which rhythmically and thematically propel [sic] both the women and the viewer down the road. (1995: 103)

It's a clever metaphor to consider songs the 'fuel' of the road movie, especially when songs are so often connected to car radios. But can songs be just background noise, like the sound of the wind and the road? And does not fuel stink sometimes, even if it is necessary, permeating the air until it becomes either unnoticeable or unbearable? Of course, this can vary by song.

Many of the songs are just background music to the action taking place. In contrast, other songs loom large, either by commenting or by putting another perspective on the action. Of particular difficulty is the problem that the songs are rarely heard in their entirety. (Healey 1995: 104)

But the abbreviation of songs is not a problem, as this is common practice in filmmaking. Music conforms to the moving picture, not the other way around; a scene would not be extended to accommodate a song's entire length. Jeff Smith has looked at 'partial uses' of cues dating back to the beginning of sound film (2013). Partial usages are worthy of commentary when the portion chosen (or rejected) bears some interesting significance.

> [O]nly the chorus of B.B. King's 'Better Not Look Down' is played in the film. [...] The stanzas do not necessarily apply to the action when the song appears, but the chorus fits perfectly. Thus, parts of some songs cleverly match the ongoing action, but to try to apply the song in its entirety, as in the case of B.B. King's tune, to the message of *Thelma & Louise* would be a mistake. (Healey 1995: 104)

Editing songs so they will work with the picture is standard practice in filmmaking. In this way, the audience need not engage too much critical thinking to rapidly interpret the songs' narrative significances. The film's music editors can selectively edit songs, perhaps upsetting their normal linearity, but achieving an appropriate synchronicity with the moving picture. In addition, the film's mixers can boost lines from songs selectively within the overall film sound mix.[6]

> Certain lines of songs come to the forefront during a scene where previously the songs had been in the background. [...] Lines and even phrases from songs are highlighted on the film's soundtrack for a variety of reasons – to intensify emotion, to comment on or complement the action, or to involve the viewer more intimately in the film. (Healey 1995: 104)

Healey identifies how Grayson Hugh's 'I Can't Untie You From Me' plays softly in the background until Jimmy and Louise kiss, at which point a selected, relevant line is pumped louder in the mix: 'For the truth that's in your heart / Is never, ever far away' (1995: 104). Selective use of song gives Healey, Gorbman, and Chion plenty to digest. But these analyses are usually weighted *textual*, less so *musical*. Songs in film are first and foremost a cultural artifact, secondarily a verbal text, and then something that is musical. Perhaps not surprisingly, much analysis of popular song in film comes from fields other than musicology, music theory, or music composition.

Song placement in *Thelma & Louise* was not just the suggestion of music supervisor Kathy Nelson. Callie Khouri, who won the 1992 Academy Award for Best Original Screenplay for *Thelma & Louise*, specifies in her script exact lines from B.B. King's 'Better Not Look Down' to be synchronized with Thelma and Louise speeding over the cliff (Gorbman 2007: 78). Ridley Scott's original cut of the ending faithfully reproduced this effect, but the ending was recut, the song replaced with Zimmer's score. Fortunately, the DVD includes the 'alternate' ending that Ridley Scott originally delivered to the studio's alarm and disapproval.[7]

The 'alternate' ending has spectacular coverage of Thelma and Louise's 1966 Thunderbird plunging 2,000 feet to the bottom of a canyon carved by the Colorado River near Moab, Utah; this dramatic footage was excised, as it left no ambiguity as to the demise of our heroines.[8] The studio felt it was too much, and preferred an ending that left some ambiguity, even if it were symbolic: the theatrical release's ending is not graphic, almost suggesting the car would rise up into the heavens, a mythological ascension, not a real life plummet to certain grisly death. On the DVD commentary, Ridley Scott says it was his idea to recut the end, even as he recounts the studio's negative reaction to the initial cut; this slight self-contradiction should demystify the production process and puncture the balloon of auteur theory.

In this 'alternate' ending, at the moment of a close up of Louise's foot flooring the gas pedal, sending the T-bird over the cliff, an upwards organ glissando leads into the chorus of 'Better Not Look Down': 'Better not look down, if you're gonna keep on flyin.' Regardless of lyrical content, the upbeat, major key excitement of this song communicates fun, imbuing this act with rollercoaster-like enjoyment as we see the car careen into the canyon. If this cut makes their death more explicit, the music also makes it more enjoyable, a celebration of suicidal self-determination.

The ending, of either the theatrical release or alternate version, may rightfully be perceived as dark or revolutionary within the context of Hollywood cinema, *Bonnie and Clyde* (1967) notwithstanding. But an ending featuring romantic suicide, death by love, or double suicide is a longstanding classical tradition, frequently seen in 'Greek tragedy' or baroque literature; consider Shakespeare's *Romeo and Juliet*, or Jean Racine's seventeenth-century dramas *Andromaque* or *Phèdre*. Henry

Purcell's opera *Dido and Aeneas* anchors Dido's final, minor key aria 'When I am Laid in Earth' upon a ground bass with a descending motive, a staple musical indicator of tragedy.[9] As Heather Love discusses in *Feeling Backward: Loss and the Politics of Queer History* (2007), there is a queer affinity with and celebration of the tragic. *Thelma & Louise* reaches beyond queer affinities to the bedrock of romantic classical literature, to a universality that may have been rejected by happy-ending Hollywood but is part of all human cultures.

To combine romantic suicide with the happy jauntiness of 'Better Not Look Down' creates a challenging juxtaposition. The lyrics and conventions of the road movie no doubt made this song choice an irresistible temptation to Khouri, but the choice spins deep-seated societal conceptions of suicide on their head. The song accentuates the joy and impulsiveness of driving over the cliff, something also seen in *Harold and Maude*, and privileges them above literal death or sadness. Hence 'Better Not Look Down' encourages a mythological reading of the film's conclusion; while the rest of the film feels plausible and realistic, the ending 'jumps the shark' to supernatural the moment Louise floors the gas pedal. Subsequent flashbacks to happier times emphasize the supernatural, as if life is passing before our eyes, or we are heading into an afterlife with happy times eternal. But in lieu of making an entirely theoretical reading, let us remember that it is also a Hollywood convention to employ flashbacks, reuse the best footage, and avoid showing bodies in excessive graphic detail. Zimmer's score can be tailored to nuance the reading we (director, studio, test audiences) wish to achieve, whereas 'Better Not Look Down' is pre-recorded and more difficult to manipulate. Here score replaces song, although not through any 'queering' of convention; the theatrical release's ending, while also jarring, is more conventional than Ridley Scott's initial cut in the larger landscape of art and culture.

Transamerica: use of song

Nicole Richter uses *Transamerica* as an example of what she calls 'New Trans Cinema' (2013: 162–63). Features of New Trans Cinema as described by Richter include the necessity of living a double life for a period of time as an obstacle to finding love; a quest for identity of an indefinable self; constructing new conceptions of personhood; and contesting heterosexual romance as constructed fiction. Dramas of romance and identity are complicated through spaces of gender transition and identity construction, and these films extend the question of identity formation to all audiences.

Musicologist Susanna Välimäki notes the film's opening features vocal exercises that defy gender stereotypes, accompanied by the incantation, 'This is the voice I want to use.' The exercises imply choice and empowerment, and relate that agency to biology, audition, and to the creation of sound, the building blocks of music itself. In this way, gender presentation is marked not merely by visual aspects, such as choice of clothing, but also by sound, and by logical extension, music. The vocal glissando that begins the film can be read as a form of music. Välimäki writes, 'the search for a voice of one's own is the main theme of the film,' and sees these vocal exercises as an allegory for the film's story (2013: 373). The exercises' smooth transition through vocal registers defies the binary construct of gender. It is this defiance of the binary that queers gender and transfolk; those who are able to release fixation with the binary are open to accept myriad possibilities, genders, and identities.

In *Transamerica*, Bree Osbourne, formerly Stanley Chupak, discovers he has a son, Toby, age 17, a hustler in jail in New York City. Bree, 'living stealth' as she describes it, journeys across the country with Toby who is unaware that Bree is his biological father. It is on this journey that both characters evolve. Välimäki sees *Transamerica* as queering or 'transgendering' the road movie.

> [T]he classic road movie structure is adopted as the means for depicting the culmination of the protagonist's gender transition, a transgender person's 'coming home' to her/his/hir true self (and new, true body). [...] [T]he journey trope – 'departure, transition, and the home of reassignment' – is common in transsexual autobiographies and other discourses of transsexuality. In *Transamerica* Bree has already undertaken a long journey [...] which also includes accepting her parenthood and coming out to her son as his father and a transgender person. (Välimäki 2013: 375)

Transamerica, like *Thelma & Louise*, makes use of a compilation score idiomatic to the road movie genre. And like the songs in *Thelma & Louise*, the music in *Transamerica* is not merely 'driving music,' but connects with the intentions and nuances of the film.

> [*Transamerica*'s] music – most of which is archetypal 'road music' mixed with travel montages in conventional ways – is appropriated to construct transgender meanings and subjectivity: an auditory version of the transsexual journey trope of traveling and border crossings. (Välimäki 2013: 375)

'The journey' is an important archetype for a film about transfolk. Much contemporary discourse concerns issues of identity, discovery, transition, and empowerment; the 'journey' is a romantic, appropriate, *universal* allegory in which to wrap the story and sell it to a wide audience. The 'journey' is fertile subject matter in popular music, and it is easy to find songs that lyrically address the 'journey.' Välimäki identifies and discusses three

> musical transgender (queer) strategies in *Transamerica*: (1) the use of American, country-based roots music to symbolize an identity in transition; (2) the use of music encoded in terms of ethnic or 'racial' identity to highlight transgender people's social status and to create a potentially progressive social space of intersectionality and multiculturality; and (3) the play on the human voice. (Välimäki 2013: 376)

Välimäki argues that American country, bluegrass, folk, and gospel music are used to construct transgender subjectivity because they 'inflect in various ways themes of travel, questing, soul-searching, and transformation, and the idea of redemption from a present burden' (Välimäki 2013: 376). It is no struggle to find lyrics that fit these themes and read a double meaning as applied to transfolk: Välimäki posits that lyrics about 'chains,' taken from a biblical context, can also refer to the weight of the 'wrong' body, for example, as in the Old Crow Medicine Show song 'Take 'em Away.'

Rootsy music performed by Lucinda Williams, Nitty Gritty Dirt Band, and Old Crow Medicine Show in *Transamerica* emphasizes its characters and setting as 'American,' a localization Välimäki sees signposted directly in the film's title. Emphasizing an 'American' quality through music makes the film more marketable to a domestic audience, and builds audience affinities with otherwise outsider characters. (Bree is trans, but she's American!)

Not all the music bears the same stylistically 'American' connotative markers, yet still ties in to Bree's story. The first song Bree plays on her home stereo, somewhere in Los Angeles, is 'Jol'inkomo,' written by Gibson Mtutuzeli Kente and Letta Mbulu, performed by Miriam Makeba, recorded and released in 1967 in the United States on the *Pata Pata* LP on Reprise Records. Makeba (1932–2008) was a South African singer and civil rights activist. In 1966 Makeba shared a Grammy Award with Harry Belafonte for *An Evening With Belafonte/Makeba*, an album with African music and anti-apartheid themes. The use of Makeba's music ties Bree's gender transition and personal struggles to a greater civil rights movement with a broad, international history. To those who do not recognize 'Jol'inkomo' or Makeba's backstory, the music nevertheless situates Bree within a multicultural environment that will be reinforced throughout the film in an interesting counterpoint to the 'American' quality frequently represented by white performers such as Williams and Old Crow Medicine Show.

Bree works as a humble dishwasher in 'Papi's Kitchen,' a storefront 'Latin Caribbean – Mexican & Sea Food' restaurant. This Latino-coded, Angeleno, working class environment is flavored with the song 'Maldito Cabaret,' written by Luis Bernardo Saldarriaga and performed by Los Pamperos, a Colombian group active in the 1950s and 1960s. This music signifies ethnicity, class, and social status for the film's presumptively white, middle class, American audience; Välimäki argues that 'Latin music affirms the Hispanic setting of Bree's life, but it also draws parallels between racism and transphobia' (Välimäki 2013: 379). 'The use of Latin music aligns Bree's identity with marginal whiteness, deviance, and social displacement' (Välimäki 2013: 380). The sequential usages of 'Jol'inkomo' and 'Maldito Cabaret' early in the film emphasize Bree's 'marginal' whiteness, her proximity to the margins of society, and her struggles to succeed financially and emotionally under adverse conditions. Latin music also cannily pulls the transgender story away from the clichéd domain of 'white people's problems' and 'first world problems.' Välimäki notes that 'It is precisely Hispanics as well as Native American people, not white people, who accept Bree as she is' (Välimäki 2013: 380). In as much as *Transamerica* addresses issues of ethnicity, music is used to outline cultural identifications.

Music continually leverages identities and affiliations in *Transamerica*. Briefly, Bree and Toby battle over the car radio (DVD 0:19:35); Toby favors hard rock, while Bree prefers a calmer, rootsy Americana. This common vignette, also seen between Luke and Jon in *The Living End* described in Chapter 2, brings music to the narrative forefront in order to clarify generational and cultural divides between Bree and her son. Although the story is told from Bree's point of view, Toby's character adds complexities and exposes cycles of abuse that give the story an added weight of family drama beyond the initial struggle for Bree to qualify for her surgery. One might argue that the surgery is the film's 'McGuffin,' and the real story is Bree's resolutions and reconciliations with her family and son. While the surgery holds more importance than a standard 'McGuffin' plot device, it is nevertheless the ensuing drama and interaction with Toby that give the film its full depth and richness.

Toby is initially presented as a juvenile man-boy street hustler, so inconsequential and worthless that his bail is set at one dollar. Toby aspires to move to Los Angeles, become a blond, and work as an actor in homosexual pornographic films. While this glib introduction seems to paint Toby as both simple and comical, there is a definite independence and pragmatism behind his plan. As Bree hides her trans identity, so Toby also hides his recreational drug use. Toby's motive is clear, to get to Los Angeles, while Bree's motive is ulterior, as she does not reveal why she is giving Toby a free ride. Bree is more opaque than Toby, although they both have secrets.

Bree concocts a plan to dump Toby back 'home' with his stepfather in the fictional Appalachian town of Callicoon, Kentucky. In this context 'Take 'Em Away,' written by Christopher Day Fuqua, projects its meaning, playing as Bree drives over country roads into the tiny town. While the audience knows Bree's plan, Toby does not. The lyrics project Bree's thinking that bringing Toby back to Callicoon will offer him safety or salvation: 'Open up your gate now, let me put down my load / So I can feel at ease and go back to my home.' Alternatively, these lyrics could imply that Toby is Bree's load, and if she drops him off, she can go back to Los Angeles alone; but the stronger implication is that this is Toby's return home to the small town where he grew up.

But while Toby grew up in Callicoon, it is no safe haven. *Transamerica* rapidly discards its light, comedic tone as audience and Bree are confronted with Toby's violent stepfather and backstory of abuse and molestation. The film plunges into a dark place that explains Toby and rationalizes his situation in New York and his demi-monde survival strategies. Toby's awkward reunion with his stepfather and the stepfather's brutal eruption are not scored with any music, only realistic ambiences of crickets and what might be a distant radio or conversation in an adjacent home. This scene is shot with hand-held camera, the visual shakiness adding to an overall cinéma vérité effect. An African American neighbor, who helped raise Toby, witnesses the scene; she also seems shocked, perhaps clued in but unaware of the extent of the domestic abuse. While it's a minor role, her presence reinforces the ties to communities of color that both Bree and her son have.

The entire Callicoon visit sequence is introduced and prefaced by 'Take 'Em Away.' Välimäki's reading that the song's 'chains' refer to Bree and her relationship to her body is intriguing but flawed. 'Take away these chains from me / My heart is broken 'cause my spirit's not free / Lord take away these chains from me.' While 'Take 'Em Away' could hold a double meaning, these proverbial chains are not Bree's as much as they are Toby's. When Toby left home for New York, he broke the chains that had held him in bondage and trapped him in Callicoon. When Bree realizes the full extent of Toby's situation, she becomes genuinely remorseful, not the least because she had suffered her own familial abuse from parents who hired private detectives and tried to have her committed. The song musically is part of the Americana stitchery that holds the film together, while the lyrics accentuate themes of home and bondage.

The Callicoon sequence establishes a counterpoint between abusive and absent fathers, underscoring Bree's own failings as a parent. In a mirror to this sequence, Bree and Toby later go to Phoenix, Arizona, to visit Bree's parents, who are also manipulative and dysfunctional. Similarly to the scene with Toby and stepfather, there is no music used for Bree's reunion with her parents. While Fionnula Flanagan leans a bit over the top in her role as Bree's mother Elizabeth, the lack of music underplays any comedy, whether intended, unintended, or augmented by acting style at this reunion. Similar to *The Living End*, dramatic moments are left dry to heighten realism and to balance or contrast moments of comedy or whimsy.

Despite making bold challenges to heteronormativity, *Transamerica*, like *Thelma & Louise*, features conventional use of song and compilation score. This usage becomes part of the craft that seduces the audience, as D. A. Miller argues of *Brokeback Mountain*, discussed in Chapter 3. *Transamerica* likewise deliberately courts mainstream audience affinities. Songs are not used where they would interfere in dramatic scenes, but are employed liberally throughout to draw the audience into the film.

> The mainstream audience is not alienated from the film's transgender protagonist, but rather can identify and sympathize with the protagonist thanks to the appealing, demystifying music. [...] There might also be some gentle queer irony in the choice of American country music, traditionally considered very conservative and normative, as the music of transgenderness. Indeed, the film manages to address two distinct audiences at the same time, the mainstream and the transgender. (Välimäki 2013: 382)

The film would lose credibility if it did not appeal to a trans audience, and it would not likely recoup expenses or show a profit if it ignored a mainstream audience. Music helps bring in the mainstream, but there is no reason a trans person might not also enjoy such Americana country music, 'queer irony' notwithstanding.[10]

The film's signature tune, Dolly Parton's 'Travelin' Thru,' is held in abeyance until the end of the film, but is cleverly presaged by 'I Am a Pilgrim' (traditional), arranged and performed by Duncan Shiek on acoustic guitar and voice.[11] 'I Am a Pilgrim' appears quietly and briefly when Bree first takes Toby to lunch in New York City after bailing him out of jail (DVD 0:11:50). It plays softly as background music; the performance is ragged enough to suggest that it might be an offscreen live performer in the restaurant.[12] The audible refrain, 'I am a pilgrim and a stranger, travelling through this wearisome land' foreshadows their trans-American road trip and models the lyrics for Dolly Parton's own original song: 'Like a poor wayfaring stranger that they speak about in song, I'm just a weary pilgrim trying to find what feels like home.' It would be reasonable to suspect that 'I Am a Pilgrim' or its lyrics may have been presented to Dolly as a guide or demonstration of what director Duncan Tucker was looking for. According to Parton, Tucker offered direction and 'he wanted the song to be about redemption and about people's feelings' (Cooper 2006).

Parton's 'Travelin' Thru,' which she wrote and recorded specifically for *Transamerica*, plays at the end of the film when Bree and Toby have finally reconciled at Bree's home in Los Angeles, and it leads into the end credits. Therefore 'Travelin' Thru' comments on the whole movie, not any particular scene. These two lyrically similar songs about pilgrims, strangers, and traveling, 'I Am a Pilgrim' and 'Travelin' Thru,' serve as bookends for Bree and Toby's story. As such, this narrative arc begins with the traditional and concludes with the new. 'I Am a Pilgrim' is a public domain folk composition presented in a simple rendition. 'Travelin' Thru' is a bright, contemporary, catchy, original song, musically optimistic and hopeful.

'Travelin' Thru,' beyond the 'journey' metaphor, adds on a 'puzzle' metaphor, wherein Dolly sings of trying to 'figure out where all my pieces fit.' This line can be read as an identity struggle and a reference to the film's transgender theme, yet it is also self-referential to Parton herself, who occupies a liminal space between traditional, conservative country music and self-made, self-empowered gender construction.

Transamerica: Dolly Parton and constructed femininity

The intertextual deployment of Dolly Parton imparts, with sugary sweetness, multiple messages about the film and, by extension, about trans people to the audience. A mainstream audience is likely to know and like Parton. Part of Parton as 'text' is her self-constructed presentation of gender, her self-creation as an entertainer and busi-nesswoman, and her openness about surgery.[13] These factors all have subjective or relative parallels in the trans community; therefore, issues that must be addressed in a film about trans people can be suggested or spoon-fed through referencing Dolly as text. I would like to reiterate that it is important *not* to equate cosmetic surgery with transgender surgeries; the parallel is that Parton, although not transgender herself, is also situated within a broader cultural debate on gender, body modifica-tion, and bodily ownership.

In 1995, Pamela Wilson published an extraordinarily prescient and relevant critique, 'Mountains of Contradictions: Gender, Class, and Region in the Star Image of Dolly Parton' that analyzes the complexities of Parton's image, public perception of that image, and Parton's exer-tion of control thereof (Wilson 1995). Wilson notes that

> Dolly Parton's appearance, notably, the images of her body and espe-cially her breasts, has become the terrain for a discursive struggle in the popular press over the social meaning of the female body and the associated ideologies that compete for control over the meaning of 'woman' in our society. Parton has consciously and strategically created a star persona that incorporates and even exploits many of the gender contradictions that currently circulate in society. (Wilson 1995: 111–12)

Wilson carefully unpacks how Parton has managed and manipulated her sexual image, her identification with working-class women (like Bree), and 'contested meanings of gender – the social construction of "woman"' (Wilson 1995: 120). While Wilson does not bring up trans-folk or directly address surgery, this is essential groundwork that estab-lishes why Dolly Parton is so apropos to *Transamerica*.

One aspect of transgender narratives and experiences is an exposi-tion of how gender is internalized, externalized, and performed by *everyone*; most people are unaware of these performances and accept cultural gender normativities without question. Transfolk question gen-der assumptions and performances, and make us aware of them. Dolly Parton, although not trans herself, has likewise made people aware of the artifice and performative aspects of gender.

> Parton's carnivalized country femininity is a paean to the erotics of artifice. Every facet of her body has been exaggerated to match the outlandish dimensions of those infamous breasts: hair, cheekbones,

lips, hips, height. [...] their grand sum has attracted as much attention as her accomplished musical talents (and increasingly, excep-
tional business savvy). More than any other legendary country
female performer, Parton *is* body, although one that appears to both
epitomize and defy the laws of nature. (Fox 1998: 257–58)

Gender is, of course, *more* than body; it is identity, culture, politics,
and performance, to name a few; it encompasses physical, sociological,
and anthropological constructs. It is essential *not* to conflate the body
or its genitals with gender; to do so reduces the complexities of gender
to body parts, and even bodies can be subject to naturally occurring
variances.[14] Likewise, 'Dolly Parton' as performer and as text touches
upon more than body as well; she has a depth and complexity people
know, and the audience can extend those associations to the film's
trans subjects, rendering them equally deep, complex, and human.
Dolly's personal narrative has a thematic connection to the film on
multiple levels.

Recent feminist cultural critics have made laudable efforts to understand the body politics of Parton's image, envisioning it as a deliberate parody of dominant cultural norms for women. [...] [I]s 'Dolly
Parton' an explicit invention with subversive under currents? Her
autobiography provides another means of reading her performative gestures specifically in the context of country music discourse.
Country metanarratives of Loss and Desire have particular salience
here, as Parton's impoverished Smoky Mountain childhood so markedly pales beside her current material excess. At this point, which
is the fiction: her past, or present, incarnation? According to the
dictates of country authenticity, Parton must make good in both
her stage performance and in the example of her 'real' life story one
of the autobiography's central tenets: 'Although I look like a drag
queen's Christmas tree on the outside, I am at heart a simple country
woman.' (Fox 1998: 257–58)

The tortured concept of 'authenticity' resonates with both Parton and
transfolk, who are often attacked for challenging presumptions of their
'true' gender. Parton's persona encompasses both 'Christmas tree' and
'simple country woman'; Bree can also be read as a 'simple' woman
who works in a restaurant. This false dichotomy, of outlandish presentation and simplicity, suggests questions of *musical* authenticity. What
music are we supposed to like or listen to? What music are we allowed

to perform?[15] Can we appropriate Americana music for a film about a transwoman? The counterbalance to 'authenticity' is 'artifice,' or the act of willful creation. Why would we value one over the other? Dolly Parton's persona, in containing both authenticity and artifice, becomes an allegory for transfolk and for musical appreciation.

> Parton's life story verifies her own authenticity by recuperating abjection – allowing it to take another, more Desirable, form. That form may be an explicit construction, both in terms of her intangible image and very real body. She is in fact quite candid about her efforts to deliberately reshape and augment the latter through cosmetic surgery [...] 'Dolly Parton' becomes a separate, almost reified persona which her body literally creates. Yet in the end, it does not quite function as a means of critical parody. Parton understands that gender is performance: achieving the right hair color, conforming to a seemingly impossible hour-glass bodily ideal. [... Parton] exchanges the class-based objectification of her past for a gender-based one in the present. The Dolly character represents the literal embodiment of her own personal 'dream.' (Fox 1998: 259–60)

The notion of 'transformation' is central to 'the Dolly character': from rags to riches, from unknown to celebrity, from backwoods to mansion, from submissive wife to powerful businesswoman, from singer to theme park. These transformations create a lattice of complexity that becomes 'Dolly'; while it is easy to be dismissive of Dolly's 'carnivalized' (Fox 1998: 257) image, 'Dolly' is a monument to self-creation and self-realization, from Dollywood in Pidgeon Forge to Dolly's ability to handle the popular press.

Dominic Clarke in *Indiewire* makes the connection between Parton and transfolk, seeing Parton's inclusion in *Transamerica* as a way to indicate irony and injustice:

> It's highly problematic that a woman can go to a plastic surgeon and get FF sized breasts implanted in her chest without question but someone searching out gender conforming surgeries is required to undergo psychiatric evaluation and be deemed mentally ill before they can receive surgery. (Clarke 2014)

Clarke suggests that *Transamerica* uses Parton to critique inconsistencies in public policy and sentiment around issues of body and gender. These inconsistencies certainly exist, and yet, in fact, Dolly *has* answered many questions from the press about her breasts and surgery, and this may be another point in common with transfolk. From a theoretical standpoint, Parton is highly relevant to transgender studies, a field that examines

> anything that disrupts, denaturalizes, rearticulates, and makes visible the normative linkages we generally assume to exist between the biological specificity of the sexually differentiated human body, the social roles and statuses that a particular form of body is expected to occupy, the subjectively experienced relationship between a gendered sense of self and social expectations of gender-role performance, and the cultural mechanisms that work to sustain or thwart specific configurations of gendered personhood. (Stryker 2006: 3)

This describes Parton well, who has disrupted many assumptions, social roles, and statuses. Such disruption is not only seen in Parton's image, but has been heard in some of Parton's best-known songs. George Lewis discusses Dolly Parton's contributions to the 'Sex-Role Conflict in Modern American Country Music' through songs like '9 to 5' and 'To Daddy.'

> By conflict, I mean problems arising from the clash of perspectives of differentially socialized individuals, whether this difference is a result of differences in gender, social class, age, region, or other major demographic differences. Such conflicts involve different views of the world and what is appropriate, or involve conflicts between mutually incompatible expectations and values, especially in the area of male-female sex roles, as in the Dolly Parton hit song '9 to 5,' in which social class, gender and sex role conflict are reflected. (Lewis 1989: 232)

Dolly's social disruptions include her music; one can argue that songs like '9 to 5' 'transition' beyond country western to mainstream 'top 40' popular music. In this case, it is one more journey that makes Parton symbolic of transition and transgression. '9 to 5' also incorporates a typewriter as part of the rhythm section, placing the song within the secretarial world of the film *9 to 5* (1980). While 'Travelin' Thru' does not contain that kind of highly signposted musical-narrative connection, it does feature a sumptuous melisma on 'thru' during the breakdowns; this can be read as an emphasis on, or 'word painting' of, journey and transition. Parton also word paints 'fly' with an octave-wide ascending glissando. These vocal ornaments are idiomatic to Parton's country style; she is, after all, by her own account, a 'simple country woman' (Fox 1998: 258).

Boys Don't Cry

Boys Don't Cry was made for $1.7 million, financed by the independent production company Hart-Sharp, and sold to Searchlight Pictures for $5 million (Vachon 2006: 93, 101). After struggles with the MPAA, it was released with an R rating (Vachon 2006: 103–7). Director Kimberly Peirce's first feature is an adaptation of the true story of Brandon Teena, a transman raped and murdered by acquaintances threatened by the unintended exposure of his biological sex. The film was a critical hit; Hilary Swank won the 2000 Academy Award for Best Actress for her portrayal of Brandon.

Peirce devoted five years of research to the film, initially making a short called 'Take It Like A Man' while pursuing an MFA in film at Columbia University in New York. Feminist scholars such as Elizabeth Schewe have criticized *Boys Don't Cry*'s erasure of Philip DeVine, an African American man murdered alongside Brandon; Schewe also emphasizes the theme of the unsafe 'home' and the tradition of 'gay migration' to find a new home (Schewe 2014). These themes can also be read in *Transamerica*, with its uncomfortable visits to Toby's abusive stepfather and to Bree's manipulative mother. And like *Transamerica*, *Boys Don't Cry* can be considered a queer twist on the road movie. Peirce discusses how the process of editing the film helped to frame it within the road movie genre:

> What's interesting was that the dream of a highway had always been there in the writing, in the script, but that really in the editing, because of the way the film had been photographed, it became such a central piece in terms of the beginning, the middle, and the end, visually. Dreams of escape. Wanting to get out of these circumstances. The highway being the one place that you could go to that would lead you out. And also the road in American culture being the place where people have sex, where people are raped, where we're all teenagers, where we're free. So we start the movie on the highway, inside Brandon's dream of himself, and follow as he takes to the highway to make that dream come true. Meets a girl he wants to escape onto the highway with, and who ultimately takes to the highway. (Peirce 2009: 1:41:20)

Similar to other road movies examined in this chapter, *Boys Don't Cry* uses a compilation score, a selection of appropriate songs, in addition to original music composed by Nathan Larson, guitarist for American indie-rock band Shudder to Think. Larson would go on to score other films including *The Woodsman* (2004) and *Palindromes* (2004).

Much of Larson's original score feels improvisational; the score features lots of little guitar bits, flourishes, atmospherics, and 'tones' as described by Kimberly Peirce, instead of formal symphonic arrangements. Larson's music can be compared favorably to similar guitar scores such as Gustavo Santaolalla's score for *Brokeback Mountain* (2005) and Neil Young's music for *Dead Man* (1995). The avoidance of an orchestral score helps ground the film in the humble, earthy, Americana expanse of rural Nebraska, and in the working class backgrounds of the characters. Larson's score also matches and blends well with the guitar-oriented songs and source music placed throughout the film.

Boys Don't Cry: use of song

Although copiously researched, *Boys Don't Cry* intentionally avoids the story of Brendan's gender transformation, and starts at the beginning of his romance with Lana (Peirce 2009: 0:02:00). The title sequence encompasses the first night that Brandon has the courage to dress up as a boy, and goes out on the town to Broadway Skateland. The music is The Cars' 1978 debut single, 'Just What I Needed.' Peirce originally placed Boston's 'More Than A Feeling' here, but that song proved unaffordable. Peirce wanted a 'teenage fantasy' song, and settled on 'Just What I Needed.'

> I was worried about The Cars early on, because I thought it was going to be too hard and repetitious. If you listen to that song, it has a great deal of repetition in it. But the great thing about a good sound mix is you can do what we call 'soaking it.' You can put a lot of the sound into reverb and you can echo it out so it's a lot softer and more romantic. (Peirce 2009: 0:03:50)

Inside the skating rink, as Peirce describes, the music becomes reverbed and placed in 'perspective,' transforming it into a delicate, pulsating bed beneath dialogue. The song disappears across a dissolve to an exterior shot where Brandon, having escorted home a girl he met at the skating rink, kisses her in the dark street in front of her house.

> At this point, we actually pull all the music out. Let it go to silence. And the memory of the music, hopefully, [is] echoing in the audience's mind. Then when we bring it back, the sound is much harder, and then we throw it into reverb and we soak it, so that it's echoing out into the future that Brandon is walking into. (Peirce 2009: 0:04:25)[16]

As discussed previously, songs can easily be tied diegetically to locations like skating rinks, bars, and cafés where music occurs naturally, and this music can be selected to establish audience affinities or emphasize narrative elements. Songs can be substituted or swapped out, if they can do the same job for a better price. For a drive down the highway after Brandon meets his new friends, Candace, John Lotter, and Tom Nissen, Peirce uses 'And It's All Right' by the Dictators because she couldn't afford AC/DC, Black Sabbath, or Megadeth; The Dictators offered the same basic raw metal sound but at a more affordable price (Peirce 2009: 0:10:35).

Brandon soon meets up again with his new friends at a roadside bar with karaoke. Lynryd Skynyrd's 1973 southern rock anthemic ballad 'Tuesday's Gone' plays in the bar.

> The use of Lynryd Skynyrd was important because that was the guys' song to introduce the bar, but then it also had to be romantic enough and steamy enough to get this moment, when Lana stares at Brandon and asks, 'who are you,' which is the question of the movie. (Peirce 2009: 0:14:50)

The next song in the bar is Lana and her friends' karaoke performance of Ruthless Heart's 'Bluest Eyes in Texas,' which the real life Lana actually sang to the real life Brandon. Much later in the film, after Brandon's murder, a guitar plays 'an echo of "The Bluest Eyes in Texas," Brandon's anthem' (Pierce 2009: 1:51:00). 'Bluest Eyes' does not hold any particularly salient *lyrical* reference (other than to the color blue, a visual motif for the film, further discussed below), but an *historical* one, preserving a factual detail of Lana and Brandon's true life romance; it becomes Brandon's 'anthem' by virtue of its historical connection to the real story.

Although Lana sings to Brandon, the singing is not reciprocated. Brandon will later tell Lana that 'I can't sing to save my life' (DVD 00:27:45). An audience member could reasonably surmise that this could be part of Brandon's cover, for if he *did* sing, it might reveal a biologically high-pitched voice. But there may be other sociological factors at play as well. Kalinak has correlated singing with socialization, as noted in Chapter 3 on *Brokeback Mountain*; I noted that singing can be a reinforcement of masculinity, based upon performance practices, even as some films connotively portray singing as sissifying. In either case, singing as social practice reflects gender traits. Peirce has said that Brandon adopts John as a male role model and father figure (Peirce 2009: 0:09:30). While John and Tom *observe* women singing at the bar, they do not participate in it themselves; this establishes a norm within their circle of man as observer (and evaluator) of singing. It would make sense for Brandon, who wants to fit in with his new male friends, to emulate John's behavior with regard to singing.

The film's upbeat eponymous title song plays when Lana bails Brandon out of jail, and the two run out of the building together.

> We tried using the Cure version of ['Boys Don't Cry'] and I love it so much, but it just sounds very '80s and British pop. And it takes you right out of this world. So Nathan redid it in the style of the Replacements. And it's another one of those examples where the song is actually binding all these scenes together in a way that, if you broke them apart, it would just slow the momentum down. (Peirce 2009: 1:12:30)

A filmmaker can selectively prune intertextual references by having a composer or other performer cover an existing song. Having Nathan redo the song preserves its title, lyrics, upbeat tempo, and energy, but gives it a more American flair, jettisoning the '80s British feel, and making it more a part of the film's rural Nebraskan setting. Covering the song also may have made it cheaper; Peirce would only have to pay for one of two 'sides': a synchronization license from the publisher for the underlying composition, but not a master use license from the record label for using the original Cure recording.

Boys Don't Cry: overlaps, tones, and use of score

Boys Don't Cry reinforces introspective, dreamy, and suspended moments with ethereal atmospherics and 'tones,' composed by Larson, that often meld with source music or effects tracks. Peirce describes one scene at a factory with John smoking and watching Lana from afar.

> The fun part of areas like this for me was that we got to have visual scenes that didn't have dialogue and that allowed the music to do interesting things. Like sometimes the music was reaching into a prior scene and pulling you forward, as it does in this one, using reverb to pull you forward. Nathan composed a lot of great stuff. Tones. (Peirce 2009: 1:05:30)

These 'tones' are possibly from guitar, but are of ambiguous instrumentation and heavily reverbed to give them a dreamy, abstract quality.

They blend with the sound effects and ambience tracks, making them appear as environmental as the diegetic sounds. Nathan's 'tones' appear throughout the film in dreamy or suspended moments.

At a flashback to Brandon and Lana's outdoor sexual assignation and apparent sexual insertion (DVD 0:58:10), the sounds are abstract and indeterminate, neither the sounds of the river nor the factory in the background. Similar sustained tones and ambiguous sounds also occur at the courthouse interior, when the Cop says to Brandon, 'You tell me' (1:08:40); when Brandon is in his cell in an orange jumpsuit (1:09:00); when Candice finds Brandon's tampon (1:09:35) and his court summons (1:10:10); and when Lana asks John, 'Do you trust me enough?' (1:20:00).

Nathan's music is at times used to complement existing source music tracks. As Brandon and his friends speed down a dirt road, there is a shot of a pursuing cop car seen through a dust cloud (0:40:45). The source music track phases (a swirly effect also sometimes called 'comb filtering'), and is reverbed to unintelligibility; what sounds like original score – Nathan's guitar – is layered on top of it. This blends and maximizes the potential of both song and score; the overlaps are ambiguous.[17] This similarly occurs when Brandon makes out with Lana at the riverbank (0:54:38); what is presumably Larson's guitar leads into a psych rock track.

There are brief incidental guitar cues, presumably by Larson, that accent similar moments. The electrical tower time lapse features a guitar intro and brief rock number (0:46:30); when Lana tells Brandon, 'Don't be scared,' this leads into a little guitar cue, and a flashback to the electrical tower (1:20:45); Lana and Brandon lie on Lana's bed, discussing a fantasy of living in a trailer park and having an Airstream, and a touch of tremolo guitar acts as a 'prelap' or 'sound advance' to the Hunt County courthouse daytime exterior (1:06:47).

Peirce uses not only music, but also sound effects to work as a 'prelap' or 'sound advance.' Following Brandon's forced bodily exposure before Lana, we see a close-up of Lana in a blue jacket. We don't know where she is yet, but we hear the sounds of the police station *before* we see a clear establishing shot.

> We're soaking the sound advance with the police station, so that you're inside Lana's mind. And as the sound is clearing up, then the scene is clearing up, and the audience is being brought into the present. (Peirce 2009: 1:24:05)

The washed-out sound, in combination with the ambiguous location, gives an effect of distraction; Lana seems distracted, and as the sound clears up, things gradually come into focus narratively. We recover from the shock of the violence of Brandon's forced exposure at the same time as Lana.

Peirce makes strategic use of absolute silence, a striking effect when used in cinema.[18] John violently and forcibly exposes Brandon before Lana; what follows is a stylized, frozen moment of Brandon surrounded by his abusers and observers in the bathroom, with severe, interrogation-like pinspot lighting on Brandon.

> The real horror for Brandon is becoming conscious of what's been done to him. That's where everything slows down. It's a moment out of time. That was the first time we went to absolute silence – the silence that we didn't go to during the car race. (Peirce 2009: 1:23:25)

The silence not used in the car race was an earlier opportunity to use this effect, but Peirce decided absolute silence should be used only once in the film. The effect of absolute silence is to make everything stop, and freeze; the audience can hear themselves in the theatre, and can become self-conscious of their own participation in the film.

Boys Don't Cry: visual color

A striking feature of *Boys Don't Cry* is the visual look of the film, and how it connects to narrative and to sound. The bright primary colors of *Boys Don't Cry* were a reaction to the popularity of the bleach bypass process at the time, and a conscious step away from it (Peirce 2014). The bleach bypass process for developing color film allows silver to be retained in the emulsion, giving the image reduced saturation, increased contrast, and some of the arty qualities of a black-and-white image as well as the normal colors. Peirce consciously avoided this technique, preferring to use bright colors and increased saturation to show Brandon's 'version of reality and what he wanted' (Peirce 2014). The film features brilliantly exaggerated, dominating blues and contrasting accents of bright oranges, with almost Technicolor-like brightness. This idealized view of the world through Brandon's desire is 'not intellectual, but of the heart' (Peirce 2014). What Brandon wanted was to be one of the guys, to get the girl, and to participate in an uncomplicated, idealized American masculinity, and the use of primary colors, most notably blue, was intended to help communicate his desires and outlook.

Boys Don't Cry surrounds us in a blue landscape with blue horizons, blue sky, and blue light. The title sequence's skating rink has a magnificent blue disco globe. Candace lives in a blue house with blue lawn chairs, blue pillowcases, and wears a blue bathrobe. Lana has blue drapes at home and wears a blue uniform at work in a blue factory. The bar pool table has blue felt. Blue streetlights light the blue highway. Inside the blue gas station convenience store are blue racks, the cashier's blue uniform, and blue products: Stayfrees, Kleenex, Hefty bags, and the blue ring case. Brandon's 'anthem' is the 'Bluest Eyes in Texas.' There is lots of blue clothing: blue jeans and blue jackets. Says Peirce, 'it took a lot of effort to get the color of the jeans right' (Peirce 2014). Peirce wanted to depict an 'American landscape,' an 'idealized version of the Midwest' through 'aesthetic control' and the use of color.

In contrast to the blue, Tom Nissen wears a yellow hoodie. Brandon wears an orange jumpsuit as he sits on his blue bed in jail. Lana's blue eyes and jacket are offset by a red shirt. Brandon's 'failure to appear' court notice is red. Brandon wears a red jacket when he is murdered; there's red blood and Lana's red fingernails. After the murders of Brandon and Candace, a red sky turns to blue.

Blue has a wide range of connotations in addition to Peirce's own explanation of a stylized look that conveys Brandon's idealized view of reality and desire. Blue gives the film a cool look, a cool temperature; it suggests sadness, as in 'the blues'; it suggests expansiveness, like the sky and the ocean, not to mention the gendered cliché of identifying blue as a 'boys' color.'

A body of existing theory and research connects visual color to music or sound. I will briefly outline some of these correlations and theories in order to establish a context for my ensuing discussion on how the striking approach to visual color in *Boys Don't Cry* is reflected in the use of music and sound.

In 1912, Italian Futurist Bruno Corra devised and built a contraption he called a 'chromatic piano' with 28 keys that illuminated 28 colored light bulbs to 'create a music of colors' which he also called 'chromatic music' (Corra 1912). 'Chromatic' here as used by Corra does *not* refer to musical chromaticism or half-steps, but to visual chroma and visual color. Corra was trying to treat color as he imagined music; the device allowed one to mix colored lights, which Corra called 'chromatic harmony.' Regardless of his results, Corra was at the very least thinking of color in musical terms.

The uncommon sensory phenomenon of synesthesia, or 'color-hearing,' whereby some individuals 'see' or associate visual colors with specific musical pitches, has long been studied, and has influenced the work of composers including Alexander Scriabin and Olivier Messiaen. New Age musician Steven Halpern has a 'Spectrum Suite' (1977) based upon color-coded movements. Research on synesthesia has been published by biologist Otto Ortmann (1933), developmental psychologists Simon Baron-Cohen and John E. Harrison (1997), musicologist Kenneth Peacock (1988), art theorist B. M. Galeyev (2007), cinema scholar Joshua Yumibe (2009), and art historians Greta Berman (1999) and Brian Evans (2005).

Film historian Russell Merritt (2008) notes a correlation of Technicolor with certain film genres, including musicals, during a time when there were several available commercial color processes from which to choose. This correlation connects a particular color film process and its corresponding visual color palette with music; the brightness of Technicolor is associated with the vibrancy of the musical.

Film scholar Clark Farmer (2008) postulates that animators for Walt Disney's *Fantasia* (1940) selected visual colors to track certain musical instruments; violins are yellow, for example. (This differs from synesthesia, in which specific *pitches* are associated with colors.) In this case, the visual color used by animators follows after and takes its cues from the pre-recorded music in *Fantasia*.

I argue that the reverse is possible: a composer or sound designer might tailor their music or sound design to complement or emphasize onscreen visual colors or to suit the visual look of a film. In such cases, music and sound design would respond to a film's existing colors or visual palette. But how might a composer score for onscreen visual color?

A precedent lies in the work of composer Bernard Herrmann, who used only string orchestra to score *Psycho* (1960, dir. Alfred Hitchcock). Herrmann explained, 'I felt that I was able to complement the black and white photography of the film with a black and white sound' (Zador 1971: 31; Steiner 1974: 34). This shows a composer responding to the *visual* look or style of a film by scoring a certain way, describing the sound of the string orchestra as being similarly 'black and white.' Composer and author Fred Steiner interpreted Herrmann's remark:

> [B]lack and white photography is capable of infinite gradation, especially in the hands of a master such as Hitchcock. In fact, there are many for whom the expressive range of black and white cinema is greater than color. When the expressive range of the string orchestra is compared to the expressive range of black and white photography, Herrmann's analogy becomes clear. (Steiner 1974: 35)

Another way to describe Herrmann's *Psycho* score and explanatory remark is thus: Herrmann limited the orchestral 'color' palette of the orchestra by eliminating winds, brass, and percussion, for example, in the same way that Hitchcock eliminated colors such as reds, yellows, and blues. There is no lack of expressive possibility in either case; but in Herrmann's mind, there is a corresponding artistic or aesthetic approach.

A different approach to scoring for visual color is to handle scoring in terms of contrasts. If a composer is presented with a particular scene with a radically different look than the rest of the film – for instance, the overall film has an orange sepia tone to give it a dated feel, but one scene bursts with color – she might treat that particular scene differently. Or, she might handle it the same, so it doesn't poke out *too* much, and can be better united with the rest of the film.[19] This approach links color and music without considering pitch-based synesthesia: it might function in terms of brightness and darkness, warmth and shadow, and how those might translate from visual aspects into musical direction. If a particular color seems very 'loud,' like a bright red, that might translate musically into loud, brash, brass instrumentation.

These approaches have considered pitch, volume, contrast, and other allegorical features to correlate visual color and music or sound. I wish to emphasize that I am not necessarily discussing orchestral 'color,' nor black-and-white cinema, as these issues might confuse the discussion of how a composer might respond musically to visual color. These examples I have presented provide context for my further analysis of *Boys Don't Cry* and its use of visual color.

Boys Don't Cry features a striking visual color palette, and in applying this analytical thinking to *Boys Don't Cry*, I argue that its American pop music soundtrack is the primary color blue. Blue is flat, patriotic, uncomplicated, direct, and conventionally 'masculine' in an adolescent way.

In order to conform to this scheme, the title song, The Cure's new wave hit 'Boys Don't Cry,' was modified and rerecorded by Nathan Larson because its '80s Britpop *sound* was not the right *color*. The signature colors of The Cure are white, black, and red: Robert Smith's pancake makeup, jet black dyed hair, red lipstick, and black nail polish. The Cure's visual image and graphics bridged Goth, New Romantics, and '80s noir-inspired monochromaticism, as exemplified in cover art for the 'Let's Go To Bed' 12-inch single (1982) and *Concert: The Cure Live* album (1984). Larson updated the song, removed Robert Smith's childish whine, and changed the color to a solid American blue. It became a reflection of Brandon's vision of the world and who he wants to be.

By contrast, the film's visual oranges are analogous to Larson's weird 'tones,' sickly, mesmerizing, and oscillating in a liminal space between fluorescent yellows and angry reds. The 'tones' offset the blue of the American popular source music and act as a foil and contrast to it. When the blue American songs play, events and emotions are clear and unambiguous. When there is ambiguity in emotions or events, Larson's tones or little guitar cues appear.

Such color analysis is subjective, but in *Boys Don't Cry*, where color selection and visual design are so pronounced, it is necessary to consider ways that music might have its own corresponding part in that grand, albeit visual, design. Whereas *Boys Don't Cry* lacks the consistent, repetitious, melodic, *musical* themes that provide cinematic glue or unity in many classical Hollywood pictures, some of that broad conceptual design is transferred to other aspects of the film; here, *color* may serve the purpose of a recurring musical theme.

Go Fish: avant-garde aesthetics

Of all four films examined in this chapter, *Go Fish* had the lowest budget and most humble beginnings. Two aspiring filmmakers sent producer Christine Vachon a script and a videotape. Vachon recalls:

> I had twelve minutes. Just twelve minutes of a very rough experiment called *Ely and Max*. It was a real garage production made by two twenty-eight year old gals in Chicago named Rose Troche and Guinevere Turner. [...] The movie was a mix of documentary, overreaching art film, and dramatic narrative about, as Rose called it, 'what it's like trying to meet cute girls in Chicago.' Rose and Guin, who were girlfriends at the time, burned through their life savings of $15,000, getting twelve minutes down. (2006: 64)

The 'overreaching art film' had promise; it showed lesbian life without the angst of a coming out story. It was fun, fresh, and genuine. It was about 'life and romance and hanging out and having sex' and Vachon 'just knew there was an audience hungering for it' (Vachon with Edelstein 1998: 21). John Pierson of Islet fronted $53,000 for completion funds. Pierson sold the film to Tom Rothman of The Samuel Goldwyn Company for $400,000. The film grossed $3 million theatrically the summer it was released, a remarkable return for a black and white, 'DIY' first feature, which has proved itself an enduring classic.

Go Fish features extensive use of B-roll and highly stylized visual editing. Interstitial imagery inserted between narrative scenes includes book pages flipping, kids running, falling papers, spinning tops, flaring stage lights, gesturing hands, and paint dripping. An experimental aesthetic informs *Go Fish*, and although the film eschews any 'Hollywood' type of narrative formula, it is fun, endearing, and easy to follow.[20] *Go Fish* may be persistently self-conscious,[21] but it's not using avantgarde techniques to hide a lack of content; rather, director Rose Troche has a lot to say, making brutal honesty a near affectation, giving a scripted film with stiffly recited lines a convincing feeling of cinéma vérité. Some critics mistakenly thought the film had been improvised. Guinevere Turner wrote:

> It was June of 1994 and Rose and I were in L.A. promoting the movie. [...] 'How much of that was improvised?' (Half of one scene. The question always offended me for some reason. I guess because it implied that we were just a bunch of gals goofing around with some camera equipment.) (Turner and Troche 1995: 25–26)

Troche and Turner co-wrote the script, which features supporting actors commenting on the action in recurring vignettes (something like a Greek Chorus), and various poetic monologues. The experimental aesthetic that informs the script, visual editing, and interstitial imagery extends to the film's artful use of sound.

> In film school I was dedicated to experimental film. I felt narrative was not art. So all my early work is images and sound and perhaps the occasional VO. *Go Fish* came out of that tradition. I did not want to leave my experimental roots. (Troche 2014)

B-roll helps pace the film and slow the narrative, allowing for comfortable digestion of dialogue-heavy scenes and socio-cultural commentary. 'The interstitial imagery is there to sort of check-in on the main narrative. The top is a sort of barometer of whether [Ely and Max's] love connection is working or not' (Troche 2014). The fluttering books and papers can be seen as relating to Kia, a college professor, and Max, a young lesbian student.

Structurally, the film balances love story, interstitial imagery, dramatic vignettes, and various commentaries on love, social relations, and negotiating Chicago's urban lesbian community. Who is worthy of the title 'lesbian,' and who is a pretender? What is acceptably butch and what's too hippie? What's the best word for female genitals? What is proper dating etiquette?

> I was very influenced by Todd Hayne's *Poison* (1991), a film in three parts with three different narratives handled in three different styles. I remember going to the Music Box in Chicago and seeing the film. Todd was there to talk about it and I was just smitten with it. I decided *Go Fish* should be in three parts: (1) Experimental, (2) Documentary (shot in color), (3) Narrative. When [producer] Christine Vachon came on she nixed the doc portion and we thankfully followed her advice and the film was left with parts (1) and (3). (Troche 2014)

Troche's resulting hybrid of experimental and narrative elements makes effective use of sound and music. Pierson's infusion of completion funds provided further encouragement for sonic experimentation, simply because it was enabling.

> I was (am) so interested in the building of scenes, the construct of the experience of cinema. How I could affect the audience through sound was always on my mind. You have to remember we made this film for so little money that when given the opportunity to put some pristine [sound] elements into the film I took it. (Troche 2014)

Many of *Go Fish*'s sequences highlight sound design. Musically, *Go Fish* offers a wide variety of contrasting styles without prejudice: jazz, samba, trip-hop, and singer-songwriter fare. The original score is by Brendan Dolan; Jennifer Sharpe with Scott Aldrich contributed songs. Dolan had been a sound designer for Todd Hayne's *Dottie Gets Spanked* (1993). He would go on to compose the department store music for Todd Hayne's *Safe* (1995), and compose the 'Prologue' music for *Girls Town* (1996). Missy Cohen was sound editor, and director Troche worked on the sound, as well as a crew at Sound One.

> I was like a kid in a candy store. I was cutting at Sound One (now closed but a rather famous location in NYC) and I would go up to the sound department and make the engineer play me all these different effects from the library. I would sometimes ask to slow them

or reverse them. At this time we were dealing with mag [film] and I was cutting on a two track flat bed, so I had to keep the main dialog track on and cut in my effects one track at a time. Sound is incredibly important to me and I think it is often overlooked. (Troche 2014)

Missy Cohen was tasked with cleaning up production audio, the sound recorded during filming on the set. During post-production, many onscreen sounds are recreated and recorded separately, footsteps and clothing sounds for example, so they can be recorded cleanly and treated independently of dialogue; the post-production recordings of these sounds are called 'Foley.' Troche recalls, 'Foley was fantastic. I remember the foley artist [Brian Vancho] used a watermelon and his fist to simulate a sex scene.' Troche was happy to experiment with unorthodox sound possibilities: 'There is a backward whale cry that occurs when Evy is kicked out of her mother's house.' The final completed audio track pleased Troche: 'The mixer was excellent and I had such a good time during the mix' (Troche 2014).

Four exemplary scenes

Four scenes in particular exemplify Troche's savvy, progressive integration of sound techniques with narrative filmmaking. These scenes are the haircut scene, Ely's morning-after victory dance, the jury sequence, and the wedding dress vignette.

In the haircut scene, Ely, a longhaired, Michigan Womyn's Music Festival attending lesbian, updates her look with a fashionable, butch crew cut. As women's music moved towards a more punk, riot grrl aesthetic, so the crew cut became an important marker of urban lesbianism. (Max: 'What if people think I'm just cutting it so that I'm like … look more like a "real" dyke?' Ely: 'Yeah, but if you don't cut it, because you want to, aren't you falling into the same trap?' (Turner and Troche 1995).

For the haircut scene, the audio track is entirely music and sounds of scissors and clippers; the sounds are placed and timed to compliment the *music*, and thus they are *not* in sync with the *picture*. This is an unusual handling of sound effects. The music has a cheesy element to it with playful marimbas, percussive bangs, and goofy organ. It's not quite jazz, it's not quite comedy music, it's not in any way orchestral, and while it sounds cheesy and cheap, it's done in a confident, intentional way. The 'sounds' of the haircut are embedded in the music, not the production track. Troche credits Dolan with using the scissor and clipper sounds as part of the music track.

> [Composer] Brendan Dolan was the genius behind the music of the film. I have to say, I don't recall whose idea it was to use the [scissor and clipper] effects as a percussive element, but something tells me I should hand this one to Brendan. He was amazing. We went to his apartment and he just played us music until we found the right sound. (Troche 2014)

It was not always Dolan who combined effects with music; Troche and Cohen added spice to Dolan's work as well. After successfully hooking up with Max, Ely performs a happy dance to an upbeat song with yells and brass; the audio track features overlays of a car horn's 'beep beep beep,' passersby 'congratulations,' dog barks, all placed in time to Dolan's music. The scene is fun and celebratory, and, like an earlier coffee shop scene where a harp comically accents the line 'contestant number one,' it hits a light, playful note.

> The music always came after [the film was shot and edited]. The only scene I knew I wanted a particular feel for the music was when Ely skips home after hooking up with Max. I really wanted an old band Latin song here and got one; the effects were lovingly laid in by me and Missy Cohen. What a good time. It was [...] really fun to punctuate the score with effects. (Troche 2014)

In some scenes, like Daria's jury vignette, Troche's sound effects support the film without any music at all. Following a sexual assignation with a man, Daria finds herself surrounded by a jury of dykes who question her identity as a lesbian. Troche assembled sound elements that include gavels, indeterminate whooshes, and wind-like ambiences, as Daria answers accusers who question whether or not she is a 'real' lesbian.

> That scene is based on a Disney cartoon where Pluto chases a cat and falls down a hole to find himself in a court of cats. He will never win. It was how I felt about the conversation of sexual fluidity in the '90s. I didn't know why you had to call yourself something different if you fucked a man but felt like most of you wanted to be with women. That's what I thought then, and since [then] I have an even looser idea of a definitive definition of sexuality. (Troche 2014)

Troche describes the sound design for this scene as 'sound effects' (Troche 2014), even though there is a musical quality to it, a dark, threatening, industrial quality, something that could be interpreted as ambient music or musique concrète. As K. J. Donnelly notes, 'there is an increasingly musical conceptualization of sound design in such films, where sound elements are wielded in an artistic manner, manipulated for precise effect rather than merely aiming to duplicate and complement screen activity' (Donnelly 2014: 126). But within the division of labor on *Go Fish*, this sound palette was created by Troche from sound effects. 'I really wanted to create a mood, like she had fallen down a hole' (Troche 2014).

An abstract, poetic 'wedding dress' sequence features Max and other women in wedding gowns in an industrial space, accompanied by Max's voiceover; Max imagines waking to find herself married to a man and raising children, and ruminates on this. A whispering overlay quietly and eerily echoes Max's voice. Guinevere Turner performs both voices.

> Honestly, I feel like I overworked that. I'm not sure I needed the second voice. I did it and at the time liked it. I was working on a flatbed so the sound was on a mag track. I simply offset the same recording by a number of frames and, in the mix, recorded the two tracks at two different levels, creating the [delayed] whisper. (Troche 2014)

The whispering echo has a musical quality to it, similar to the effect of Jim Morrison's whispered parallel vocal track in 'Riders on the Storm' from The Doors' 1971 album *L.A. Woman*. The effect may be 'overworked' or gratuitous, but it has a hallucinatory, dreamlike effect, and nudges the film towards the experimental. Troche also has a philosophical justification for the whisper track.

> It was supposed to be a sort of, 'I'm admitting this to myself and then saying it again to really take it in.' I'm still trying to wrap my head around subtext. I definitely see it as voice over, but the whisper was part of this idea that it would get in you more if repeated. If said [aloud], then whispered to oneself. (Troche 2014)

This emphasis on repetition is also a musical quality, whether as a musical feature, or the way music is learned through practice and repetition.

The use of sound and music in these four scenes shows a progressive, experimental aesthetic unusual for a mass-market film. Its $3 million gross is a testament to what an audience can enjoy and assimilate.

Because *Go Fish* was made independently for a small budget, its film-makers were not entirely forced to use conventional techniques, even if they did drop the 'documentary' segments. Troche wrote, 'Back then we thought there was indeed a lesbian community, and it was that community to which we wanted to give *Go Fish*. Not only for them, but for us' (Turner and Troche 1995: 5). This echoes Gregg Araki's statement that *The Living End* was made for himself and his friends. Large studios pressure filmmakers to aim for the lowest common denominator, and to use cinematic techniques that are obvious and easily read. *Go Fish* was able to employ adventurous techniques and still capture a relatively wide audience in a competitive market.

Conclusion

Motion pictures can reveal commercial ambitions through the use of sound and music; films aiming for big box office or a wide audience will prioritize techniques that are easily understood. Smaller, independent, art-house films are freer to employ experimental or avant-garde techniques.

Picking apart the lyrics of popular songs placed in films can reveal narrative connections, but scholars and filmmakers often fail to question overuse of this technique, or to notice how facile and obvious it can be. While popular music can reinforce audience affinities, lyrical recitation of narrative elements risks becoming unintentionally cartoonish, especially given its history in animation (Goldmark 2005: 22).

While film music scholars have parsed lyrics to uncover meaning and studied genre connections to audience affiliations, a further line of inquiry is an examination of other musical alternatives. As we have seen, an arguably 'queer' film does not necessarily have a 'queer' soundtrack. A conventional soundtrack does not necessarily indicate a conventional film. Music supervision is frequently driven by marketing concerns or the desire to seduce a wider audience. With greater confidence or daring, other alternatives might be welcomed.

Transamerica and *Thelma & Louise* employ conventional use of sound and music to draw in a wide, mainstream audience. The placement of Dolly Parton's song 'Travelin' Thru' in *Transamerica* is subversive in that Dolly herself as text has an added cultural weight relevant to the film. *Boys Don't Cry* occupies a space where there is conventional use of song and score, but some room for experimentation with tones and ambiences to create eerie sonic environments. These three films all rely heavily on the compilation score, using known or radio-friendly genre specific tracks to establish and encourage audience affinities and help pull in a mainstream audience.

The filmmakers of *Go Fish* did not try to pull in a mainstream audience, and they were the most experimental of all four films studied in this chapter. Freedom from studio financing and marketing allows more freedom to experiment; there are fewer (or no) executives giving notes on rough cuts, and less money to recoup. The audience finds itself lucky to see films like *Go Fish*, a gripping, personal film that rings true and may not be entirely polished but does not pander to the crowd in an effort to provide 'something for everyone.' All of these four films are powerful and were groundbreaking in their own way; analysis of music provides insight into how filmmakers desired to position their work within greater commercial and cultural contexts.

Part III
Queering of Genre

6
Queer Monster Good: *Frankenstein* and *Edward Scissorhands*

The 'Queer Monster' has been studied extensively by cinema scholar and critical theorist Harry Benshoff, notably in *Monsters in the Closet: Homosexuality and the Horror Film* (1997). The archetypal cinematic monster is an outsider figure opposed to a requisite heterosexual romance embedded in the horror film; the monster can be understood as a racial, ethnic, sexual, political, or ideological Other. Benshoff based his work upon essays by Robin Wood, who suggested that the horror film was thematically based upon three variables: *normality*, represented by heterosexual patriarchal capitalism; the *Other*, embodied by a 'monster'; and the *relationship between them* (Benshoff 1997: 4).

The AIDS epidemic made this framework especially trenchant at the time of Benshoff's writing; common perception saw gay men as emblematic of death and disease, morally reprehensible, emaciated, or hideously disfigured with Kaposi's sarcoma. But the coding of the monster as queer existed long before the epidemic, and will remain part of the genre's formal structure and canon. In classic horror films, the monster is routinely given more dramatic weight than characters coded for societal normalcy; everyone wants to watch the monster, and the 'straight' couple is a foil. Benshoff notes:

> The heterosexualized couple in [horror] films is invariably banal and underdeveloped in relation to the sadomasochistic villain(s), whose outrageous exploits are, after all, the raison d'être of this genre. [...] It is usually the heterosexualized hero and heroine who are stereotyped – painted with broad brush strokes – while the villains and monsters are given more complex, 'novelistic' characterizations. (Benshoff 1997: 11)

Horror films have long held special appeal to many queers, given the genre's bridging of camp and masquerade as well as its placement of power in the outsider. Consider the popularity among queers and outsiders of the ritual of the *Rocky Horror Picture Show* (1975) and of horror movie revival series such as 'Midnight Mass' in San Francisco, promoted by filmmaker and drag personality Peaches Christ. Benshoff relates how horror films and their relationship to masquerade are seen as a celebration of deviancy:

> The experience of watching a horror film or monster movie might be understood as similar to that of the Carnival [...] allowing otherwise 'normal' people the pleasures of drag, or monstrosity, for a brief but exhilarating experience. However, while straight participants in such experiences usually return to their daylight worlds, both the monster and the homosexual are permanent residents of shadowy spaces [...] Queer viewers are thus more likely than straight ones to experience the monster's plight in more personal, individualized terms. (Benshoff 1997: 13)

The creation and coding of the monster as queer has been clearly understood in narrative terms, as well as reinforced by study of script, performance technique, acting, makeup, direction, and even marketing. This study needs to be extended to music for the queer monster.

There is a temptation to argue that atonal or dissonant music represents the monster, and to unpack the musical coding of the monster in these terms. Atonal music is an established horror movie convention with obvious associations to psychosis, madness, tension, conflict, and fear. I am far more fascinated by directors and composers who, knowingly or unwittingly, employ music that makes a more nuanced set of references. Many horror films rely exclusively on the conventional musical trope of dissonance to represent the monster. Fortunately, there are other canonical horror films whose directors, either by knowledge or intuition, create a more complex rendering of the queer monster through music.

James Whale, openly homosexual British expatriate and renowned Hollywood monster movie director, brought a tender, humane side to Frankenstein's monster.[1] His queer perspective is most famously notable in *Bride of Frankenstein* (1935), scored by Franz Waxman, particularly in a musical 'seduction' scene where the monster, hearing a violin in the woods, is led to befriend a blind hermit. Music telegraphs the monster's humanity to the audience; the monster loves violin, has a soul capable of empathy, and forms a tender relationship with the hermit.

Homoerotic undertones of this scene were parodied by Mel Brooks in *Young Frankenstein* (1974).

As a contrasting contemporary example, Benshoff identifies Tim Burton's Edward Scissorhands as a similarly queer monster. *Edward Scissorhands* (1990) features Danny Elfman's celebrated score, laden with celeste and harp, music highly reminiscent of gay composer Tchaikovsky's fruity *Nutcracker* ballet.[2] Stylistically and historically queer musical markers and references incorporated into Elfman's lauded and much-imitated score reinforce Benshoff's reading of Edward Scissorhands as a queer monster. This chapter uses an examination of Waxman and Elfman's scores to further identify, analyze and describe the 'Queer Monster' posited by Benshoff and others.

Bride of Frankenstein and *Edward Scissorhands* share structural and thematic sensibilities that encode their monsters as innocents, fugitives, attacked and maligned by an ignorant, intolerant, larger society. *Edward Scissorhands* is an extension of classical Hollywood cinema traditions fostered in *Bride*; it is a post-modern recontextualization of the monster movie. Both films are presented as morality plays, fables with cautionary warnings against nonconformity; *Edward* is framed as a fairy tale with 'present day' bookends. This chapter will first examine both films as queer texts, and then further scrutinize their music, in particular where it informs or accentuates a queer reading.

Both *Bride* and *Edward* have highly emotive, traditional, symphonic scores. The music in both films is an essential part of the creation and management of a highly nuanced subtext. Both films use music to enhance queer coding, incorporating signs and references within the musical score that reinforce readings of 'Otherness.' I will look at references to Schubert, Tchaikovsky, *Rudolph the Red-Nosed Reindeer*, and other musical and intertextual references that code the music as queer, as well as how Waxman's Jewish background in Nazi Germany and Elfman's marginalization as a composer of popular music, wrongfully derided as musically illiterate, enhance their own sympathetic 'Otherness.'

The queerness of *Bride of Frankenstein*

The queerness of Whale's monster is bound with his innocence. There has been fervent critical analysis of sexuality, gender, desire, and racial representation in *Bride of Frankenstein*,[3] but the underlying queerness is related to the monster as outsider, innocent and tormented by an oppressive heteronormative mainstream that does not and cannot understand him. The portrait of the monster as innocent is repeated in

Edwards Scissorhands; the 'innocent' monster is forced by circumstance to commit heinous crimes.

Bride of Frankenstein seemingly forces a heterosexual identity on the monster. The title, though ambiguous, titillatingly implies the *monster*, not his creator. Posters and lobby cards publicizing the film clarified the matter with the lurid tagline, 'The Monster Demands A Mate!' This marketing slogan might have drawn in the crowds, but it does not reflect the real propulsive drive of the film, the otherness and the moral complexity of the monster. The failure of presumed normative heterosexuality is one of the hallmarks of the film. The monster is a queer or innocent who will ultimately challenge all kinds of norms presented by society. Feminist theorist Elizabeth Young argues that the monster 'stands outside of normative male sexuality,' but this does not make him homosexual, as he challenges both heteronormativity and homonormativity.

> The monster, like the cultural stereotype of the homosexual man, is an 'unnatural' creation, an analogy to which the film gives form in significant ways. When the monster learns to speak, for example, he indiscriminately links the word 'friend' – his only term for an affective bond – with the hermit who first befriends him; then [...] with Dr. Praetorius [sic]; and finally with his future female mate. He has no innate understanding that the male–female bond he is to forge with the bride is assumed to be primary or that it carries a different sexual valence from his relationships with the two men: all affective relationships, with women and men, are as easily 'friendships' as 'marriages.' (Young 1991: 410)

This innocent equivocation of 'friend' and 'mate' repeats in *Edward Scissorhands*, where Edward does not understand Joyce's sexual advances, and his innocent relationship with Kim is perceived as a love triangle by Kim's jealous boyfriend, Jim. The conflation of 'friend' and 'mate' is more complete in *Bride*; in *Scissorhands*, matters are slightly more complicated. *Scissorhands* stars teen heartthrobs Johnny Depp and Winona Ryder and was marketed with the tagline, 'Innocence is what he knows. Beauty is what she sees.' (This does imply, accurately, that Kim is more sexually developed or aware than Edward.) Furthermore, the film alludes to a sexual or romantic awakening in Edward, even though this is only implied and never consummated. In both *Bride* and *Edward*, the negotiation of the spectrum of innocence and desire is carefully nuanced and manipulated through the musical score.

Frankenstein's monster's identity as Queer or as Other transcends mere sexual orientation, if the monster even has any sexual orientation at all. The monster's queerness aligns with an expanding definition of what it is to be 'Queer.' An expanded definition of queerness can include any perceived innate Otherness to which larger society responds by bullying or oppression; this potentially includes introversion, race, ethnicity, gender, religion, different abilities,[4] as well as other possibilities. This expanded definition also provides a wider audience that can relate to the queering of the monster. Young, picking up on the mob brutality and references to lynching presented in *Bride*, unpacks some of the possibilities:

> Keeping in mind this link between the horror of lynching and the horror of the monster movie, we can read *Bride of Frankenstein* initially as intervening in lynching discourse in order to present the plight of the monster sympathetically. Counterposed to the unjust pursuit by the frightening lynch mob are the actions of the kind hermit, blind to the monster's appearance, who teaches him language, literally enacting 'color-blind' liberalism. [...] When the old man comforts the monster to sleep, a crucifix remains brightly lit above their heads even after the camera fades to black. With the monster recognizably coded as a Black fugitive, this religious symbolism translates, via *Uncle Tom's Cabin*, into the Christian abolitionist narrative of slave humanity, misery, and redemption. (Young 1991: 425)

The presentation of the monster as a fugitive from an angry lynch mob at the climax of *Bride* is repeated in *Edward Scissorhands*. Burton interestingly invokes Christian iconography only with a creepy neighbor, Esmeralda, who plays organ and, mistakenly or maliciously, tries to warn the neighbors that Edward is evil and 'a perversion of nature.' Where Whale uses a glowing crucifix (after the hermit's prayer, DVD 0:40:25) to signpost the monster's goodness, Burton uses a glowing crucifix (DVD 1:19:35) in conjunction with Esmeralda to warn of the potential evils of dogmatic or superstitious Christianity. Musically, this warning is negotiated by an accompaniment of bizarre and creepy hymnic organ music, initially performed as a diegetic 'visual instrumental'[5] performed by actor O-Lan Jones herself. In contrast to Esmeralda's suspect religious fervor, *Edward* is set during a comparatively secular Christmas; Edward's adoptive family, the Boggs, have the requisite tree, while their home's rooftop has fake snow and lights that simply read a secular 'Happy Holidays.'

Both *Bride* and *Edward* give the monster a character arc from birth or creation to fugitive. Along this arc, the monster struggles to learn or negotiate socialization, friendship, and conflict with a broader dominant culture that largely fears him. At varying points along this arc, music informs the awkwardness of Edward's 'etiquette lesson,' Frankenstein's monster's curiosity about children, his relationship to others, and interactions with society.

The queerness of *Edward Scissorhands*

Edward Scissorhands is posited as a fairytale revolving around a lovable, innocent, boyish monster. The film is bracketed by a whimsical bedtime story of how snow is made. The Christmastime setting and snow mythology relate *Edward* not just to monster movies, but also to Christmas television specials like the stop-motion animated Rankin/Bass production *Rudolph the Red-Nosed Reindeer* (dir. Larry Roemer, 1964). This invocation of the Christmas special accentuates Edward's queerness.

Rudolph was among the most successful American 1960s Christmas specials, and would have been familiar to Tim Burton and Danny Elfman, who both grew up in the Los Angeles area, Tim Burton in Burbank, California. Burton describes the syndicated prevalence of *Rudolph* and its impact on his work:

> The initial impulse for doing [*Nightmare Before Christmas*] was the love of Dr. Seuss and those holiday specials that I grew up watching, like *How the Grinch Stole Christmas* and *Rudolph the Red-Nosed Reindeer*. Those crude stop-motion animation holiday things that were on year in, year out make an impact on you early and stay with you. I had grown up with those and had a real feeling for them, and I think, without being too direct, the impulse was to do something like that. (Burton 1995: 115)

While Burton discusses *Rudolph* in relation to *Nightmare Before Christmas* (1993), it is nevertheless clear *Rudolph* made a strong childhood impact on the director and its influence is applicable to *Edward Scissorhands*.

The Rankin/Bass Christmas special casts Rudolph as a bullied outcast who is forced by family, friends, and Santa's professional reindeer colleagues to hide or 'closet' his blinking red nose. Rudolph runs away with an Elf named Hermey, also an outcast, who wants to become a dentist rather than make toys.[6] Continuing this theme of the banished outcast is the Abominable Snow Monster, who really just has a toothache, and the inhabitants of the 'Island of Misfit Toys,' a group of unwanted or differently-abled toys looking for loving homes and understanding. A bevy of catchy musical numbers is the icing on the cake.

Rudolph's many queer codings make it a subversive piece of children's entertainment. While the surface message is a benign and simple 'it's OK to be different,' actively queer themes occur consistently throughout the show. Alphie Scopp's fey and tearful performance as Charlie-in-the-Box, one of the misfit toys, gives a strong indication of effete male as banished outcast. Rudolph, Hermey, Charlie, Abominable, and all the misfits are happily redeemed in the end, allowing the queers a clear victory, with Santa cast as the heteronormative straight man who learns to appreciate differences. The music has a light, bouncy, infectious Leroy Anderson meets Tchaikovsky tip throughout.

Edward Scissorhands employs much of the whimsy of the animated television Christmas special, but also features moments that fall close to pure horror (Edward's dramatic entrance before Peg in the attic of the old house), or even magical realism (the Ice Dance sequence, or Edward's covering the town in snow from the window of the old house). *Edward*'s most powerful reference is to the Frankenstein myth: Edward is created by 'The Inventor' (Vincent Price), but is flawed or 'unfinished,' without the final set of hands; Edward does not understand sexual advances; Edward is misunderstood; Edward becomes a fugitive. Edward's flight from an angry lynch mob at the film's climax is a repetition of *Bride of Frankenstein*. These multiple references paint Edward as innocent and code him as queer. Benshoff notes how Edward is a far cry from the psychopathic serial murderer of slasher movies, and is instead imbued with a cuddly warmth we also see in the harmless Rudolph:

> [Edward] has no interest in dispatching promiscuous teenagers – he just wants to be loved. Although never marked as explicitly gay, the film does posit the leather-wearing Edward's special talents as hedge-trimming, poodle-grooming, and hairstyling, trades with which gay men have been stereotypically associated. (Benshoff 1997: 266)

Benshoff contends that Edward, like Rudolph who conceals a congenitally blinking nose with dirt, is accepted as long as he closets some part of his true identity, a characteristic that Benshoff associates with homosexuality:

> Most of the film's 'normal' suburbanites at first welcome Edward, because he brings a tremendous amount of style to their otherwise

dull lives. Like gay hairdressers and flamboyant entertainers, Edward is accepted as long as he keeps working (and stays in the closet). (Benshoff 1997: 267)

As Elizabeth Young posits with Frankenstein's monster, what makes Edward queer is not necessarily his sexuality; perhaps the more powerful interpretation is the archetype of the misunderstood Artist, or the iconoclastic Free-Thinker. Undoubtedly there is *something* within Edward that ordinary townsfolk find threatening. It would be possible but difficult to cast Edward in racial terms, as Young does with Frankenstein.[7] Part of the broad appeal of *Edward Scissorhands* lies in the ambiguity or open-endedness of Edward's otherness, and how Burton invites the audience to identify with Edward rather than fear him.

The climax and finale of *Edward Scissorhands* do not work out terribly well for Edward. Violence and misunderstandings erupt, and a mob chases Edward back to the old house from whence he came. The lynch mob at the end of *Edward Scissorhands* has a non-fantastical danger; it connects back to the mob that chased Frankenstein's monster. Elfman's score successfully plays this level of danger. Likewise, Waxman would have related to the monster having been beaten and chased by a mob, as he himself shared this same experience on anti-Semitic streets of Berlin. *Edward* repeats the archetypal Frankenstein narrative, but *Edward* ends with a happier, if surreal, conclusion: Edward, presumed dead, disappears from the town forever, but makes snow from giant block ice every winter.

Both *Edward Scissorhands* and *Bride of Frankenstein* exemplify Benshoff's queer monster, although separated by more than five decades. The music of these films needs to be considered in the analysis of the queer monster. Both films use classic, symphonic orchestra style scoring; this ties *Edward* to the classic horror genre as well as to the television Christmas special. Both films incorporate musical references that give depth to the queer monster; these include references to classical period composers Schubert and Tchaikovsky that add a further inflection to readings of the films.

The music of *Bride of Frankenstein*

Composer Franz Waxman, né Wachsmann, was born 24 December 1906, in Koenigshutte, Upper Silesia, Germany, now part of Poland. Franz was the youngest of seven children in a prosperous Jewish family; his father was a steel company sales executive. At the age of three, Franz climbed on a stove and overturned a pot of boiling water, scalding his eyes; for the rest of his life he wore thick glasses with lenses of greater than ten diopters. Later, the family moved to Dresden; Franz studied at the Dresden Music Academy, but soon transferred to the Berlin Music Conservatory (Cook 1968: 415; Neumeyer and Platte 2012: 1).

Waxman worked in Berlin at UFA as an orchestrator and conductor; among the films he worked on is *The Blue Angel* (1930), the cautionary tale of a schoolteacher's moral decline, produced by Erich Pommer. In early 1934, Waxman, after being beaten by a mob on a Berlin street, moved to Paris to join Pommer, who was producing Fritz Lang's only French film, *Liliom* (1934). It was for *Liliom* that Waxman composed his first film score. Waxman used an ondes Martenot, an early electronic instrument favored by Olivier Messiaen, as well as a large choir. Pommer brought Waxman to the United States later that year to work with him as music director on a film version of a Jerome Kern–Oscar Hammerstein II musical, *Music in the Air* (dir. Joe May 1934) (Cook 1968: 416–17; Handzo 1995: 48).

James Whale, resident director at Universal and director of *Frankenstein* (1931), had been impressed by Waxman's score to *Liliom*. In early 1935, during the filming of *Bride of Frankenstein*, Waxman met Whale at a party at the home of actress and screenwriter Salka Viertel, another Jewish émigré from central Europe.[8] Whale invited Waxman to his set to observe the filming (Cook 1968: 417). Whale told Waxman, 'Nothing will be resolved in this picture except the end destruction scene. Will you write an unresolved score for it?' (Curtis 1998: 245; Cook 1968: 417; Rosar 1983: 407). Whale did not mean 'unresolved' in musical terms, but rather in dramatic terms. This oft-repeated quote emphasizes the essential kernel of the film: the monster and narrative are shrouded in moral complexity. There is no absolute moral conclusion, nor any clear black-and-white binary of good and evil. The monster decides who lives and who dies at the film's end, with the *deus ex machina* help of a self-destruct lever that suddenly appears in the laboratory. The ending is satisfying but, as Whale indicates, all the moral and queer complexities are left unresolved.

Waxman's score proved influential and iconic, and became a standard part of Universal's music library that was dubbed into *Flash Gordon's Trip to Mars* (1938) and many other serials and horror films (Karlin 1994: 172; *Music for the Movies: The Hollywood Sound*, 00:04:30). Karlin calls the score 'extraordinary for its time, and a significant role model. As a result of this score, [Waxman] became music director for Universal' (Karlin 1994: 308).[9] At the same time, Waxman's score is highly representative of a certain period, the 'Golden Age' of Hollywood film scoring. Like other canonical work of period composers such as Max Steiner and Erich Wolfgang Korngold, Waxman's manipulation of themes became labeled as 'leitmotivs' even if the extent of their manipulation, made obvious and telegraphic for cinema audiences, was less than truly Wagnerian.[10] Waxman's score is logical, natural, and reflexive for a composer raised in Weimar-era Berlin filled with musical theatre and opera.

Waxman's ideas about film scoring were not unusual or revolutionary, for his day or today. In a 1940 speech to the Local Federation of Women's Clubs in Hollywood, Waxman discussed the balance of music and dialogue, the purpose of a film score, the logic or realism of underscore, and whether a 'good motion picture score' should be 'unobtrusive' or not. 'If it is so subdued that its only virtue lies in the fact that it is not noticeable, it can hardly be effective' (Waxman 2012: 102).[11] These debates, while persistent even today, are relatively innocuous and do not indicate any significant controversy in his work. Nevertheless, Waxman's work has been regarded as highly influential. The *Bride of Frankenstein* score has been widely discussed by critics and scholars including Page Cook, William Rosar, and Larry Timm. Cook emphasizes the use and development of 'leitmotifs':

> The most striking leitmotifs are those for Dr. Praetorius [sic], The Monster, and The Monster's Mate. Waxman varied the four-note, broken-chord theme for The Monster so that it sounds now clumsy and pathetic, now menacing and terrible. Often it is orchestrated very gently. The leitmotif for the Bride has clever variations, and the dazzling crescendo of it, as Praetorius [sic] reveals the shrouded figure, is one of filmmusic's [sic] most exciting moments. (Cook 1968: 417)

I am content to accept denotations of these manipulated themes as 'leitmotifs,' or 'leitmotivs,' primarily because film music scholars have appropriated the term and there's not too much confusion with an actual Wagnerian leitmotiv that transforms musical material in extensive or obtuse ways over long stretches of music drama. I would, however, like to bring Waxman's own ideas into the discussion, as Waxman provides a more refined explanation of the use of themes:

> Film music must make its point immediately because it is heard only once by an audience that is unprepared and didn't come to the theatre to hear music anyway. I believe in strong themes which are easily

recognizable, and which can be repeated and variated [sic] according to the film's needs. But the variations must be expressive and not complicated. (Waxman in Thomas 1973: 75–77)

This lack of complication, and the necessity of making themes 'easily recognizable' within variations, distinguishes film score leitmotivs from leitmotivs as used by Wagner. Elsewhere, Waxman elaborates on his film music compositional technique, comparing it to the classical form of Theme and Variations.

> I regard a film score as essentially a set of variations. In concert music, variations are usually written around a single theme.[12] But in film music, where there are many themes, the variations turn out to be variations on a group of themes. Another difference is that in film music the variations are not motivated by purely musical considerations, as they are in concert music. The motivations come from the screen action.
>
> The leitmotif technique is common in film scoring, that is, the attaching of themes to characters and then varying them as the situations change, and I have found this very practical in writing film music. It is an aid to composition and an aid to listening. Motifs should be characteristically brief, with sharp profiles. If they are easily recognizable they permit repetition in varying forms and textures, and they help musical continuity. (Waxman in Thomas 1991: 41–42)

While Waxman himself uses the term 'leitmotif,' it is clear that he is borrowing a term favored by contemporary film music fans and critics; his larger discussion indicates a more refined understanding of motive selection based upon melodic contour ('sharp profiles') and subsequent musical transformation based upon the concept of theme and variation.[13]

Rosar provides a lengthy description of the score in his article, 'Music for the Monsters: Universal Pictures' Horror Film Scores of the Thirties.' Rosar identifies the same 'three principal themes' as did Cook: the 'five-note motif for the monster,' a 'glamorous motif' for the mate, and a 'sinister villainous theme' for Dr. Pretorius. Rosar surmises Waxman's inspirations for various sections; he hears 'Straussian brass figures are enveloped in coloristic Debussyan harmonies and orchestral scintillation.' He notices snatches of 'the scherzo in Mendelssohn's incidental music for *A Midsummer Night's Dream*' and 'shades of "The Story of the Kalendar Prince" in Rimsky-Korsakov's *Scheherazade*.' He emphasizes the use of concert organ music in the score (Rosar 1983: 408–10). This use of organ music is also noted by Julie Brown, who notes of the non-diegetic organ used in the hermit scene, 'the instrument's clear religious associations enable it to serve as a musical sign of religious ponderings' (Brown 2010: 5).

What Rosar describes is impressive, if fairly typical, scoring of the early Hollywood 'Golden Age' period: symphonic music with strong reliance on the harmonic vocabulary of the late romantic period of Western art music. The most striking aspect of the score is the dissonant theme for Frankenstein's monster, which often incorporates the jarring use of flutter tonguing in the brass, and the variations of this theme motivated by screen actions as described above by Waxman himself. Says Waxman, 'It was a "super horror" movie and demanded hauntingly eerie, weird and different music' (Waxman in Rosar 1983: 407).

'Weird and different' succinctly but aptly describes the concept of 'Otherness'; in this case, even without any suggestion of sexuality, the composer aligns his music to a post-modern conceptualization of the 'Other.' This weirdness was crucial to the film. In its climax, says *Bride of Frankenstein*'s film editor, Ted Kent,

> The sound effects are an important factor, but in my opinion the most valuable contribution to this sequence was made by Franz Waxman for his imaginative music score. (Kent in Curtis 1998: 245)

Waxman concludes the score with 'a big dissonant chord' that was reportedly Whale's idea (Cook 1968: 418; Curtis 1998: 246). This dissonant musical ending, while not unheard of in concert music, contradicts the typically consonant *musical* 'resolution'[14] expected at the 'resolution' of a film, and it signposts for the audience, at Whale's direction, the absence of a happy, neat, morally-just conclusion. This musical complexity, reflecting the moral complexities of the film, garnered praise for Waxman's score. Whale's biographer James Curtis effuses:

> [Waxman] produced what is probably still to this day the greatest score ever written for a horror movie. Three distinct themes, representing the Monster, the Bride, and Thesiger's Pretorius, weave leitmotifs throughout the film. The score is alternatively romantic, exciting, and horrifying as it builds to a clamorous creation scene in which the rhythmic thumping of a kettledrum suggests the newly beating heart of the Bride. (Curtis 1998: 246)

This 'heartbeat' effect telegraphs narrative information on the success of the creation of the Bride. The imitation of a heartbeat has been used in other classical repertoire, such as Tchaikovsky's Sixth Symphony, with which Waxman would have undoubtedly been familiar.

Curtis mistakenly states, 'Franz Waxman's score, conducted by Constantin Bakaleinikoff, was recorded with 22 musicians in one marathon nine-hour session' (Curtis 1998: 249). While a single marathon recording session may have been possible or even characteristic of Universal, the photo of the recording session (Curtis 1998: 246) clearly shows more than 22 studio musicians. Film historian Scott MacQueen's audio commentary on the *Bride of Frankenstein* DVD claims that there were between 32 and 40 musicians, depending upon the cue being recorded.

Although scholars have paid great attention to the 'leitmotifs,' dissonance, and ending of Waxman's score, I wish to focus upon a brief but important moment: the emotionally pivotal scene where the monster meets the blind hermit in the forest. The documentary video, *Music for the Movies: The Hollywood Sound*, superimposes the blind hermit playing violin to the monster with audio commentary by Hollywood composer David Raksin who says, 'Music, you know, can seduce nearly anyone. It does this on a subliminal level, and it worked' (00:04:05). Raksin may not have been discussing the blind hermit scene, but it's clear that the directors of the documentary used this voiceover to indicate music's seduction of the monster. Just as the violin tune 'seduces' the monster, it also serves as a barometer of the monster's humanity. It further references religion, holiness, the text associated with the tune, and the brief life of the tune's original composer, Franz Schubert.

This tune, Schubert's well-known art song 'Ave Maria,' exists as both diegetic music and underscore, emphasizing its importance as text. The religious aspect provides the most readily accessible, superficial reading of the tune.

> Waxman cleverly takes the source music (Franz Schubert's 'Ave Maria') being played on the violin by the lonely man and converts it to dramatic underscoring [...] The blind man cannot see the hideous monster's face and the monster cannot talk. The hermit thinks that the monster is an answer to his prayers. He had prayed for a companion. As he tells his story to the monster we hear the 'Ave Maria' again, but this time as dramatic underscoring with religious overtones played on the organ. (Timm 2003: 98)

Schubert's 'Ave Maria' makes poignant lyrical references. Schubert used Adam Storck's German translation of Walter Scott's 'Hymn to the Virgin' (Schubert 1894–1895). Storck's lines 'Wir schlafen sicher bis zum Morgen, Ob Menschen noch so grausam sind' literally reference the cruelty of man, something the monster experiences with regularity; Storck's translation prioritized matching rhythm and meter over the preservation of literal meaning. Scott's corresponding original lines, 'Safe may we sleep beneath thy care, Though banish'd, outcast and reviled,' reflect the monster's precarious situation. In either case, the prayer to the Virgin for safekeeping and pity is apropos for the fleeing creature seeking refuge.

Things take an interesting turn when we give a close reading to the inclusion of the Schubert in the score. To seasoned musicologists, there is an obvious sand trap here, one that I will explain in a minor digression. After this elaboration on Schubert and contemporary musicology, I will resume my own unpacking of the use of Schubert in *Bride of Frankenstein*.

Schubert's sexuality has been the subject of intense debate and rigorous academic research. Maynard Solomon presented a paper at the 1988 American Musicological Society meeting; this paper was subsequently published in 1989 in the journal *19th-Century Music* as 'Franz Schubert and the Peacocks of Benvenuto Cellini,' the title a reference to authentic period innuendo. Solomon argued that Schubert was homosexual, basing his argument upon readings of historical documents and surviving correspondence. In 1993, Rita Steblin countered with 'The Peacock's Tale: Schubert's Sexuality Reconsidered' in the same journal, an effort to debunk Solomon's research and conclusion. Many other musicologists jumped into the fray: Agawu, Byrne-Bodley, Clark, Gramit, Kramer, Muxfeldt, Tellenbach, Webster, Winter, and Susan McClary, author of the landmark book *Feminine Endings: Music, Gender, & Sexuality*.

Solomon's 1989 article considers not just the question of Schubert's sexuality, but also considers the question of representation: what homosexuality might have represented in Schubert's time and how such representation might have impacted Schubert's life and creative work.

The bohemian-homosexual community represented freedom from the restraints of family and the state, freedom from the compulsions of society and the strait-jackets of heterosexuality, freedom from the imperative to raise a family and to make a living in a routine job – in short, freedom to ignore the reality principle in favor of the pursuit of beauty and pleasure. These were temporarily adequate, if ultimately insufficient, indemnities for a precarious existence on the margins of society. (Solomon 1989: 205)

Schubert has often been considered to have been on the 'margins of society,' *regardless* of his sexuality. Schubert died at the age of 32; many secondary sources attribute his death to syphilis, based upon primary source descriptions of his affliction and deterioration. Schubert's *popular image* carries a connotation of young dandy, a sissified creature, a genius of lieder and parlor entertainment, whose symphonic works were inferior to those of more masculine, Teutonic masters. This image has a distinct lineage dating from critic and composer Robert Schumann, and extending well into the following century.

Musicologist David Gramit studied Victorian-era perceptions of Schubert and his music. In Britain, these perceptions largely stemmed from George Grove's article for his *Dictionary of Music and Musicians*, 'the standard English-language account of Schubert's life from the time of its appearance in 1882 until well into [the twentieth] century' (Gramit 1993: 66). The implication to my work is that James Whale would have been familiar with popular perceptions and biases extended or perpetuated by Grove's account. Grove's article paints Schubert as feminine in no uncertain terms.

> Grove did not invent the analogy comparing Beethoven to Schubert as man to woman – Schumann did in his 1838 review of Schubert's Grand Duo – but while he acknowledges his debt, he expands the metaphor well beyond Schumann's original use. [...] Grove shows no [...] moderation: 'Another equally true saying of Schumann is that, compared with Beethoven, Schubert is as a woman to a man.' (Gramit 1993: 72)

Victorian-era music critic Joseph Bennett explained Schubert's popularity and image at the time in Britain, emphasizing his 'mystery' and 'beauty,' two feminine qualities, but also the tragic element of Schubert's short life.

> In his 1908 memoirs, the English music critic Joseph Bennett recalled the impact of the Victorian discovery of Schubert on audiences in the 1860s. [...] 'The charm of his simple nature, the freshness and beauty of his music, and the mystery of his tragic life, drew our eyes to him brimming with love and pity, and we could offer him naught but praise.' (Gramit 1993: 67)

The tragedy of Schubert's early death from syphilis would have further resonated with a sympathetic audience fascinated by the romanticizing of illness, death, and bohemia; consider Puccini's opera *La bohème* (1896), Verdi's *La traviata* (1853), and Offenbach's *The Tales of Hoffman* (1881). This romanticizing of illness and death is easily relatable to a homosexual underworld present not only in Vienna but in Britain as well.[15] Even if Whale's generation was unaware of Schubert's *actual* sexuality, they would have been sensitive to his unconventionally masculine *outsider image*. Schubert's transgressive image and reputation were well-established by Whale's time, dating to nineteenth-century criticism. Musicologist Lawrence Kramer argues:

> What worried nineteenth-century critics was not Schubert's own sexuality, but the effect of his music on the sexual identity of his male listeners. It is worth revisiting Lenau's remarks in this connection: 'Schubert's compositions are wearing thin. There is a certain coquetry, an effeminate weakness about them.' (Kramer 1998: 98)

The 'effeminate weakness' of Schubert's *music* has been noted by contemporary analysts as well; consider McClary's 'Constructions of Subjectivity in Schubert's Music' (2006). Posits Kramer in redux, 'Whatever his sexuality, Schubert was constructing models of masculinity that went against the grain of his age' (Kramer 1998: 99). To pin 'gender' onto *music* itself, as opposed to associated cultural signs, is a controversial and slippery slope. Musicologist Suzannah Clark defends McClary's musical analysis:

> McClary's main point is incontrovertible: Schubert's music depicts a markedly different version of masculinity from the prevailing norm of masculinity – a 'norm' which, incidentally, is equally a construction. (Clark 2011: 187)

My point is not to discern Shubert's sexuality or the gender characteristics of his music, but to emphasize how James Whale would have seen him: a beautiful monster who died young. Schubert would have been seen as 'effeminate' or as an outsider in Whale's day, even without the ensuing twentieth-century arguments about his sexuality. Schubert's actual sexuality is not at stake here; rather, his queerness or 'otherness' encouraged Whale to associate the hermit, the monster, and their affectionate bond to the outsider status of Schubert himself. The hermit is 'holy' by virtue of his blindness, seclusion, and generosity. The monster registers as 'human' by virtue of his reaction to the hermit's violin; through his interactions with the hermit, the monster is depicted as innocent. The incorporation of 'Schubert' as text serves as a knowing nod to the oppression of the outsider.

Unfortunately, spotting notes for *Bride of Frankenstein* could not be found in the Waxman Archive at Syracuse University. I strongly suspect that Schubert's 'Ave Maria' was suggested by director James Whale himself, in the same way that Whale suggested the ending's dissonant chord. This would reinforce my argument, but is not a necessary condition. 'Ave Maria' is *not* a massive signpost to 'homosexuality' inappropriately placed in *Bride of Frankenstein*. There is some subtlety in the use of Schubert here; to decode the reference requires a modicum of historiography and sensibility. In the same way, the feyness of Dr. Pretorius is also a tip of Whale's hand.

The music of *Edward Scissorhands*

Edward Scissorhands, with its eponymous monster, deliberately modernizes both the fairy tale and the horror film. While being steeped in artifice (the exaggerated suburbia, topiaries, the old house, the caricature of the loving inventor), the film is also poignantly realistic – its observations and dynamics on family relations, the 'black sheep' outsider artist, jealousy, teen bullying and delinquency ring true. Music helps the film balance the poles of artifice and realism, horror and whimsy.

Musically, *Edward Scissorhands* breaks the mold of stereotyped dissonant scoring for the monster. The film's music, to a large degree, represents a 'queering' of conventions, just as other aspects of the film are queered throughout; one could easily unpack the queering of makeup, narrative, casting, lighting, and so on at length. The film does away with the typical gore, female shrieks, and monster of minimal intelligence, replacing them with punctured waterbeds and tires, and monster as sensitive artist and auteur. Correspondingly, whimsy has overtaken the usual musical markers of the horror film: jarring atonal stabs and dissonant atmospheres are replaced by delightful musical bon-bons.

These whimsical musical moments help *Edward Scissorhands* negotiate liminal spaces between genres and degrees of artifice and realism. Consider the efficacy of the Czardas inspired solo violin accompaniment to Edward cutting Joyce's hair. Actor Johnny Depp's prop department 'scissorhand' gloves looked great but were incapable of such fine work. In the period before expeditious VFX, the hair cutting effect is achieved by a combination of an off-screen leaf blower and music itself.

Rapid-fire violin bowing with great accuracy indicates how proficiently and fast Edward cuts hair. A similarly whimsical moment is Elfman's 'Ballet de Surburbia' accompanying choreographed cars leaving pastel homes for morning commutes; here Elfman's music imparts playfulness to the mundane.

Elfman reinforces Burton's vision with a musical score that defies not only horror conventions but also expectations and preconceived notions of Elfman's own style and influences. Elfman, former rock star with Oingo Boingo and consummate interviewee, has encouraged a mythos that casts him as proponent and emulator of Bernard Herrmann. But the *Scissorhands* score does not follow a Herrmanesque style of angular, cellular music. Existing musical analyses of Elfman within film musicology and fan communities align him with Bernard Herrmann, Gustav Mahler, and Richard Wagner, painting Elfman as a motivic composer of the Germanic late romantic school. This may be true in other films, but in *Edward*, the significant, overarching musical reference is Tchaikovsky's fruity *Nutcracker* ballet, childlike and luxuriant with celeste, harp, and intertextual Christmas references. *Edward* uses sweeping themes that are lush, romantic, Christmassy, and Tchaikovsky-like, expertly transformed as needed. While Elfman discusses Herrmann, but not Tchaikovsky, on the *Edward Scissorhands* DVD composer commentary audio track, he has recently acknowledged the importance of *The Nutcracker*.

> [*Edward Scissorhands*] was just going to my other influences – you know, strong Russian influences, bits of Tchaikovsky and Prokofiev. They're so deep in my psyche, and as soon as I got to that part of the world, I dipped into the Eastern European part of my musical soul. [...] Frequently when I'm writing, I'll hear bits of *Lieutenant Kije* or *Alexander Nevsky* or *Romeo and Juliet* – or, in this case, *The Nutcracker*. In the same way *Pee-Wee* took me to Italy, *Edward Scissorhands* took me to snowy Eastern Europe. It's just my sense of a fantasy or fairy-tale character. It takes me right back to my ancestral side of my roots, which is Poland and Russia. Even though I don't know either of them personally, as I started growing up and hearing music from that part of the world, it immediately felt like it was from my own blood. (Elfman in O'Neal 2014)

It is this sense of fantasy, fairy tale, and snow that connect *The Nutcracker* to *Edward Scissorhands*, as well as the Christmastime setting. *Edward Scissorhands* incorporates not only horror tropes, but also genre conventions of, or allusions to, the television Christmas special and the fairy tale. Scholars have noted that Elfman has a strong capacity to score for genre, and to cannily create musical environments that strongly evoke a film's generic situation and referents.

> [Elfman] is able to concentrate existing signifiers into a musical form that captures the tone of the film so well that it effectively redefines the music of an entire genre, as happened in particular with [...] *Edward Scissorhands'* post-Disney redefinition of the idea of fairy tales and fantasy. (Halfyard 2004: 35)

Elfman's approach is 'classical' in terms of a return to the sound of the symphony orchestra and to tropes of highly dramatic orchestral music, with an emphasis on sincere, ardent emotion in a seemingly timeless, formal orchestral palette. Elfman employs a limited number of main themes, rather than theme-tagging every major character (Figures 6.1 and 6.2). Elfman's main themes then become identified with the movie itself, and more memorable through greater repetition. Scoring emotions, rather than characters, allows for a musical interpretation of the queer monster that is finely nuanced with multiple variations. This is

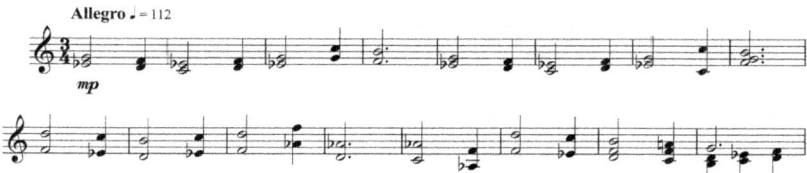

Figure 6.1   Edward Scissorhands 1M1A 'Titles' from Bar [18]. Excerpt extracted from full score by the author

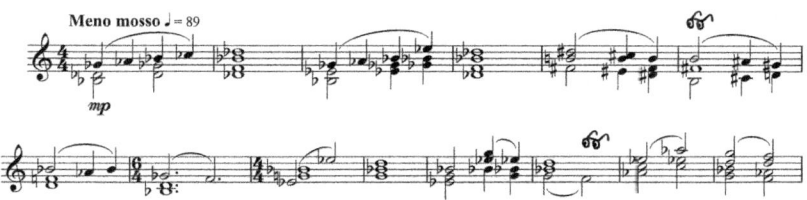

Figure 6.2   1M1B 'Storytime' at Bar [33]. Excerpt extracted from full score by the author

a contrast to horror films that deploy a consistent character theme to signpost the monster's presence.

Fan communities and some film musicologists have expressed opinions in which Elfman is sometimes seen with great respect, but sometimes dismissed as a 'hummer' or a dilettante, an autodidact rock star; he is seen as a disciple of Bernard Herrmann, or as a continuation of Wagnerian stylings of film scoring's 'Golden Age.' *Edward Scissorhands* shows that Elfman's strength is an intuitive grasp of story, emotions, and genre. He has recaptured many older sounds that date to film scoring's Hollywood 'Golden Age' period, but selectively so. Elfman is best seen as a tastemaker and dramaturge; he has a gift for melody, and even if his scores are sometimes derivative, his execution makes them uniquely his. The *Edward Scissorhands* score is relatively simple, old-fashioned, and romantic, emphasizing Edward's internal drama.

> With *Edward Scissorhands* everything happened very organically and simply, quite the opposite of *Batman*. What I loved about writing that score, and it's one of my favorites, was that it was a very simple through-line. [...] It was a pleasure to do *Edward Scissorhands* where this simple storyline was told from an internal standpoint of this one character, and musically I simply had to follow that. I think the film was clearly an old-fashioned, sweet fairy tale and I think I played it just as I saw it. Also the music was very sappy and romantic and emotional and I enjoy doing that. (Elfman in Russell and Young 2000: 159)

Existing analyses of the score honor its wide appeal but do not recognize it as subversive. Its subversions are easy to miss. The score is a charming throwback to Hollywood usages, with no exteriorizing meta-perspective nor winking-at-the-audience jokes (as found in John Morris' score for *Blazing Saddles*); it offers little to add to old arguments about diegesis and functionality.

> Elfman's score is used nondiegetically and follows Gorbman's principles of film scoring in the classical Hollywood film. The music signifies emotions with Edward's two themes reflecting his emotional states; it works to establish setting and characters as well as to interpret and illustrate narrative events; and also provides unity as the tone of the film changes. (Reay 2004: 37)

Such analyses and criticisms are slightly if unintentionally dismissive and overlook the score's subversive elements in defiance of genre, employment of whimsy, and referential allusions to Tchaikovsky and television Christmas specials. Elfman's score is one of the elements that enables Burton to 'queer' the genres of horror and fantasy, and to position Edward as a 'queer monster.'

Excerpts of the score have been published in Russell and Young's colorful, over-sized volume *Film Music* (2000). In 2006, Hal Leonard published a collection of 'Themes from Edward Scissorhands' for level-3 string orchestra, arranged by Larry Moore. In 2013, Omni Publishing released a limited edition of the original full orchestral score; the examples and reductions used in this chapter I have extracted myself from this edition. Various unauthorized piano transcriptions can be found on the Internet; these are not always reliably accurate.

Elfman and perceptions of music literacy

Pertinent to the queerness of *Edward Scissorhands'* score, and to a queer reading of the film overall, is composer Elfman's marginalization as a rock star, a pop musician, wrongfully derided as musically illiterate, one who arrived late to film scoring without requisite conservatory training and who is somehow inferior or outside of the film scoring establishment, such as it might exist or be imagined. This marginalization, instead of recognizing that every successful person in Hollywood has a unique path, 'others' Elfman by placing him outside of various educational and vocational structures which were apparently not necessary for his success.

Discourse in *Keyboard Magazine* from October 1989–January 1990 (also discussed in Halfyard 2004: 10–13), an article by music reviewer Steven Wright (2006: 1032–33), and popular opinions posted in fan blogs have claimed outright that Elfman is musically illiterate. This charge has been leveled at other film composers like Hans Zimmer, and Gustavo Santaolalla as discussed in Chapter 3. In the case of Elfman, this charge has been debunked, but deserves a brief overview and some commentary on music literacy in general, as well as an unpacking of this charge's place and purpose within critical and fan communities.

Elfman discusses his music literacy in Richard Davis' *Complete Guide to Film Scoring*, saying, 'I wrote down everything, I didn't start using MIDI notation until '96' (Elfman in Davis 1999: 279). Elfman learned orchestration techniques in order to work with the performance troupe Mystic Knights of the Oingo Boingo, who later became the rock band Oingo Boingo. The Mystic Knights had winds, reeds, brass, and a rhythm section, totaling about eleven or twelve players, with whom Elfman worked, composed, and arranged for eight years (Halfyard 2004: 5; Elfman DVD commentary 0:58:44). Elfman also claims he transcribed early jazz by Duke Ellington and Django Reinhardt, something that would require a good amount of ear training to do accurately, even if it were self-taught.

Elfman has been consistent in his own defense and in describing his own literacy skills and development as a musician; his accounts have appeared in letters and interviews in *Keyboard Magazine, Film Score Monthly,* and elsewhere (Elfman 1990; Kendall 1995b; Lustig 2005). Mystic Knights guitarist and longtime Elfman orchestrator Steve Bartek has corroborated that Elfman writes things down with a pencil, as well as marking-up computer printouts by hand (Kendall 1995c). *Film Score Monthly* printed two pages of hand-scrawled autograph scores, one from *Batman Returns,* another from *Black Beauty* (Kendall 1995b). Mark Russell and James Young's *Film Music: Screencraft* shows several pages of orchestrated score to *Edward Scissorhands,* all handwritten. These pages are almost definitely in Bartek's hand, but they are clearly not from a computer. Orchestration and copying were increasingly computerized as time went on, but examples from the early 1990s show a lot of work by hand.

Additionally, Elfman doesn't conduct, and, admittedly, will stay in the control room to listen and follow the picture rather than burying his nose in the score.

> I also like watching the screen. I don't want to watch the music. I'm not concerned with what's on the music at that point. I'm more concerned with the screen and so my eyes have to be glued to the screen. And I want the director sitting right next to me and I want to be looking at his expression. (Elfman in Braheny 1990)

It would be easy to attend an Elfman recording session, see the *conductor* field players' musical questions, and presume that Elfman himself is illiterate. This is not the case, but this scenario may explain some of the gossip within the Hollywood industry and fan communities. I consider this matter settled; Elfman can read and write well enough for his work. However, I do see the existence of this very controversy as a matter of importance and relevance to my arguments.

Music literacy is a huge and problematic subject to survey. Who reads? Who doesn't? What qualifies as sufficient evidence of competence in literacy? How do we judge or evaluate literacy or weight its importance in music making? Some work has been done in these areas by Lucy Green, who studied pop musicians and their acquisition of musicianship (Green

2007). There is a wide spectrum of music reading ability; it is not a simple can-or-cannot read situation. Sight reading is a different skill than reading slowly for memorization. Different instruments use different clefs, transpositions, and notation practices. A guitarist who reads tablature at sight might be lost reading a viola part in alto clef, for instance. A French horn player doesn't like to see notes high in the bass clef; a bassoonist doesn't want to see notes that sit low in the tenor clef. Some pianists are good with transpositions; some not at all. There are a variety of accepted notation practices, such as 'standard' musical notation, tablature, figured bass, jazz or rock chord charts, lead sheets, piano reductions, and so on; the acceptance or preference of a particular system within given genres suggests a hegemony of notations and subjective cultural and musical hierarchies. The more this issue is broken down and dissected, the less it appears to be about literacy or musical competence, but rather about something else: where and how knowledge was acquired, under whose tutelage, and ultimately, about the authenticity of authorship itself.

The Elfman literacy controversy easily crossed over into an attack on authorship, as noted in Kendall's interviews with Elfman and orchestrator Steve Bartek (1995b, 1995c) published in *Film Score Monthly*. Elfman's interview features a lengthy section entitled 'He Writes His Own Music, Already,' and a following section, 'Look, Scores!' (1995b). The issue's table of contents boasts, 'Danny Elfman's Actual Sketches: Feature Article part 2 – in which we print some of Elfman's actual sketches to prove he writes his own music' (1995b). I emphasize that these interviews aim to convince the reader that Elfman not only *notates* his own music, the old literacy issue, but *composes* it as well.

If music is seen as a 'language,' to be written and read, then a composer who cannot read music becomes cast, like Frankenstein's monster, as an outsider who cannot speak, or speaks poorly. (Mel Brooks parodies the monster's poor language, musical, and motor skills in a song-and-dance number, 'Putting on the Ritz,' in *Young Frankenstein*.) This projects Elfman further into the role of outsider, a stranger, from an uncouth rock establishment, improperly groomed, who crashed the film music industry on the coat tails of his friend, director Tim Burton. Those who argue that Elfman is illiterate seek to demean, not to glorify. Complaining that composers cannot read music is an attack couched in intellectual terms on musical or cultural background. We can anecdotally relate this to literacy tests that were used to prevent people of color from voting in the United States. Would we institutionalize musical literacy tests to prevent people from composing music for films? What would such a test ask? And to what end? Questions raised by the Elfman literacy controversy are germane to a book on queerness in film music when rephrased in these terms. If the *copyist* cannot read, we have a real problem. If the composer cannot read, perhaps we will see some sloppy voice-leading. But what of it? If people still love the music, to what degree is that an issue?

Elfman on his influences

Part of Elfman's fan mythology is the idea that the composer comes from a European, Germanic tradition of 'Golden Age' Hollywood film scoring, traceable to Mahler, Strauss, and Wagner. This sounds impressive and makes for good PR, but obscures the driving influences of Tchaikovsky and television Christmas specials behind the *Edward Scissorhands* score. Elfman discusses Wagner but not Tchaikovsky in his *Edward* DVD commentary. Elfman has emphasized the Germanic lineage in other interviews as well.

> After *Batman* a lot of people asked me about my Wagnerian influences and my answer was that I never really listened to Wagner. On the other hand I was very influenced by other composers such as Korngold, Tiomkin and Steiner and I think they were probably very much influenced by Wagner, so I probably was indirectly. Many of my musical influences are classical which have in fact been filtered through other film composers. (Elfman in Russell and Young 2000: 156)

Wagner, Steiner, and Korngold are also seen as being filtered through Bernard Herrmann on their way to Elfman; Herrmann is seen as Elfman's primary influence. Elfman has encouraged these perceptions.

> Even now I often go back to stuff that I heard in movies when I was a kid, and I know when I'm doing bits of Bernard Herrmann and Nino Rota, Max Steiner, Franz Waxman or Erich Korngold. It's all this vast repertoire to pull from. (Elfman in Braheny 1990)

Those bits of 'Nino Rota' are evident in oompah, circus-like cues rampant in Elfman's scores for *Pee-Wee's Big Adventure* (1985) and *Beetlejuice* (1988), and have become an Elfman trademark, combining energy, humor, and slightly sinister dissonances. Elfman has consistently credited Herrmann with being a 'model' for his film composition:

> Bernard Herrmann was the composer who really made me understand and appreciate film music. And Bernard Herrmann is still, I

think, my model, my idol, in terms of (I believe to me) the best film composer of the twentieth century, although that, I'm sure, would be a hotly debated item. And a lot of people would disagree with me. To me, he was the most consistently inventive and brilliant. (Elfman 2000 00:57:38)

Fan communities have seized upon Elfman's connection to Herrmann; some have accused Elfman of outright stealing. Academia has ignored some of the observations and opinions generated by fan communities. Halfyard's book on the *Batman* score neglects to mention the indebtedness of the main theme to Herrmann's *Journey to the Center of the Earth* (1959) that was widely noticed by fans (Filmtracks 1997; 'Have you heard it before' 2009). While fan communities tend to make their arguments in the heated language of lay people, this does not discount the validity of the observations. A trained musicologist or music theorist will provide notated examples of themes and discuss them in appropriate terminology. Observations from fans, even from those with inferior training and analytical skills, may be *especially* valid precisely because they are clear to someone *without* high-level training.

Accurate analysis of 'Elfman' as text needs to acknowledge fan communities and fan commentary. When Elfman speaks or gives interviews, his statements are knowingly directed to fan communities. As a former rock star, Danny Elfman has a heightened awareness of fan communities and image maintenance, and he applies his PR acumen to his career as a film composer. He may score by intuition, as has been argued by Halfyard, but he presents himself in a savvy, dignified, humble manner, tipping his hat to Herrmann and earlier composers. The *Edward Scissorhands 10th Anniversary Edition* DVD (2000) contains, as extras, two optional audio tracks: Burton's director commentary, and Elfman's composer commentary. An undeniable reason for this unusual, full-length *composer* commentary track is its commercial draw for Elfman's own fanbase. This fanbase must be part of the analysis of Elfman as a composer because it helps shape the mythology and discourse around him and his work. The connection to Herrmann may be true, but it becomes further solidified, concretized, and extended to any Elfman film score, deservedly or not.

Elfman's scoring: puzzle pieces and intuition

In spite of some notational shortcomings, occasionally poor voice-leading, and an autodidact musical education, Elfman works in a manner characteristic of classically trained composers. He will first compose themes that seem appropriate, before hanging them on a predetermined structural framework. In period classical music, the established framework might have been a symphonic, sonata, or concerto form, for example. For Elfman, the predetermined structure is the film itself. This is a process of determining what themes work well, where, and how, and what opportunities exist for the transformation and manipulation of thematic musical material. Elfman describes this:

> Here on *Edward* [...] there was this process of looking at things, and how to divide up themes, lay them out, and look at them like a great puzzle, that it was becoming how I looked at a movie. Each of these pieces of music began to become colored pieces of puzzles. They're either the blue piece, the red piece, the green piece, but they're parts of different color-coded pieces related to different themes. And they all had to fit together. [...] It is rather like setting out all the pieces in a huge jigsaw puzzle and understanding what each of the different color groups are going to do for the movie, and then breaking them down [...] knowing not quite how they're going to fit together, but knowing you've got all the pieces laid out in a way that's going to make sense. So when you need to draw from one color or the other color, you know exactly where to go, they're right there at my fingertips. And what I'm going to do with them I don't know, but I know where I need to find everything that I'm going to be looking for. (Elfman 2000 1:02:30)

Elfman makes thematic associations intuitively; Halfyard argues that Elfman might not always identify formal composition techniques, but can use them well enough on his own.

> As a composer, Elfman knows what does and does not work: even when he is surprised by the results and does not entirely understand them, he is happy to trust his instincts and leave analysis to the analysts. (Halfyard 2004: 29)

Elfman has been criticized, rightly or wrongly, for his notation, sometimes riddled with conflicting enharmonic spellings,[16] and for weaknesses in musical literacy. But notation and literacy are just one aspect of being a composer, and a rather technical aspect at that. Literacy can be taught; a more critical area of a composer's skill and technique is the ability to transform and manipulate musical material. This is where Elfman excels. As Elfman limits the number of major musical themes within each film score, the transformation and musical manipulation of those themes are a characteristic part of his style and technique.

> When I first start a score, I play around for quite a bit with the thematic ideas. And I really have to really know that they're going to play all the beats that I want them to play. And so there was a number of weeks when I was just coming up with a number of these ideas and playing them for Tim [Burton], and not really necessarily putting them against individual scenes in the picture, but it was just knowing that there were these different sides of Edward. One would play over the inventor because that's one part of the story. The other would play over the ice scene; that was Edward's emotional center. And in fact Edward's music would even play over Kim as a character, that she wasn't even going to get her own theme. And I suppose classically speaking that's kind of odd too. But I like following the emotions, not the characters, and I've always felt that way, and that I carry into the score as well. (Elfman 2000 0:07:30)

Elfman may think that, 'classically speaking,' whether in reference to 'classical' music or 'classical' Hollywood film scores, what he's doing is 'odd,' but playing around with themes to get them right before writing the actual composition is a basic conservatory, classical-training technique based upon performance and improvisation. Waxman skirted around the semantics of the 'leitmotiv' in film music; Elfman performs these types of manipulative musical operations as a result of having assimilated much film music from the 'Golden Age' period, and describes them in his own terms.

> The same themes that were innocent and tender are now going to start appearing – as I'm grabbing for these pieces as I started talking about earlier, and mixing them up, and inverting them, sometimes twisting them around, and even turning them inside-out, but always trying to keep a melodic thread through all the music, even though it's going to start breaking down into more dramatic, sometimes melodramatic type of elements. I still have to keep the same melodic threads going, even if it's subliminal. I think that's part of carrying us through a story like this: that it's going to change, the tone is going to change, the attitude's going to change, but some way or another the melodic threads are going to keep joining together. And in that way music in film becomes kind of a knitting element: it knits together, ties together. (Elfman 2000 1:06:30)

Elfman is able to point out in his running DVD commentary moments where various musical transformations occur. Edward's first major theme, a dreamy waltz sometimes called the 'storybook theme,' is introduced in 1M1A 'Titles' (Figure 6.1). It is initially heard in a mixed treble choir comprised of sopranos, altos, and boys. The corresponding choir parts in the score have no phrasing and no marked rests or places to breathe, details that must have been worked out by the choral conductor during rehearsal or the recording process itself. This is an example of a continuum of music literacy; much canonical published choral music is highly marked, but Elfman's choral parts were evidently clear enough for the recording session.

The 'storybook theme' reappears transformed in 1M4 'Castle.' Elfman describes this moment, 'As you can hear, we're playing the entire opening theme, very darkly this time' (Elfman 2000 00:11:15). The theme is reintroduced again in 4M2 'Etiquette.' The theme reappears ethereally in 7M1 'Heist' at [63] in wood flute. In various places in the score, the theme is fragmented or used as the basis for constructing new material with similar intervals or melodic contour.

Music editor Bob Badami's spotting notes for 1M4 'Castle' reveal how this sequence, although scary, is tempered with mystery and magic. The spotting session, held between composer, director, and music editor, records where music should be placed. At this point, there is no record of what particular theme should be used; but the director's musical intention is recorded and serves as a guideline for the composer.

> We talked about this cue being in three parts. 1. Driving section should be creepy scary with weight but understated. 2. Garden section – creepy magical. 3. Interior – wonderment but still scary. (Badami in Karlin 1994: 10)

Badami's 1M4 spotting notes conclude, 'Music is out when Edward thrusts his scissors forward' (Badami in Karlin 1994: 10). Elfman's music does reach a cadence and resolution at this point; but the music extends even further, with a cadential extension. This is a means of extending the music beyond the specified out-point, but allows for the opportunity to have a music editor or sound mixer fade it out unobtrusively where its ending was originally specified. The entire cue is left in the film, so evidently Elfman's later out-point satisfied the director.

Edward's second theme, sometimes called the 'emotional' theme, initially appears in 1M1B 'Storytime' (Figure 6.2). It sounds both beautiful and delicate, perhaps a reflection of the fragility of emotion or of Edward's own sensitivity. Careful inspection reveals some of the quirks of voice-leading and harmony characteristic of a self-taught composer. Notice the incomplete chord in the sixth bar; the omission of the third is uncharacteristic of the classical style Elfman endeavors to emulate. Elfman's handling of 7ths also shows some rather unclassical, rock-and-roll style. Notice, in the twelfth bar, the failure of F to resolve down by step to Eb, and the resulting awkward parallel motion upwards. Between bars 8 and 9 are some particularly unclassical parallel fifths that sound just fine to the rock-and-roll ear. (Notice also in Figure 6.1, the 'storybook' theme, in the 8th bar, the unprepared leap into the dominant 7th.) These voice-leadings are not inherently 'wrong' nor do they establish illiteracy; rather, they indicate a lineage from a popular music tradition and some independence from the strictures of the 'classical' era even as it is being emulated.

In 5M2 'Kim at the Mall,' as Edward sees Kim and her physical relationship with boyfriend Jim, Edward's second theme is stated and passed between celeste, harp, and shakuhachi, implying Edward's emotional awakening and growing attraction to Kim. The theme reaches its grand, sweeping, majestic, full realization in 8M4A 'Ice Dance' from bar [16], where Kim sees Edward carving a giant angel out of ice in the Boggs' front yard, and she dances with her hands up in the resulting falling snow. Elfman has saved the full realization of the theme for the film's most romantic, dramatic, narratively essential moment. It is a savvy recognition of an important internal climax within the film.

Orchestration: music box, harp, and celeste

Stan Link discusses 'The Monster and the Music Box' in the anthology *Music in the Horror Film* (Link 2010). Link relates the 'music box' trope to a nineteenth-century musing on morality through children, as seen in Mahler's creepy *Kindertotenlieder* (1904), for example. Link sees sound and music in cinematic horror as stemming from this tradition of morality through children, and relates this to music's performance of innocence and simplicity.

The coding of the music box, typically via harp and celeste, to childhood and innocence is often nuanced, subverted, or demented in movies; consider the embedded mischief in John Williams' main theme for *Home Alone* (1990), featuring a prominent celeste. *Home Alone*, coincidentally, is also set during Christmas and was released the same year as *Edward Scissorhands*. Williams' *Home Alone* theme uses excessive chromaticism in an otherwise simple theme to indicate the playfulness and deviousness of the child.

There is an *archetypal* quality to the music box *sound*, since children and nurseries rarely have actual music boxes anymore. Tinkly, high-pitched, and delicate timbres make strong associations to children and children's music; children's television shows and children's music albums continue to employ instruments or sounds that, if not from a genuine music box or toy piano, still have high-pitched, quickly-decaying sound qualities. It is easy to relate these sounds to high-pitched voices, little pattering feet, and the transience of childhood.

If there were a musically coded 'child' in *Edward Scissorhands*, that child would be Edward. When Peg Boggs first meets Edward in the attic of the old house, she asks him, 'Where are your parents? Your mother, your father?' This immediately signposts to the audience that Edward is still a child, or not yet an adult. There is an obvious dissonance here, given that actor Johnny Depp was a 27-year-old teen heart throb in tight leather regalia. This is one of the conceits of the film, and characteristic of its position in a liminal space between reality, artifice, and the fantastic. Nevertheless, Edward is an innocent who, if not an actual child, inhabits a not-fully formed adolescent sexuality (evident by his awkward encounters with Kim and sultry neighbor Joyce), and a wide-eyed innocence about everything as a result of his isolation (as seen in his curious reactions to the suburban quotidian and his unfamiliarity with various commonplace objects).

Celeste and harp, employed extensively throughout Elfman's score, do far more than code innocence. Music box gestures give the soundtrack a whimsical element of foofiness, as well as associations to winter, falling snow, Christmas television specials, and Tchaikovsky's *Nutcracker* ballet. The *Nutcracker* ballet connects to Christmas television specials through the work of composer Maury Laws.

Harp and celeste serve to generically locate *Edward Scissorhands* in a lineage of Christmas television with queer subtexts like *Rudolph the Red-Nosed Reindeer*. In the Rankin/Bass television special *Santa Claus Is Coming to Town* (1970), these sounds permeate scenes with a letter-reading postman voiced by Fred Astaire, the baby Claus, and various bits referencing children. While the songs are a nod to Broadway, the arrangements and underscore, like Elfman, ascribe to a classical, traditionalist sound. Maury Laws, composer of the Rankin/Bass specials, said, 'I never went for the "flavor of the day" in my background scores. Maybe that's why people still enjoy them' (Laws in Ehrbar, 2002: 197). Laws credits his

work arranging music for Christmastime television advertising for securing him his longtime composing job with Rankin/Bass Productions.

> The thing that probably got me the *Rudolph* job. I had done the
> Christmas commercials for GE for a couple of years. I didn't do all
> the composition. That was given to me. But I did the orchestrations.
> You're talking about orchestration when you talk about sounds and
> the Christmas sounds. [...] That sound, I think I hit on, doing these
> GE commercials. [...] When I wrote that stuff, I think I tried to con-
> jure up sounds from *The Nutcracker*. [...] Not to lift it or to steal it, but
> I would try, way back then, try to get in a frame of mind. I figured
> it ought to have some brightness. There should be bells at times, it
> should be bright. And once I hit on it, and it worked, I guess without
> really knowing it, I stayed with it. (Laws 2006)

The 'bright' Christmas sound described by Laws is characteristic of *The
Nutcracker*; this particular orchestration style can also be heard in iconic
compositions like Leroy Anderson's 'Sleigh Ride' (1948). Elfman follows
in the footsteps of composers like Laws and Anderson in borrowing
orchestral sounds and textures from *The Nutcracker*.

Figure 6.3 is an idiomatic celeste passage from *The Nutcracker*'s 'Dance
of the Sugarplum Fairy,' a well-known representative example of
Tchaikovsky's celeste writing and voicing.

For comparison, Figure 6.4 is a 'quasi solo' celeste passage from
Edward Scissorhands, 1M4 'Castle' from bar [53] (Elfman 2013: 34). It
coincides with DVD 0:09:47, and can be heard as Peg opens the old
metal gate and enters the topiary garden.

The sound of this solo celeste passage evokes Tchaikovsky's *Nutcracker*;
additionally, the notation graphically imitates the cross-beaming used

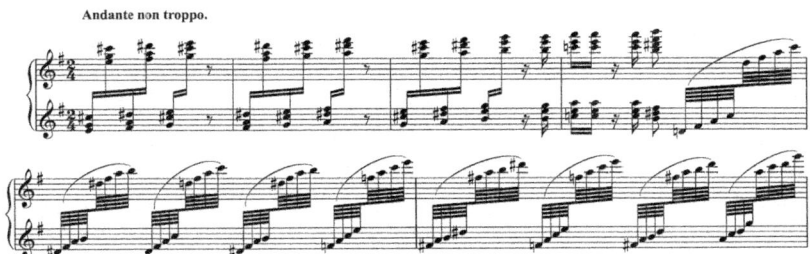

Figure 6.3 'Dance of the Sugarplum Fairy' celeste excerpt. Extracted from full
score by the author

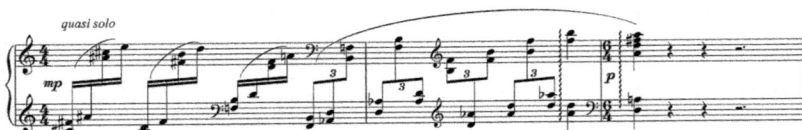

Figure 6.4 1M4 'Castle' celeste part from [53] extracted from full score by the author

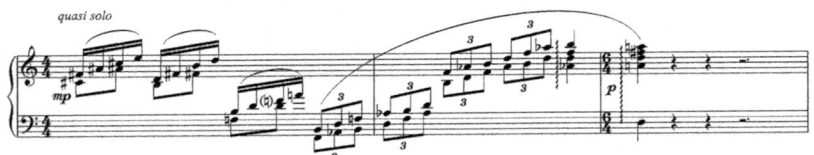

Figure 6.5 1M4 'Castle' celeste part from [53] renotated by the author

in the *Nutcracker* example (Figure 6.3), emulating the look and fingering of the Tchaikovsky excerpt. On close inspection, however, the *Nutcracker* excerpt is beamed this way because of an octave displacement between left and right hands. While it is *possible* to play the Elfman excerpt with alternating hands, as suggested by Elfman's notation, the part makes more sense and is easier to play as I have renotated it in Figure 6.5.

Elfman's original notation, while it looks idiomatic for celeste, implies more a nod to *The Nutcracker* than an engraving that will read quickly on the scoring stage, which is the usual concern. I suspect that, given the marked tempo of qu=104, the player performed the part as I have renotated it. The celeste is a keyboard instrument played with the fingers, as a piano is played, but the hammers strike metal bars rather than strings; I encourage readers to try this excerpt out for themselves on piano or keyboard.

Elfman's score has other connections to the *Nutcracker* ballet beyond the use of celeste and harp. The balletic aspect of *Edward Scissorhands* is made explicit in the names of cues: 8M4A is the 'Ice Dance' sequence, and 3M1 is 'Ballet Suburbia,' in which pastel-colored, choreographed automobiles leave their driveways to head out for the morning commute. The use of dance is visually downplayed: these are not extravagant showstoppers, but the score is musically aware of the choreographed movements. Kim's exultation of Edward's ice sculpting in the 'Ice Dance' is shot to make her movements look like natural behavior, rather than a dance number. Especially within the context of the musical score, a dance number is what it is.

William Rosar, cataloguing Universal's horror film scores of the 1930s, hears quite a bit of Tchaikovsky in the horror films of that period. Rosar notes the main title of *Dracula* (1931) contains music from *Swan Lake*; he asserts the 'Cat Love Theme' in *The Black Cat* (1934) was modeled by Heinz Roemheld on the love theme from *Romeo and Juliet*. He hears foreboding music in *Dracula's Daughter* (1936) that resembles the opening of the *Pathétique Symphony* (Rosar 1983: 393, 403, 404). In these cases there may be little symbolic or coded about these associations, other than it being a common reference or culturally assimilated music; Rosar does not extend his inquiry into this direction of critical cultural analysis. But in *Edward Scissorhands*, because of *Nutcracker*'s connections to television specials with queer content, Elfman's evocation of Tchaikovsky encodes more intertextual references than these earlier films.

Treble choir

Another characteristic of Elfman's orchestration prominently featured in *Edward Scissorhands* is the use of treble choir: sopranos, altos, and boys, used in varying combinations. The wordless choir dates back to earlier scores like Alfred Newman's *Song of Bernadette* (1943), where it has religious associations. Elfman employs choir as a distinctive flavor, another sonic reference to 'Golden Age' period symphonic film scoring. Halfyard connects Elfman's use of choir to more recent films that are 'concerned with the dangerous, supernatural, or alien "others"': *The Night of the Hunter* (1955), *The Amityville Horror* (1979), and *Interview with the Vampire* (1994) (Halfyard 2004: 33). Halfyard argues that these films

> have children as important characters and, on one level, the children's voices in the soundtrack are specifically linked to and representative of the children in the narrative. However, in all these films, the apparent innocence of the child's voice is positioned against the threat implicit in the film's title and genre and, by association, the child's voice itself comes to represent that threat, conveying a sense of mystery and immanent evil. (Halfyard 2004: 33)

As discussed above, the 'child' in Burton's film would be Edward; the treble choir is *not* used to accent the children in the classroom show-and-tell scene, for instance. In *Edward Scissorhands*, sometimes the choir sounds frightened, sometimes soothing. It is not necessarily Edward's voice or perspective, but can be. The choir trembles, afraid, when Peg enters Edward's 'Castle,' representing Edward's fear of an intruder, not

Peg's fear of the creepy old house. There are subtle, flitting scissors sound effects in this scene as Peg mounts the stairs, before we even meet Edward. Edward is hiding; Peg is intrepid and curious, even if she is trespassing on Edward's territory.

From a production standpoint, music editor Bob Badami's spotting notes say to make this scene 'wonderment but still scary'; it is not specified who owns the fear, just that it is the desired musical effect. One can inject theory and narratological interpretation into a close reading, but here, all the director specified was 'scary.' Furthermore, Elfman's choir is not just boys, but women as well: it is more an *effect* than a coherent semiotic device. Elfman scores by intuition rather than theoretical consistency. Not all musicologists share the same view on Elfman's use of choir.

> In *Edward Scissorhands* [...] the wordless boys' choir [sic] lends the film a sense of warped Disney scoring, managing to evoke something of the use of choirs in films such as *Pinocchio* (1940), on which the film as a whole is clearly modeled, and *Sleeping Beauty* (1959), with its Tchaikovsky waltz rhythms: but this is Disney seen through a glass darkly, the major keys of the voices in those films replaced with the minor-key waltzing of Elfman's main title. (Halfyard 2004: 33)

I would not agree that *Edward Scissorhands* is modeled on *Pinocchio*, or that the music or narrative is a direct reference to Disney. Halfyard misses references to queerness and television specials, as well as existing scholarship on Tim Burton that traces his lineage and inspiration to Vincent Price, Edgar Allen Poe, science fiction, and horror films. Burton did have an early gig with Disney working as an apprentice animator, but Disney is not a primary touchstone, even with regard to *Edward* as 'fairy tale.' Burton's aesthetic and fixations are far darker.[17] The lynch mob at the end of *Edward Scissorhands* has a non-fantastical danger to it; it leaps over the fairy tale aspect of the film and connects directly back to the mob that chased Frankenstein's monster. Elfman's score successfully plays this danger, as well as magical Christmas tropes that permeate the film.

Conclusion

When these analytical threads, historiographies, and arguments around Edward, Frankenstein, Schubert, Tchaikovsky, Waxman, Whale, Burton, and Elfman are sewn together, a queer musical tapestry emerges. Whale's biographer James Curtis argues that queer readings are 'revisionist' and are digging up mere 'subtext.' I argue that the queerness of the Monster is not subtext; rather, it is the essence of these stories, what has made them timeless and archetypal.

> As James Whale's homosexuality became widely known in the nine-teen seventies and eighties, revisionist criticism found a gay subtext to the isolation and scorn endured by the monster in *Frankenstein*. [...] [A]nalogies drawn from Whale's life as a homosexual presume he must have seen himself as a societal misfit on the same scale as the monster, and there is no evidence to support this. Whale never went to any particular trouble to conceal his homosexuality. (Curtis 1998: 143)

But analogies and queer readings of Frankenstein do *not* presume that Whale saw himself as a societal monster. In fact, a deeply closeted director would not have embedded such flamboyance (consider Ernest Thesiger's Dr. Pretorius!) into *Bride of Frankenstein*. Despite Curtis' objec-tions, Whale must have related to the monster as an archetypal outsider. Likewise, composer Franz Waxman would have related to the monster having been beaten and chased by a mob, as he himself shared this same experience on the anti-Semitic streets of Berlin.

In mid-1930s Hollywood, there was a European expatriate circle that included James Whale, David Lewis, Franz Waxman, Erich Pommer, Billy Wilder, Peter Lorre, Salka Viertel, and others. These expatriates would form their own 'island of misfit toys' to borrow an expression from *Rudolph the Red-Nosed Reindeer*. Through this expatriate circle we have an expanded notion of queerness that is beyond mere sexuality or homosexuality. Queerness here encompasses myriad forms of 'other-ness': nationality, ethnicity, religion, gender, ability, sexuality, asexual-ity, but above all, an experience of isolation and societal oppression. It is in this context and milieu that queerness is also expressed through music; hence, Schubert and Tchaikovsky join that circle as well.

As noted by Benshoff, Edward can be read as a queer monster. Edward's accompanying music is largely based on Tchaikovsky, who, like Schubert, is his own little queer monster. This has been over-looked in favor of a mythology that Danny Elfman emulates Bernard Herrmann. But *Edward Scissorhands* aligns more directly with *Rudolph* and *Bride* in a celebration of the oppressed, the misunderstood, the queer outsider, voiced musically in the form of dainty queer Christmas ballets. The music of the queer monster is not the clichés of atonal dis-sonance, but of references to goodness and humanity. Because the queer monster is good.

7
Blazing Saddles: Music and Meaning in 'The French Mistake'

Many motion pictures challenge audiences with narratives and meanings that are not perfectly clear-cut, suggesting titillating alternative interpretations. Could *Dune* really be about dependency on oil from the Middle East? Could *Borat* really be about American ignorance and xenophobia? Could *Avatar* really be about global ecopolitics? If such interpretations are possible, then things are not as simple as they appear to be onscreen. These examples align with a leftist politic, but conservatives have made their own observations. Televangelist Jerry Falwell contended that purple, purse-toting Tinky Winky from the children's television series *Teletubbies* represents a gay agenda, and a North Carolina pastor, Joseph Chambers, claimed that *Sesame Street*'s Ernie and Bert represent a gay male couple despite routine denials from Children's Television Workshop (Zekas 1994).

There are many ways to deconstruct and parse a film's thematic 'message.' Film score often operates as a non-verbal, subtle commentary on more obvious visual or literary cues. Film music can serve as an allegorical sign of alternative narratological interpretations to surface readings, revealing contrarian interpretations to onscreen narratives often taken at face value. Film music wordlessly reveals director biases and perspectives often couched behind expected genre conventions.

Mel Brooks' cowboy comedy *Blazing Saddles* (1974) appears to mock homosexuals, when it may be the first feature Hollywood Western film to cast homosexuals in an empowered, visible light, and unite them romantically and happily at the end. The film's 'French Mistake' musical sequence appears troublesome since it features overt mockery of stereotyped, disposable gay characters. However, analysis of the music reveals a surprising reversal of perspectives, showing the most readily apparent interpretation to be inaccurate. The results of this musical analysis are corroborated by other analyses from traditional aspects of film scholarship, including unpacking narrative, script, visual elements, director statements, and production practices.

Blazing Saddles is an intentional subversion or modification of the traditional Hollywood Western. *Blazing Saddles* is not merely a Western, but a comedy that knowingly mocks and parodies the Western genre. It exploits narrative and philosophical opportunities afforded when infusing portrayals of homosexuality into the mix, and it is their interpretation that is at stake.

In a further genre twist, *Blazing Saddles* features a handful of musical numbers, and Warner Bros.' original 1974 *Pressbook* for the film includes advertising art with an alternate tagline: 'from the people who gave you "The Jazz Singer"' (Warner Bros. 1974: 8). This tagline, an alternative to the primary, more commonly seen, Western-oriented 'or never give a saga an even break!', was a nod to the radical racial humor and musical sequences in *Blazing Saddles*, and related the film to the historically problematic 1927 musical that starred Al Jolson, a Jewish vaudevillian who appeared as the son of a Cantor, rebelling against his orthodox father to sing jazz tunes in blackface. Visually, these advertisements still use standard Western imagery and iconography, thus making the reference to *The Jazz Singer* a comic tease.

Conventions of the Western provide fertile ground for parodist and satirist Mel Brooks, who has also lampooned other genres including science fiction (*Space Balls*), silent film (*Silent Movie*), the sword-and-sandals epic (*History of the World: Part I*), horror film (*Young Frankenstein, Dracula: Dead and Loving It*), and Hitchcock thrillers (*High Anxiety*), to name a few. Brooks' formula includes a tight script, likable characters, Borscht Belt humor, vaudevillian song and dance numbers, deliberately Brechtian fourth-wall jokes, intertextual references to other films and personalities, provocative innuendo, and colorful language, creating films that are outré yet have wide audience appeal.

Blazing Saddles is, in these regards, a typical Mel Brooks film. While it may not be a typical Western, it is clearly knowledgeable of and *referential* to the typical Western in all its conventions. In this sense, *Blazing Saddles* exemplifies an 'ultimate' Western, replete with comic exaggeration of the appropriate stereotypes.

Two characters are central to the film. Jim, also known as The Waco Kid, is a washed-up gunslinger and outlaw played by Brooks regular Gene Wilder. Bart, the new African American sheriff, played by Cleavon Little, comes unexpected and unwanted to the Old West frontier town of Rock Ridge. Considering the centrality of Bart, whose race drives much of the conflict and dissonance, *Blazing Saddles* appears to be an 'outsider' film, with Bart cast as the mysterious figure whose arrival changes everyone's life. Yet the rapport of Bart and The Waco Kid suggests the film is a 'buddy movie,' with equal weight given to both men. The story of their developing friendship is the essential thread of the picture, and the film's finale puts a deliberately romantic twist on the buddy movie formula, well in advance and in excess of the more recent 'bromance' genre.

The final romantic ending is prefaced by an important fourth-wall song-and-dance sequence, 'The French Mistake,' that seems to belong to another film entirely. This unexpected sequence contains layers of interpretive meaning in an incisive commentary on the 'closet.' I will first present a brief overview of this crucial scene, then take a careful look at its introduction, the problematic character of Buddy Bizarre, the ensuing melee, and the connection to the closing scene.

'The French Mistake': overview

As *Blazing Saddles* accelerates towards a Western showdown with a chaotic, in-town, daytime exterior fight scene, the film is strangely interrupted. A magnificent crane shot lifts the camera high enough to reveal the Warner Bros.' studio lot, taking us out of the artifice of the Rock Ridge locale. The camera pans to a nearby soundstage building, creating a new establishing shot. Inside this soundstage, director Buddy Bizarre, played by actor Dom DeLuise, supervises the filming of a cliché Hollywood musical number, 'The French Mistake,'[1] with a chorus of male dancers.

> Throw out your hands
> Stick out your tush
> Hands on your hips
> Give 'em a push
> You'll be surprised
> You're doing the French Mistake, Voilà!

(Brooks 1974)

In this sequence, Buddy, in a parody of Busby Berkeley, abuses and corrects an errant dancer, demonstrates the proper execution of the routine, and calls for a new take, which is interrupted by the collapse of a soundstage wall and the abrupt entrance of cowboy combatants from

Mel Brooks' picture also being filmed on the Warner Bros. lot. Buddy tries to evict the cowboys, telling them, 'This is a closed set.' A cowboy replies, 'Piss on you, I'm working for Mel Brooks.' Buddy takes a punch, and the dancers join in a melee. This brawl results in several male couplings, and segues into a massive pie fight in the studio commissary. *Blazing Saddles* will return to its Old West setting for its ultimate conclusion.

The lead-in to 'The French Mistake' is an exterior, chaotic, cowboy fight scene in the 'fake' decoy town of Rock Ridge. This fight is musically underscored by 'The Big Fight' (Morris 1974), comprising upbeat variations of the 'Blazing Saddles' main-title theme (see Figure 7.1). This main theme features a descending major triad arpeggio; this motive will figure prominently throughout the film's score. The fight music is a typical use of variation to add to the excitement of conflict using familiar, existing musical material. This music, in a perfectly conventional manner, then follows the camera's ascension on a crane via a rising, modulating sequence, using a fragment of the main theme (Figure 7.2; note top line).

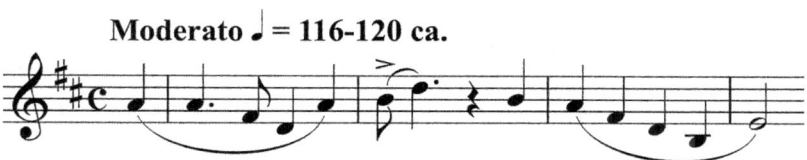

Figure 7.1 *Blazing Saddles* titles and end titles main theme. Transcribed by the author

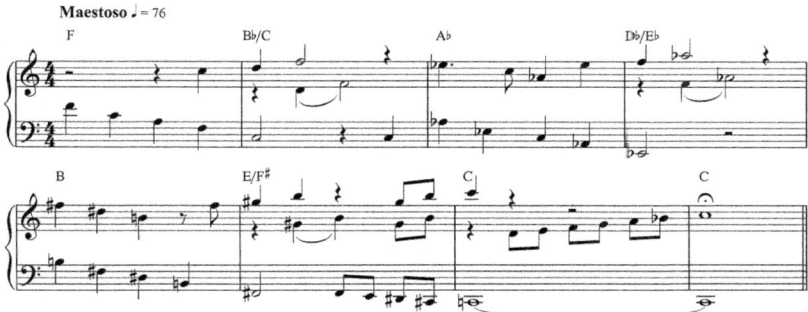

Figure 7.2 'The Big Fight' excerpt. Music by John Morris. Transcribed by the author

Following the fermata, this modulating sequence resolves to the downbeat of 'The French Mistake,' which is suddenly quick and peppy. While it was likely intended to be seamless, the resolution to 'The French Mistake' is a tad forced to the sensitive ear, indicating a likely edit, an indication that these cues were recorded separately. When we first hear 'The French Mistake,' it functions as a 'sound advance'[2] over the exterior shot of the soundstage, and pulls us into the scene inside.

Initially during this sound advance, 'The French Mistake' music briefly seems to be underscore; however, it is soon clearly revealed as diegetic music, the 'Playback!' used by Buddy and his dancers. Within the film world, this music exists as a 'pre-record' for the dancers' synchronized routine. When it needs to be restarted on Buddy's set, it begins, logically, with a series of count-off clicks that establish tempo and facilitate the dancers' proper entrance. In this way, we understand the diegetic function of the music on Buddy's set.

Mel Brooks has made recurring gags about diegesis in film music; consider Count Basie's orchestra on the prairie, also in *Blazing Saddles*, and the symphony orchestra on the bus in *High Anxiety* (1977). While handled more subtly, the 'playback' function of 'The French Mistake' uses the same music placement technique, where ostensibly non-diegetic underscore becomes revealed as diegetic music.

Basie's orchestra mocks the improbability of underscore itself and the lack of logical source for such music. Basie's orchestra is itself synchronized to playback of a pre-recorded Basie track, further layering the effect for the initiated. Basie's anachronistic big band swing accentuates Bart's inappropriately stylish Western outfit that mashes up frontier cowboy and urban African American fashions and codes. The delightfully incongruous and inexplicable presence of the orchestra on the nearly empty prairie helps push the moment over the top.

Within the context of Brooksian humor, these music diegesis jokes fall into a larger category of jokes about the production process itself; consider Dark Helmet bumping into the camera lens or knocking over a boom operator in *Spaceballs* (1987). While certainly unconventional for a Western, this fantastical meta-perspective is a recurring part of Brooks' cinematic humor.

'The French Mistake' is credited, music and lyrics, to Mel Brooks, an established song-and-dance man. Jonathan Tunick, the orchestrator credited on *Blazing Saddles*, also worked on Brooks' *Young Frankenstein* (1974) and *Twelve Chairs* (1970). 'The French Mistake' is orchestrated as a bright, peppy, show tune, driven by trap drum kit with tight hi-hat, gleeful clarinet, and bright trumpet jabs. The orchestration places the tune within the stylistic era of light, white, Tin Pan Alley popular swing that would be idiomatic for an early Busby Berkeley sound musical such as *Gold Diggers of 1933* (1933) or *Footlight Parade* (1933). This orchestration style helps make the Busby Berkeley parody robust. The 'whiteness' of the dance routine and musical style of 'The French Mistake' is another relevant aspect that could be further unpacked, since *Blazing Saddles* is dedicated to mocking racism, and the stiffness of 'The French Mistake' can be seen in opposition to Count Basie's hipper big band swing.

Visually the parody is equally clear; Buddy Bizarre's set itself, let alone the movie he directs, seems to exist in Busby Berkeley's earlier time period. Buddy speaks through a megaphone, and wears a dated pair of jodhpurs. Buddy and his world reject any connection to the contemporary world until Brooks' cowboys break their own time period. The dated orchestration of 'The French Mistake' fits right in to Buddy's apparent time period.

Musically, 'The French Mistake' is closely related to the 'Blazing Saddles' title song and corresponding main theme; the title song is credited to John Morris (music) and Mel Brooks (lyrics). Both 'The French Mistake' and the 'Blazing Saddles' themes are based around a descending arpeggiated root-position triad of the tonic major key. This descending major triad is the basic motivic element of the *Blazing Saddles* film score. While there is a clear melodic relationship between 'The French Mistake' (Figure 7.3) and the 'Blazing Saddles' theme (Figure 7.1), to an untrained ear 'The French Mistake' likely appears as new and unrelated music.

'The French Mistake' lyrically refers to two other texts related to Brooks' show business knowledge and parodic sensibilities. 'The French Mistake' in its complete rendition was recorded with a

Andante vivace ♩ = 108 ca.

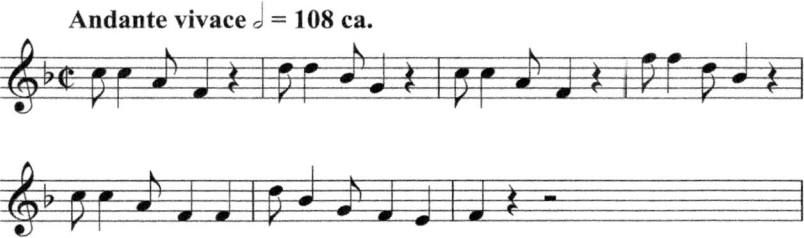

Figure 7.3 'The French Mistake.' Music and lyrics by Mel Brooks. Transcribed by the author

B-section that went unused in *Blazing Saddles*, and this full version makes explicit those references. The lyrics to the unused B-section, 'Come on try and move those feet along, Fifty million Frenchmen can't be wrong! Whee!' (Brooks 1974) reference a 1929 Cole Porter musical, *Fifty Million Frenchmen*, and, more directly, a popular 1927 'singing fox trot' called 'Fifty Million Frenchmen Can't Be Wrong' with lyrics by Billy Rose and Willie Raskin, and music by Fred Fisher. The song, recorded at the time by singers including Sophie Tucker, Frank Harris, and Ted Lewis, predictably paints Frenchmen as carefree and epicene, and mocks their taste in food and fashion, but also comparatively mocks American conservativeness, censorship, and Prohibition. This comedic musical attack would have certainly resonated with Brooks, whose films often celebrate hedonism and freedom; *Blazing Saddles* itself escaped studio censorship through a contract favorable to Brooks. The song features such relevant couplets as, 'They have a reputation of being very gay / I just got back from Paris and I just want to say' and 'They shake a ze hand, they shake a ze feet / They roll ze eyes and kiss each other on the street' (Fisher, Rose, and Raskin 1927). In this way, 'Fifty Million Frenchmen Can't Be Wrong' establishes a reference point and precedent to the Frenchified homosexual comedy of 'The French Mistake.'

An obvious surface reading of 'The French Mistake' sequence is that Buddy and his dancers are gay men, and that audience members can take pleasure in laughing *at* them. Such stereotyped portrayals, whether mean-spirited or not, have been shown to threaten the self-esteem of gay youth (Herdt 1989; McKee 2000), who might see these effeminate caricatures and think, 'That's not me, that offends me, I will stay in the closet and make myself believe that is not who I am.' So, with this type of comedy, there is actually something at stake. While a superficial reading of 'The French Mistake' accentuates homophobic humor, a close reading reveals a more positive bias.

While there are multiple possible interpretations of 'The French Mistake,' musical analysis helps indicate better readings. Before tackling a close reading, I would like to establish the existence or prevalence of the superficial one, as this discernment between readings requires evidence of misinformed or shallow interpretations. The World Wide Web has much anecdotal evidence of audience perceptions.

Websites such as Yahoo! Answers and Urban Dictionary indicate a popular understanding of the term 'French Mistake' as an accidental, unintended lapse into male homosexual behavior. Yahoo! Answers' 'best answer' claims that 'The song they sing is overtly gay, and hints at anal sex.'[3] The most popular answer on Urban Dictionary gives this definition: 'When an otherwise straight male is persuaded to, or on a whim in the heat of the moment, engages in a homosexual act of which he later regrets and is ashamed.'[4] These definitions are by no means authoritative, but serve to illustrate and document some audience perceptions. These online comments suggest that it is the film's more homophobic *surface* reading that is most clear to users of these particular websites.

However, these online interpretations easily derive from a viewing of 'The French Mistake' scene, not from any a priori knowledge of the term. It may be that Brooks independently coined this expression himself, albeit in reference to 'Fifty Million Frenchmen Can't Be Wrong,' and following the success of the film, Brooks' expression has moved into popular culture on its own. No interviews are available in which Brooks discusses the etymology or definition of the term, but this popular interpretive definition is relevant to my argument, as it serves as anecdotal evidence of audience perceptions.

The way 'The French Mistake' scene is interpreted by a mass audience corroborates a superficial interpretation that reinforces expectations of patriarchal, macho, homophobic Western genre conventions. In this reading, the musical scene is inserted into the Western to be funny because it is *out of place*. An ensemble of tuxedoed gay dancers, like Count Basie's band that appears on the prairie earlier in the film, is funny because it is unexpected and pleasantly co-opts the genre. 'Faggots' and 'sissy Marys,' as Buddy Bizarre calls them, don't belong in a Western, so the audience laughs at their presence. This interpretation, however, while it certainly has some validity, is not the joke that Brooks intended. A better interpretation of Brooks' humor is revealed by the music, but is also corroborated by a deeper analysis of visual, narratological, and contextual elements.

Buddy Bizarre: 'This is a closed set!'

On the surface, 'The French Mistake' sequence is a mocking, facile parody of affected, sissified homosexual dancers and their effete routines. But in this brief vignette lurks a sophisticated commentary on Hollywood, sexuality, and identity politics. 'The French Mistake' sequence is highlighted by the imposing presence of Brooksian regular Dom DeLuise, a married actor long rumored to be homosexual (Musto 2009), renowned for over-the-top portrayals of effeminate characters. Brooks similarly employs DeLuise in *History of the World: Part I* (1981) in the role of Emperor Nero, who is likewise pompous, effeminate, and over the top. Mel Brooks' subversive 'French Mistake' song-and-dance sketch parodies the way Hollywood film was *itself* a closet, specifically within heteronormative films that became high camp and especially those made by 'flamboyant' (Hanley 1976) choreographer and director Busby Berkeley.

Buddy Bizarre is a recognizable parody of Berkeley, who was known for a neurotic, controlling, dictatorial nature as well as successes in colorful escapist fantasies from the 1930s–1950s. Berkeley had six wives and no children, but was a paragon of what might jocularly be called the 'control queen.' Frank Sinatra found Berkeley 'too epicene and flamboyant to take seriously' (Quirk and Schoell 1998: 35), a reputation that persisted even as his films were successful box office hits. Such a character is ripe for parody by the entertainment business-savvy Brooks, who, for example, also lampoons actress Marlene Dietrich with the character Lili Von Shtupp in *Blazing Saddles*. Brooks frequently uses show business personalities as the butt of jokes; the character name of Hedly Lamarr in *Blazing Saddles* is an obvious reference to actress Hedy Lamarr, a light pun with transsexual connotations. The real life Hedy was not amused, and sued Brooks; Brooks and Lamarr settled out of court (Daly 2000).

Buddy Bizarre can also be seen as a showcase opportunity for DeLuise to act out as an outrageous effeminate gay man, an act some believe reveals DeLuise's true self (Musto 2009). In 'The French Mistake' sequence, Buddy Bizarre is the ringleader of a situation where queerness is freely expressed *on the set*, although it will be presumably silenced in the imagined mainstream final studio release. DeLuise's role lies oddly between queer empowerment and mockery (Figure 7.4). When Buddy calls for a new take, forgetfully still standing in front of the cameras on the set, he ironically shouts, 'Action! OK! Oh, Wait 'til I get out! Wait 'til I get out!' This line can be read as either getting out of the way, or getting out of the closet.

Ultimately, it is not Buddy Bizarre who reclaims queer space; it is the resulting liaisons between cowboys and dancers. Yet it is Buddy who makes the clever insinuation that begins to reveal Brooks' true underlying commentary and comedy: 'This is a closed set!'

Puns feature prominently in the films of Mel Brooks, from 'comb the desert' and 'the radar appears to be jammed' (*Spaceballs*) to the recurring 'walk this way' routine (*Young Frankenstein, Spaceballs, History of the World: Part I, Robin Hood: Men in Tights,* and the stage adaptation of *The Producers*). Puns are an important element of Brooks' humor; they

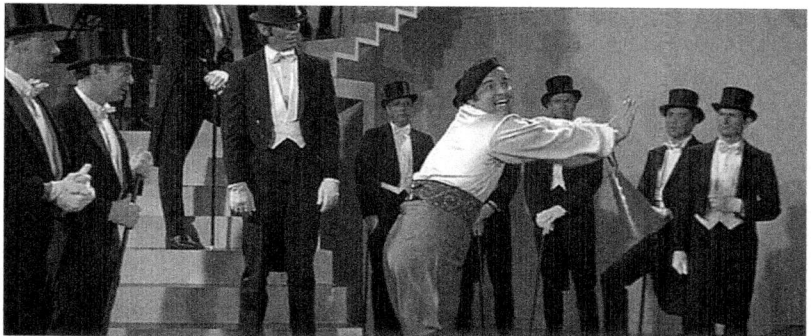

Figure 7.4 'Stick out your tush!' Buddy Bizarre in jodhpurs with megaphone

connect him to his Borsht Belt roots and to vaudevillian traditions. Puns function because they logically connect seemingly disparate elements; these connections can be silly or revelatory.

When Buddy exclaims 'This is a closed set!' he enunciates the words 'closed set' in such fashion as to suggest that those words should be carefully considered. 'Closed set' can be understood as a pun on the expression 'closet.' This pun establishes a connection between the Hollywood closed set, a private filming environment closed to outsiders in order to preserve the secrecies of the film, and the 'closet,' a well-known idiom referencing homosexuals who attempt to hide their sexuality.[5] Brooks equates classical Hollywood cinema with the homosexual 'closet' on a variety of levels.

Gay words, gay language, and effusive nelliness occur on the closed Hollywood set as depicted by Brooks, yet the final product, we presume, is heteronormative mass market entertainment. Escapist Hollywood films like Busby Berkeley's musicals were white-washed fantasies devoid of gays and people of color. They were whitebread illusions, enchanted worlds of beautiful white women, happiness, heterosexual romance, wealth, and prosperity.[6] Ironically, these heterosexist films became high camp because of their unapologetically skewed worldview.

It is easy enough to shine a bright light on the queerness of the Busby musicals; this has been done by Alexander Doty (1993: 13), Richard Dyer (2002: 51, 59), and others. But Brooks, in *Blazing Saddles*, shows not only the dancers as gay, but also a number of the macho cowboys. While this may be played for comedic effect, Brooks' fundamental message is that Westerns were *also* home to homos even though their end product was an image of rugged, manly American machismo.

Brooks would have been highly cognizant of queer situations and closeted actors in Hollywood Westerns. These would include Montgomery Clift and John Ireland comparing guns in *Red River* (1948); Westerns starring Rock Hudson, such as *Gun Fury* (1953), *Horizons West* (1952), and *The Lawless Breed* (1953); and Westerns featuring actors such as Tab Hunter, Anthony Perkins, and William Haines. Brooks' message of gay presence applies both in the context of predominantly male communities in the American West and in the context of the Hollywood acting community. In both cases, Brooks realizes that to paint these communities as exclusively heterosexual is an ironic fallacy; this duality of context allows the opportunity for humor. Of course there are gay actors. Of course there are gay dancers. Of course there are gay cowboys. Let's put them together and see what happens!

Brooks consistently breaks period Hollywood invisibility with recurring gay jokes, humor, and references, ranging from the subtle to the obvious. Maurice Yacowar identifies gay jokes or humor throughout Brooks' work: *The Producers* features director Roger DeBris and his 'bitchy valet, Carmen Giya' (Yacowar 1981: 76); *Young Frankenstein* has the lonely hermit (Yacowar 1981: 130); and *Silent Movie* features 'a running gag that has two spinsters mistake [James Caan and Dom DeLuise's] tumble as a homosexual orgy' (Yacowar 1981: 148). These are not the only examples. In *History of the World: Part I*, Brooks shows us the 'first homosapien marriage,' quickly followed by the 'first homosexual marriage'; both feature a caveman subduing his mate with a club before dragging them into his cave. While certainly a 'gay joke,' calmly narrated by Orson Welles, the 'marriage' gag elegantly implies a philosophy that beneath it all, gay and straight men are all the same.

There are further indications that these jokes are not mean-spirited; Brooks commonly uses hyper-stereotypes,[7] slurs,[8] and outright provocation[9] to further a liberal agenda. Brooks discussed gay jokes with *The Guardian*:

> Brooks was also warned that *The Producers* might be construed as homophobic, since it makes fun of a certain kind of high camp. 'They said the gay thing would come down on me hard. I said noooooo! The gay community will love it! I checked it out! I've done all my auditions, with all my gay friends and gay bars and gay places to make sure that I wasn't stepping on anybody's toe. They love it, they love it.' (Brockes 2004)

I do not argue that Brooks' jokes are inoffensive, or that *all* gay people will appreciate his humor. My point is that Brooks expresses a certain cultural sensitivity and research, and makes this claim to a straight, mainstream paper that would not likely have required any such disclaimer at the time. If Brooks is truthful, he vetted his own material with various gays before releasing it onscreen. If this is the case, then the intention is not to laugh *at* the gays; the gays are in on the joke. In this case, surface readings allowing homophobic mockery of gays are completely missing Brooks' intentions.

Within the overarching context of *Blazing Saddles*, gay humor can be read as either pure outrageousness, or as an analogous counterpart to a steady stream of racist language designed to attack racism as stupidity. Mel Brooks himself describes the film, '*Blazing Saddles*, with its black sheriff and racial jokes, is really a long sugar-coated tirade against bigotry' (Brooks in Bauer 1980).

The melee

When the cowboys burst onto Buddy's set, there is a shift in the meta-context of the film. *Blazing Saddles*, Mel Brooks' film, becomes a film within a film, *Buddy's* film, which is itself in the process of being filmed. As we watch this Brechtian interruption unfold, we gain the meta-perspective that both *Blazing Saddles* (Brooks' film) and Buddy's film are part of a hypothetical *third* film that contains the rivalry between cowboys and dancers. This is established by lines of dialogue that belong to neither *Blazing Saddles* nor to Buddy's film, such as 'I'm parked over by the commissary,' and 'Piss on you, I'm working for Mel Brooks!'

The conflagration between cowboys and dancers results in several happy male couplings. With 'I'm parked over by the commissary,' a dancer and a cowboy hook up and leave, taking the narrative from the liminal space between the two films in production and away to the third meta-film. Another petit dancer's exasperated 'You brute!' while not as obviously romantic, has a burly cowboy providing a reassur-ing, supportive masculine presence. Two dancers doing a water ballet together suggests a playful improvisation *not* choreographed by Buddy, who ironically dreads getting wet, that serves only to show two men having fun together and to parody *Footlight Parade* (1933). Furthermore, the fountains on Buddy's set squirt thin, white, particulate streams of water up into the air in what humorously resembles a continuous 'money shot' from a gay porn film (Figure 7.5).

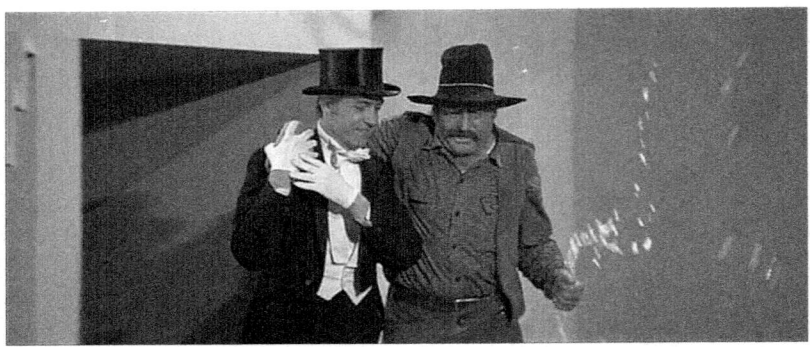

Figure 7.5 'I'm parked over by the commissary.' Notice fountain jets to the right

Support for a positive-bias reading of 'The French Mistake' relies on an awareness of these happy couplings and the weight given to them. The obviously homophobic way to play the scene would be to have the cowboys beating up the dancers. This only really happens once, when we see *Buddy* being punched in the stomach, which incites the melee; this could be read as singling out the closeted, abusive male for comeuppance. But after Buddy is punched, the potential humor of seeing gay men being beaten up is released to the humor of unexpected male couplings. It is not violence, but the male couplings that are the audience 'payoff' for the scene. The music plays a part in an accurate reading of this scene.

Music supplies prompts to properly contextualize and interpret the melee. The music that was Buddy's diegetic 'Playback!' track is now again underscore, reprising 'The French Mistake' instrumentally but at a faster tempo. It is Buddy's music, the dancers' music, but it is happy and joyous. This is not a bloodbath, massacre, or bashing. The music is not used ironically whilst blood spatters on the screen. The music marks the brawl as a happy, funny, exciting event, connecting to traditions of slapstick, yet with the playfulness of a childish food fight, emphasizing the *unity* of the cowboys and the dancers, rather than the divisiveness of combat.

When the cowboys invade Buddy's set, the dancers' music, 'The French Mistake,' stays put. Through attention to music, we can ascertain that the cowboys aren't really invading the dancers; rather, it is the *dancers* who have invaded the cowboys' previously dominant cinematic, musical, and narrative space. Eventually, the dancers' infusion of homosexuality will win over the most important male pair in the film.

The closing scene

Blazing Saddles ends with Bart and Jim, 'The Waco Kid,' riding off into the sunset together, then being driven away in a limo, a homoerotic twist on the classical romantic ending. Brooks himself lays this bare, 'In the picture, both Cleavon and Gene Wilder are searching for someone to believe in. When they find each other, it's a marriage made in heaven' (Brooks in Siskel 1977).

Although absurdist in its anachronism with the limo, this romantic ending is not entirely presented as a joke or a comic moment. Jim and Bart's 'marriage' and final exit is presented without irony or commentary as the natural, satisfying resolution to the film, accompanied by a rousing musical finale of the 'Blazing Saddles' theme. The galloping beat, harmonica, tambourine, folksy cantabile pentatonic melody with a snap-rhythm on 'saddle' (Figure 7.1, second full bar), and male chorus all function as musical markers of cowboys, determination, resolution, and the clichéd American West. These musical features have been employed in countless Westerns. While the film may be an overall parody, this musical moment is completely faithful to Western expectations; the music keeps a 'straight face' here, unlike the sequences featuring Count Basie and 'The French Mistake.'

The 'Blazing Saddles' theme is initially presented at the beginning of the film in song form, with lyrics sung by Frankie Laine, and comedic, gratuitous whip-cracks. Here, at the film's close, the theme recapitulates majestically, replete with a male chorus that is reminiscent of the ending of John Ford's *The Searchers* (1956) and other Westerns. This music is lyrically Bart's: beyond the requisite choral 'ohhs,' the only sung line reprised from the theme song is: 'He conquered fear and he conquered hate. He turned dark night into day.' Why not reprise the whole song? Why choose just one line to repeat at closure? This is where the message lies: 'fear' and 'hate' speak directly to the anti-bigotry theme of the film as explained by Brooks. In case the audience missed the point of the whole film, the music contains many effective signposts, these lyrics being the most obvious of them all.

For the grand finish, the theme modulates up from C# major to D major, a bright and resonant key for the string section of the orchestra (Prout 1899: 21). D major could be seen as symbolic of romance or coupling, with its two sharps. Einstein and Mendel suggest the key represented stability to Mozart (1941: 416), and Schubart, translated by Steblin, declares D major a key of triumph, victory, heaven, and rejoicing (Schubart 1806: 377; Steblin 1983: 238). Emphatic strings and brass push it over the top, announcing that this is the happy ending. The chauffeured 1973 Cadillac Fleetwood limousine kicks up dust as the sun sets above. The effect is complete.

Brooks has said, 'I would say that all my movies are stories of love between men, in the sense of camaraderie' (Brooks in Bauer 1980). This hardly mitigates a homosexual interpretation of the famous ending, remarkably reinforced by the deliberately romantic musical finale. Brooks also says, 'Take *Blazing Saddles*. It was about whether a black could survive in the good old West. It may seem like a silly picture but, to me, it had a strong underpinning because it was really about love' (Brooks in Parish 2007: 195–96). It *is* about love on many levels, but one of them is clearly romantic love and resolution between the two main protagonist cowboys.

While male bonding features in many Brooks films, such as *Twelve Chairs* and *Young Frankenstein*, it is this ultimate conclusion that makes *Blazing Saddles* so special. If Brooks vets his comedy with gay friends, as he has claimed, this is the kind of gay reference that could not be unintentional. Perhaps Brooks intended it as comedy or an in-joke for a select audience; but its knowing inclusion suggests a possible reality. In the context of Brooksian cinema, where Dark Helmet longs for a 'Druish Princess,' the humpback Igor lusts after 'the one in the turban,' 'homosexual marriage' was established in the Stone Age, and, in *Young Frankenstein*, 'even the monster gets a girl' (Darrach 1975), it seems plausible that Jim and Bart might live happily ever after.

Blazing Saddles pushes the Western genre with Brechtian meta-humor and outrageous comedy that, at times, is perceptibly homophobic on its surface. The music tells a different story. 'The French Mistake' musical sequence in *Blazing Saddles* reveals a joyful celebration where Brooks' male dancers and cowboys together defeat the closet of the 'closed set' and end up in a massive free-for-all, some leaving together in pairs to their cars parked by the commissary. The music at the close of the film reveals a romantic 'marriage' between Bart and The Waco Kid, an inter-racial male couple whose relationship transcends the bounds of the ordinary 'buddy' movie.

Film music can reveal biases, perspectives, and underlying messages and meanings concealed within cinematic narratives. While *Blazing Saddles* has obvious surface readings, analysis of music uncovers complex interpretations. The music functions as a wordless, hidden perspective, an allegory for the filmmakers' true intentions. It speaks a musical truth about the film, regardless of where onscreen action seems to be heading.

Postscript

This interpretation of 'The French Mistake' is filtered through an understanding of the culture and norms of the time period (1974) and through an appreciation of the work of Mel Brooks. More recently, there have been a number of television shows (*Will & Grace*, *Glee*, *Queer Eye*, for example) that have propagated homonormative stereotypes under the guise of a liberal, progressive veneer. These shows try to shoehorn gay men into binary relationships, comic nelliness, shallow portraiture, exaggerated masculinities or codings of 'normalcy,' with entertaining but problematic results. I think that Brooks, as a Jewish entertainer, or just who he was as a person, tried to celebrate diversity and differences. It has been thought provoking for me to reconcile my love of Brooksian humor with my distaste for television shows that I see as pandering crapulence, even if they are made by queers. This is a much larger discussion that I do not have the space for in this chapter, but I do see much of the recent homonormative entertainment as being somehow different to what Brooks did, which I regard as more truly progressive and transgressive, somehow. I do believe that in further investigation of these matters, music can reveal whether or not we are watching something that is holding us back, or pushing us forward.

8
Conclusion

There has been a healthy surge of interest in the study of cultural meanings and histories behind musics, giving rise to overlaps in the fields of music, film, gender, and sexuality. Musicology's interactions with cultural studies, media studies, and critical theory have revolutionized those fields. These overlaps can be theoretically complicated; competency in a variety of fields is necessary to fully dissect these issues. A queer reading in cinema requires an understanding of not only surface narrative, but of music, director, composer, target audience, associated texts, and the conventions of genre.

Where a queer reading may be subtle, it may also be glaring when overlooked. Many of the scenes and films described in this book would be preposterous without a queer reading: consider studio executives who wanted to censor *Blazing Saddles* because they did not comprehend Brooks' comedy; consider Flaherty's biographers who scratched their heads and ignored or invented hypothetical explanations of his obsession with boys; consider how antisocial and suicidal behavior is made heroic in *Thelma and Louise*.

This book endeavors to intersect three fields of inquiry: musicology, cinema studies, and queer theory. In doing so, it has examined a variety of examples in order to survey some of the broad possibilities of 'queerness' within canonical cinema, and how those possibilities are reinforced or nuanced through the use of musical score.

It is evident that music can support queer readings, as it does clearly in *Louisiana Story*, *Bride of Frankenstein*, *Rudolph the Red-Nosed Reindeer*, and *Edward Scissorhands*, but it also can undermine them, as it does in *Brokeback Mountain*, whose music emphasizes retrogressive heterosexist perspectives of the futility of male homosexuality. Music may make a film more accessible to a mainstream audience, as it does in *Boys Don't*

Cry, Transamerica, or *Thelma & Louise,* or it may align a film with a select or art-house audience by invoking experimental textures or subcultural affinities, as it does in *Go Fish* or *The Living End.*

In films that subvert or complicate genre, such as *Brokeback Mountain, Blazing Saddles,* and *Edward Scissorhands,* music can subtly but effectively situate or steer the film towards a particular genre, or negotiate generic space within an evolving narrative. This makes music an indispensable tool when it comes to 'queering' of cinematic genre. Musical genretypes, such as easy listening, Moog records, electronic industrial club music, country western, disco music, soul music, and so on, can indicate marginalization or can create subcultural identifications, as they do in *Transamerica, The Living End,* and *Young Soul Rebels.* Music is highly effective at telegraphing outsider statuses, whether connected to gender, race, ethnicity, nationality, socio-economics, or alternative sexuality.

Arguments presented in this book have constructed a lens to focus attention on particular cinematic readings. One can see *Louisiana Story* not as Cajun authenticity but as the romanticizing and eroticization of a barefoot boy. Perhaps *Rudolph the Red-Nosed Reindeer* is not simply an ordinary children's cartoon, but an inspirational story for queer youth and 'children of all ages.' *Blazing Saddles* can be seen not as racist, homophobic humor, but as a gay romance. Music is an essential part of reading film; these are not the only possible readings, but situations where musical analysis and queer theory have provided unique but compatible insights.

Some of my work has incorporated both contextualization and de-contextualization of texts, which can make analytical readings slippery, encouraging further investigation. Campy performances and musical numbers, like 'Fifty Million Frenchmen Can't Be Wrong' and 'The French Mistake,' are complicated by the veracity of period interpretation and the difficulty of accessing accurate period audience perceptions and reactions. The camp of 'The French Mistake' and other Brooksian humor may (or may not) have been offensive in 1974; today, effeminate caricatures appear regularly in 'gay-identified' movies and television shows like *Will & Grace, Glee, Queer Eye,* and the *Eating Out* franchise.

Such historical dissonances raise important questions. Who gets to 'own' performative expressions of queerness? Must we presume that performances that fulfill heteronormative or homonormative expectations and prejudices are necessarily offensive or wrong? When the presentation of texts can be simultaneously affirming and insulting, progressive and regressive, can those texts be claimed, reclaimed, historicized, reappraised, or even rejected? What is the best approach to such complicated, conflicting texts? This line of questioning naturally extends beyond male homosexuality to performative representations of lesbians, transwomen, transmen, people of color, sexual minorities and fetishists, and so on; similarly fraught characterizations and generalizations can be seen in shows like *The L Word*.[1] Music can indicate biases and prejudices as well as filmmakers' efforts to establish audience affinities, and as a result music must be part of interpretations and analyses of such texts.

Scholars and theorists must consider audience demographics, advertising, and marketing that frame these texts, but recognize when these factors contradict or present a distraction from underlying meanings. Many queers genuinely love *Brokeback Mountain*; fawning fan community support does not entirely redeem the film, even if we understand the queer love of tragedy and nostalgia. If *Brokeback* were a grainy studio product of the 1950s or 1960s, would it be received differently by contemporary gays discovering it through an online video streaming service, for example? ('Recommended because you watched *The Sergeant* (1968).') Contextualizations, de-contextualizations, fan community responses, and historicizations complicate and give different weight to different readings; music, likewise, can be subject to its own cultural contexts.

In writing this book and intersecting three disciplines with their own histories and academic cultures, I feel I have taken a very small thread and pulled it very hard; sometimes the more I pull, the more everything unravels. As I draw real (or imagined) cinematic subtexts to the surface, I am somehow reminded of iconic actor Charles Nelson Reilly, star of Broadway, *Match Game*, *Lidsville*, 'The Bic Banana,' and numerous guest appearances on *The Tonight Show*, chortling at every little bit of innuendo, amused and invigorated by each tidbit and bon mot.

Even today, audiences, scholars, and filmmakers still frequently marginalize music's place in film, where a budget–cachet–effectiveness triangle encourages directors to use off-the-shelf pop tracks rather than composed, original material. Queerness has been likewise marginalized in popular culture, yet as a discourse has surfaced as an important cultural concern. This book is not the first look at the intersection between film, music, and queerness, but it is a contribution to analytical approaches that bridge musicology, queer theory, media studies, critical theory, and cultural studies. I hope the arguments contained in this book will encourage others to undertake further research and mastication of these developing concepts.

Notes

Introduction

1. Mathematically speaking. See the work of Georg Cantor, which also inspired a musical 'set theory' promoted by Howard Hanson, Allen Forte, and Milton Babbitt.
2. I used to maintain and repair towering 35 mm mag dub machines at American Zoetrope Studios. They were loud, noisy, and sometimes finicky machines that were a marvel of mechanical engineering. These machines served the film business faithfully for many decades. It is not within the scope of this book, but there is a 'tangible' element that has been lost with the move to all-digital workflows. It would be fascinating to correlate this mechanical element with film music and queerness as well.
3. Vampires, beyond being a humorous bon mot here, have an established connection with queer fascinations, as discussed in Benshoff's *Monsters in the Closet*.
4. For more on the Code, homosexuality, and 'sexual perversion,' see Schumach (1964).
5. This oversimplification neglects sociomusicology, ethnomusicology, and comparative musicology, which predate the 1970s, and other developments; unfortunately I have not enough space here to embark on a complete historiography of the field.
6. I don't believe that we can accurately date such tropes at all; it is pure speculation. Consider that we have tropes for imitating birds during the Renaissance, as heard in 'Le chant des oiseaux' by Clément Janequin. And while clever, even that had likely been done before, even if we lack the sheet music to prove it. Tropes and imitations like this may date to the dawn of humanity.
7. Musical signification was an awkward topic for scholars who resisted the new musicology. 'Nonprofessionals are extremely adept at comprehending and even explaining affect and rhetoric in music, while professionals tend to divide into two camps: those who think they are above such nonsense and who supply formal explanations for everything they hear, and those who have not surrendered their conviction that music signifies but who have kept this carefully hidden, rather as though they were adults who still believe in the Tooth Fairy' (McClary 1991: 22).
8. Imagine the possibilities of a queer reading of Sony's *The Interview* (2014) and its surrounding political and corporate intrigue.
9. For a discussion of 'diegetic' music, the 'fantastical gap,' and 'liminal space,' see the work of Robynn Stilwell. A 'sound advance' and 'prelap' are the same thing: music (or dialogue or sound effects) begins before a picture cut, and draws us in to the next scene. 'Procedural' music, as in a crime or legal drama, marks time or keeps something 'alive' during scenes with low action but narrative necessity. 'Perspective' is any sound treatment, like reverb or EQ, used

to position 'diegetic' music into an acoustic space in the onscreen world; as music moves through the 'fantastical gap,' 'perspective' may be applied to make music less part of the 'foreground' and more a part of an 'ambience.'

10. Some of these latter arguments and criticisms are sourced, summarized, and quoted in Flinn (1992: 39).
11. I am indebted to musicologist Ben Winters for this observation, which we discussed at the 2014 Music and the Moving Image conference.
12. See Bryan Magee, *The Tristan Chord: Wagner and Philosophy*, especially discussion of Schopenhauer's influence on Wagner, Wagner's criticisms of Italian opera, and Wagner's own changing beliefs in the role of music in the staged music drama. Wagner's operas were a reaction to those wherein the importance of the orchestra had become secondary.
13. Iranian President Mahmoud Ahmadinejad, speaking at Columbia University, said, 'In Iran, we don't have homosexuals, like in your country' (http://www.cnn.com/2007/US/09/24/us.iran/index.html reported 9/24/07, accessed 13 October 2014).

1. *Louisiana Story*, Homoeroticism, and Americana

1. For a broad and reputable survey, see Reed (2011).
2. For an extensive discussion of the Motion Picture Production Code, see Schumach (1964).
3. See Hubbs (2004) for more on this circle of influential gay composers.
4. Some of these photographs can be seen in Rotha (1983: 277–78), and in *Louisiana Story: The Reverse Angle*.
5. For an extensive discussion of 'erotic age orientation' and distinctions between pedophilia, hebephilia, ephebophilia, teleiophilia, and gerontophilia, see the work of evolutionary psychologist Jesse Bering (2013: 169–208).
6. The painter Maurice Grosser (1903–1986), Virgil Thomson's most significant longtime lover and companion, was seven years younger than Virgil.
7. I wish to reemphasize that there is nothing uniquely homosexual about an appreciation of youthful beauty. From an evolutionary standpoint, reproductive ability is maximized during a youthful age (see Bering 2013: 199).
8. *Louisiana Story*'s film editor, Helen van Dongen, criticized Flaherty's script that made the boy's father seem 'simpleminded' by making his language more 'primitive,' and she questioned whether this emphasis was 'a leftover from behavior of primitive people such as the Eskimos or the natives of Samoa' that were similarly exploited or stereotyped in other Flaherty films (van Dongen 1998: 31).
9. Van Dongen recalls, 'The sounds that are used were recorded on the rig, on discs, by Benji Donniger, the sound cameraman. I asked him to record everything, the general sounds, the individual sounds – to put the microphone everyplace. Tape recorders were not yet in existence. We used a disc recorder because of the difficulty of getting constant electricity, the distance from source of power to the recorder being rather long. It couldn't be used as it was, so I had to re-record all that onto film separately in a recording studio before I could even start working with it. Some of it had to be slowed down

a little because of the unevenness of the electricity' (Achtenberg and von Dongen 1976: 51).

10. Arguably, the sound construction begins with the steady chugging of derrick machinery at 0:22:38, towards the tail end of Reel 3. For technical reasons, film sound cannot continue across a reel change, so the audio ducks out briefly and begins again at the start of the next reel. Reel 4 begins at 0:25:20 and runs until 0:35:23, running a full ten minutes. If one includes the chugging on Reel 3, van Dongen's sound construction runs roughly 12:40.

11. Van Dongen recalls, 'This sequence had to be edited in New York where I took it because we had no sound equipment in Louisiana. Flaherty was a little suspicious about that because it meant that I was out of his control' (Achtenberg and van Dongen 1976: 51). Furthermore, while it is easy to regard Flaherty as an 'auteur,' this is an example of how some of his most powerful work was accomplished within a complex, collaborative environment.

12. Musicologist Neil Lerner argues that 'only a small proportion of Thomson's score for *The River* consists of originally composed music; most of Thomson's melodies are taken from hymns, folk songs, and popular tunes with which he had become familiar through a study of the region's music' (Lerner 1999: 105). Similarly in *Louisiana Story*, much of the raw melodic material is provided through folk tunes, but this has a long tradition in Western concert music; consider Gustav Mahler's adoption of 'Frère Jacques' in his first symphony, Johannes Brahms' 'Hungarian Dances,' and Percy Grainger's 'Country Gardens.' The way the melodic material is manipulated moves it away from its folk music origins, and towards original Western art music compositions.

13. Manvell and Huntley propose seven categories of what they call 'functional music' for film. They are: 'Music and Action; Scenic and Place music; Period and Pageant music; Music for Dramatic Tension; Comedy music; Music of Human Emotion; and Music in Cartoon and Specialized Film' (Manvell and Huntley 1957: 73).

14. Hollywood film music is widely regarded as a direct descendant of German–Austrian art music, specifically Mahler, Strauss, and Brahms, via Erich Wolfgang Korngold, Franz Waxman, and Max Steiner.

15. Following established convention, bracketed figures [1D] indicate sections and rehearsal marks as indicated in the score. 'mm' indicates measure numbers as used in the score. Timings in parentheses (0:07:24) reflect timings from the commercially released DVD of *Louisiana Story*, and these timings include the bumper for film restoration credits that has been inserted at the beginning of the video file.

16. For a discussion of the bar sheet or bar chart in animation, see Dubowsky (2011).

17. Such contrapuntal textures such as the fugue have often been discouraged in film music. 'For the composer of concert music, changing to the medium of celluloid does bring certain special pitfalls. For example, melodic invention, highly prized in the concert hall, may at times be distracting in certain film situations. Even phrasing in the concert manner, which would normally emphasize the independence of separate contrapuntal lines, may be distracting when applied to screen accompaniments. In orchestration there

are many subtleties of timbre – distinctions meant to be listened to for their own expressive quality in an auditorium – which are completely wasted on sound track' (Copland 1957b: 259).

18. For a discussion of the baroque fugue form, its construction, and explanations of related terminology, see Owen (1992: 230–66), one of many good counterpoint texts.

2.   Musical Cachet in *The Living End* and the New Queer Cinema

1. In particular, note Altman's book on *Silent Film Sound*; Mera's work on *Mychael Danna's The Ice Storm* with its attention to the scoring process and computer files; Goldmark's various work on Tin Pan Alley and music in cartoons; and Wierzbicki's detailed *Film Music: A History*. Other textbooks, such as Buhler et al.'s *Hearing the Movies*, Richard Bellis' *The Emerging Film Composer*, and Richard Davis' *Complete Guide to Film Scoring*, address business and production pipeline concerns.

2. Craig O's blog makes the unsubstantiated claim that 'The Project Triangle concept was first conceived in the engineering world' (Ormiston 2011).

3. The popular website imdb.com has a 'StarMeter' rating system and indicates whether personalities' ratings are going 'up' or 'down.' This may simply judge popularity, although the ambiguous weighting of the system may be informed by other factors.

4. James continues: 'The simultaneous revival and reconstruction of the term imply both a desire for some authentically real politics and the present difficulty of actually engaging them. Occupying the space between the desire and its impossibility is the spectacle, the contemporary media system in which life as it might be lived is reflected back in the form of signs of commodities and signs as commodities. Any cultural activity that engages this media system will find its search for authenticity inhabited by irony and ambivalence' (James 2009: 58).

5. Proptarts.com, a website for independent filmmakers, estimates craft services at $150/day for 40 people, which seems very low to me. Even so, cast and crew must be fed.

6. For more on British film funding and strategy, see Julien and MacCabe (1991: 8–10, 21–23) and Peake (2000: 297–313, 337–40).

7. For a discussion of memory and why musical genres are adopted or retained from adolescence, see Smith (2012).

8. 'Inside Me,' written by William Adam Reid and James McLeish Reid, from the Jesus and Mary Chain album *Psychocandy* (1985).

9. It should be noted that 'pop song cues match visual tracks' not necessarily at the entrances, but also at chosen 'sync points' where a lyric or musical moment might have its optimum impact. One example of this is the organ glissando in 'Better Not Look Down' matching the gas pedal in *Thelma & Louise* as discussed in Chapter 5. Furthermore, music editors frequently adjust songs to better fit their placements. I have done this in my work as music editor on the CW scripted drama television series *Beauty and the Beast* (2015–2016).

3. *Brokeback Mountain* Music

1. Gary Needham's *Brokeback Mountain*; Proulx et al.'s *Brokeback Mountain: Story to Screenplay*; William R. Handley (ed.), *The Brokeback Book*; consider also the 'Special Feature on Brokeback Mountain,' an introduction and seven scholarly essays in *Film Quarterly* 60.3 (Spring 2007).
2. See articles here by Miller, Osterweil, Clover, Nealon, Rich, and others published in *Film Quarterly*'s Spring 2007 issue.
3. In this chapter, 'minimalism' refers to the actual sparse, unadorned, simplistic quality of the score, not the musical genre or movement typified by Glass, Reich, et al.
4. See especially Kalinak's *How The West Was Sung* (2007).
5. For further discussion, see Rollins and O'Connor's *Hollywood's West: The American Frontier in Film, Television, and History* (2009).
6. Gay film historian Vito Russo discusses Westerns in the *Celluloid Closet* (1981); Richard Dyer touches upon John Wayne, Rock Hudson, and other film actors in *The Culture of Queers* (2002). Many other critics and scholars, such as Kathryn Kalinak, now routinely include some analysis of gender and sexuality in their work.
7. Osterweil claims that Ang Lee admits to never having seen Warhol's film (2007: 39).
8. Consider Dimitri Tiomkin's score to *High Noon* (1952) and Elmer Bernstein's score to *The Magnificent Seven* (1960) as two iconic examples.
9. See Part Four of Rollins and O'Connor (2009).
10. Schamus had been an executive producer on *Poison* (1992) and *Swoon* (1993) (Rich 2007: 44). Schamus confirmed his own heterosexuality when receiving the 2014 Outfest Achievement Award in Los Angeles.
11. Matthew Bolton and Kylo-Patrick R. Hart have examined differences between published versions of Proulx's story in *The New Yorker* and *Close Range*, as well as changes made in Ang Lee's cinematic adaptation. I will not dwell on analyses of these small differences; it is important work, but I feel that all of the versions are adequately similar in tone, theme, and bias for my purposes in analyzing the film's music.
12. 'Conformed' is industry jargon, referring to how audio must be altered or edited or re-composed to fit changes in the picture edit.
13. Consider *The Departed* (2006), directed by Martin Scorsese with score by Howard Shore, a Boston mafia drama with plenty of Spanish guitar. *Brobeback*'s sparse guitar sound also became popular in independent cinema, not the least because of its financial economy and ease of recording. My own score for *Redwoods* (2009, Dir. David Lewis) made extensive use of guitar, which fit the film, but also the zeitgeist of the period.
14. See Rollins and O'Connor (2009) on the 'post-modernist' Western.
15. For an extended, robust, music theory discussion on these cadences and harmonic progressions, see Frank Lehman's 'Hollywood Cadences: Music and the Structure of Cinematic Expectation' (2013).
16. See Kalinak (2007) for a discussion of the inaccuracy of the portrayal of the guitar as a 'cowboy' instrument.
17. For further discussion of harmonic and melodic tension, see Fred Lerdahl, *Tonal Pitch Space* (2001: 142–49, 161); Karlin and Wright, *On The Track* (1990:

250–51; 2004: 400); and Edward G. Evans, *An Investigation of Harmonic Tension* (1950).

18. B. Ruby Rich discusses Gene Shalit's suggestion that Jack Twist is the 'aggressor' (Rich 2005).

19. It is curious to note that in December of 2005, Verve released a CD of 'remixes' of *Brokeback* music, tracks that found their way onto dance floors in gay bars and discos for a time; these remixes were a somewhat comical attempt to shoehorn the score's guitar tunes into an explicitly gay 'dance' music arena.

4.   A Tale of Two Walters: Genre and Gender Outsiders

1. The 'Prologue and Main Title' was originally composed by Malcolm Williamson, who left the project. The melancholy but optimistic pop tune 'Bright Eyes' was composed by Mike Batt, then best known as the Wombles' songwriter. The rest of the music is Morley's.

2. Kubrick 'rejected more than four hours' worth of music that Wendy Carlos and Rachel Elkind had composed for *The Shining*, retaining only their electronic version of the *Dies Irae* while employing pre-existent contemporary classical works for the remainder of the soundtrack' (Patterson 2004: 472). See also Larson (1985: 274).

3. *Switched-On Bach* entered the *Billboard 200* pop chart's 'Top 40' on 1 March 1969, and stayed in the Top 200 for over one year. Copycat albums followed, merging Carlos-inspired Moog stylings with other genres such as country western, rock, jazz, and mariachi music. Other musicians attempted their own 'Moog' classical albums; still others, like pianists François Glorieux and Mariano Moreno and arrangers Stu Phillips, Enoch Light, and Mike Curb created 'classical' or 'baroque' albums of popular music, and these mash-ups can be seen as part of a larger generic context that help popularize 'Moog' albums.

4. In the United States, 'new music' has become its own genre with implied associations to art music composed by people working within the academy and its networks.

5. Further evidence of this might be the dearth of female composers in academia, a subject that has begun to receive more attention.

6. I should note that 'Timesteps' from *A Clockwork Orange* is fairly avant-garde, as is Carlos' more recent work with micropolyphony and alternative tunings.

7. Columbia's art director Jon Berg came up with the title, a slick double-entendre with its groovy nod to Timothy Leary's counter-cultural call to 'turn on.'

8. The *Nonesuch Guide to Electronic Music* was reviewed in the *New York Times* on 28 April 1968, and so predates *Switched-On Bach* by a few months. By contrast, the *Nonesuch Guide* sounds primitive in comparison to *Switched-On Bach*; complete with booklet, it is primarily a demonstration record of what the Moog synthesizer can do in terms of making isolated sounds. There are few finished musical pieces on it, each simply titled 'Composition.'

9. Elkind and Carlos met in 1967. I do not have an exact date when Elkind signed them with Columbia.

10. A probably unrelated but curious coincidence is the title to Kraftwerk's 1977 electronic album, *Trans-Europe Express*.

11. Bell died in 1984.
12. Helen was a member of the Ambrosian Singers. She died in March 1986 in London. Bryan lives in California (Parker 2015).
13. Incorrectly, Leigh (2009) reported Angela's surgery as taking place in 'Scandinavia,' 1972; Gaughan (2009) also incorrectly reported 1972. Potter (2014) incorrectly reported 'Switzerland.' Leigh (2009) incorrectly reported that Stott's marriage to Beryl 'ended in divorce.' *The Telegraph* incorrectly dated Beryl's death to 1968. I have endeavored to correct the historical record in order to resolve inconsistencies in published accounts.
14. Morley's uncredited work as an orchestrator on *Star Wars* is discussed in Elley (1978a, 1978b). According to Williams' biographer, 'For contractual reasons, in the film credits only the principal orchestrator is mentioned. So in the case of *Star Wars* you had Morley in the orchestrators panel along with Arthur Morton, Al Woodbury, Alexander Courage and Williams himself, but only Spencer is credited in the film, none of the others (but not even Spencer is credited in the LP album, again for contractual reasons)' (Audissino 2015).
15. Martin Rosen would direct *Plague Dogs* (1982) based upon Adam's third novel, an even darker animated film that arguably ended his career as a director of movies marketed to children.
16. In prog rock, examples of I to bVI include Yes' 'Würm' (1971). New wave examples of I to bVI include Ultravox's 'Quiet Men' (1978), Talking Heads' 'Air' (1979), Gary Numan's 'Metal' (1979), and Kim Wilde's 'Kids in America' (1981).
17. Lee Holdridge scored *Mahogany* (1975) and arranged easy listening albums of John Denver and Neil Diamond songs. Stu Phillips is famous for his *Hollyridge Strings* series of easy listening Beatles albums, as well as the music for the original *Battlestar Galactica* (1978) TV series. Mancini arranged an easy listening 'Portrait of the Beatles' suite on his *Encore* (1967) LP.
18. Consider the RCA Record Club box set *50 Great Hits of the '50s for Listening, Dancing and Relaxing* CCS-0676 (undated release).
19. The 'cocktail' subgenre is another complicated matter altogether. Vapid and suave all at once, with a wry air of sophistication, it experienced a resurgence in the 1990s in conjunction with retroism, reissues, sampling, slick electronic beats, and loops, as exemplified by bands like Combustible Edison and Montefiori Cocktail.
20. Even tunes that were light enough to begin with, such as Alex North's 'Unchained Melody' from the film *Unchained*, are endlessly rerecorded.

5. Mainstreaming and Rebelling

1. This is changing rapidly; consider the recent media spectacle and reality show surrounding Caitlyn Jenner.
2. The suicide finale of *Thelma & Louise* originally used the song 'Better Not Look Down,' whose refrain was apropos to onscreen action, but whose verses could be considered irrelevant to the film.
3. *Birth of a Nation*, a seminal film well known by scholars and students alike, makes a good example, even if I lack the space to unpack its inherent racism

and problematic history, as well as the complicated history of the song 'Dixie' itself.

4. See Smith (2001a: 407–8, 415). Smith also uses the example of 'Sweet Home Alabama' in *Con Air* as an outright joke that is even discussed by the characters in the film.

5. It should be noted that musical 'diegesis' has proven to be a topic of continuing fascination and obsession within film music academia, even among practitioners in the professional field it is taken for granted or understood implicitly. The academic discussion includes 'metadiegetic,' 'extradiegetic,' and 'intradiegetic' music, while the field is more interested in music's source (who composes or licenses the music and its cost) and effect (what the music does for the film). In 2013, Kassabian extended the diegesis discussion to video games while conceding that 'we are entering a period in which diegesis is receding into the background in favor of sensory experience as the primary organizing principle of audiovisual forms' (2013: 102).

6. The sound mixers would be boosting the whole song, not just the lyrics; generally 'stems' are delivered for score, but not for licensed songs.

7. The availability of the original ending via DVD makes the film a modified text. Devoted fans are able to see it and choose their own preferred way to remember, understand, or experience the film. This encourages fans to think of the film abstractly, not as an ossified text, but one that is variable.

8. Lynda Hart discusses the verdant canyon's vaginal symbolism (1994: 445), a delightful reading that, upon further unpacking, may position Thelma and Louise's vehicular plunge as the ultimate 'muff dive.' Certainly it is the film's literal and figurative 'climax.'

9. For more on this musical trope, see Ross (2010: 22–54).

10. Queer interest in Americana or country western is not necessarily ironic; consider queer Christian cowpunk Glen Meadmore's album *Hot, Horny & Born-Again* with its hymn 'Eternal Love' and country western songs like 'I Wonder If.'

11. 'I Am a Pilgrim' has also been recorded by Johnny Cash, Merle Travis, Tennessee Ernie Ford, Willie Nelson, and The Byrds.

12. In a brief establishing shot, the restaurant bears a window neon sign advertising 'Home Cooking' that ties in nicely with an overall theme of the movie, the quest for 'home.'

13. Sources on Parton's cosmetic surgeries, and interviews with Parton discussing her surgeries, include Kearney (2012), Stewart (2011), Raphael (2014), Scordo (2012), and *People Magazine* (2003).

14. See Stryker (2008: 11–24) for a detailed discussion of gender, body, sexuality, and transgender theory fundamentals.

15. A powerful example of this is the notion of 'street credibility' and race within urban hip-hop music; much work has been done around the appropriation of African American idioms by white performers, and the movement of popular culture transnationally.

16. This is also termed an 'interrupted use' in the music licensing business. A song would need to be cleared for 'interrupted use' in these circumstances.

17. On the music cue sheet filed with performance rights organizations, the overlapping usages may be listed as 'concurrent' because filmmakers are often prohibited from altering original recordings, other than adding

effects; adding instruments would not typically be allowed without special permission.

18. Jean-Luc Godard illustrates the use of absolute silence in *Bande à Part* (1964) when Arthur, Franz, and Odile observe a minute of silence (actually less) in a crowded café; instead of just muting the dialogue track, Godard mutes all tracks, including music, effects, and ambiences. The effect is disconcerting.

19. Films that have combined black and white and color include *The Wizard of Oz* (1939), *A Matter of Life and Death* (1946), *If...* (1968), *Raging Bull* (1980), *Nostalgia* (1983), *Wings of Desire* (1987), and *Schindler's List* (1993).

20. Blake Snyder's *Save The Cat! The Last Book on Screenwriting You'll Ever Need* (2005) is a perfect example of one codification of Hollywood narrative formula.

21. *Go Fish* 'self-consciously interrogates the [romantic comedy] genre's terms and intervenes in them in minoritizing terms' (Pramaggiore 1997: 67). 'The historical absence of out lesbians is something that the film works to remedy in highly self-conscious meta-narrative motifs' (Pramaggiore 1997: 68).

6. Queer Monster Good: *Frankenstein* and *Edward Scissorhands*

1. For discussion of Whale and his sexuality, see Russo (1981: 49–52), as well as extensively in Curtis' authoritative biography (1998).

2. Recent scholarship with insights into Tchaikovsky's sexuality includes David Brown (2007) and Alexander Poznansky (1991).

3. See Young (1991), London (1993), Twitchell (1983), and Picart (2000), for example.

4. Being differently-abled might include what used to be termed a 'handicap,' but in addition, the concept of being differently-abled could also include supernatural superpowers as exemplified in the X-Men film series. This further broadens the topic of queerness. While this begins to stray from my subject in this chapter, I do believe there is much queerness to be unpacked in the X-Men series, as well as how it allegorizes different physical traits and abilities.

5. A 'visual instrumental,' abbreviated on cue sheets as 'VI,' is one of the categorizations of music used by PROs or performing rights organizations, like ASCAP or BMI, to calculate royalty payments. It is a piece of music we see performed onscreen, but it is instrumental, not vocal. If Esmeralda had sung along, it would be a 'visual vocal' performance, abbreviated as 'VV.'

6. Rudolph and Hermey agree to run away together with the resolution 'Let's be independent together.' I do not have the space to fully unpack this line, but suffice to say it is a poignant description of common homosexual experiences and twentieth-century gay communities that forged new bonds, negotiated sexualities and best practices, and worked to build bridges with other marginalized communities. Additionally, the way Hermey is forced into an unchosen profession can also be read as a stab at Soviet communism as perceived by Americans at the time.

7. Edward is about as white as can be, with pancake makeup and fair skin, and the narrative lacks the kind of 'underground railroad' references that hide

in *Bride*. Culturally, there is little to suggest that Edward might be anything other than white. The film's 'creation' flashback informs us that Edward was developed by the Inventor from a robotic cookie-making machine. Edward is transfixed by a can-opener in Peg Boggs' kitchen, and this initiates a flashback to his home with the Inventor.

8. Salka Viertel lived in Santa Monica at 165 Mabery Road, and entertained many important European émigrés. For more on Viertel, see Bilski and Braun (2005).

9. After heading the music department at Universal and supervising the music for about fifty films, scoring about a dozen of them himself, Waxman became a staff composer at Universal (1935–36), then MGM (1936–43), then Warner Bros. (1943–47) (MacDonald 1998: 119; Thomas 1973: 77).

10. For a brief discussion of the relation of film music to opera, and one which does not mention the leitmotiv, see Chion (1995: 124–25).

11. This notion of 'effectiveness' is further elaborated in Chapter 2; my postulated music supervision triangle balances budget, cachet, and effectiveness.

12. To clarify, Waxman must be referring specifically to the traditional form of Theme and Variations. Waxman would have been aware of classical period musical forms with multiple themes, counter subjects, or multiple movements, all with extensive development and variation of multiple themes.

13. Melodic contour and musical transformation are discussed in many music theory and composition texts, including Dallin (1974: 4–18).

14. Much of classical music theory rests upon the notion of alternation between consonance and dissonance, and the idea that resolution is a goal achieved by movement through various dissonances. There is not enough space here to devote to an extended explanation of Western music theory; but, suffice to say, there is typically an expectation of a nice, pretty, consonant chord at the end of a piece of music.

15. Solomon's 1989 article endeavors to describe such homosexual circles in Vienna during Schubert's time; Curtis' biography of Whale describes his circle and liaisons. Academic research into LGBT history is an expanding field, and more research needs to be done.

16. This is an increasingly complex topic, as notation practice in Hollywood has diverged somewhat from traditional Western classical notation practices. In classical music, as commonly notated, notes will be 'spelled' to preserve vertical interval relationships. Hollywood notation has seen the removal of key signatures and the notation of horizontal lines so they are easier for the individual player to read, regardless of harmonic relationships to other players around them. This can lead to some 'misspellings' in full score. In some cases, criticism of Elfman's spellings may be valid, or they may be criticisms of standard Hollywood practice.

17. For history and discourse on Burton, see especially Woods (2007), Hanke (2000), and Stranieri (2010).

7. *Blazing Saddles*: Music and Meaning in 'The French Mistake'

1. Music and lyrics by Mel Brooks, *Blazing Saddles Original Motion Picture Soundtrack* CD.

2. For a discussion of the sound advance, see Buhler et al. (2010: 18).
3. Quote supplied by 'top contributor' 'Marilyn B'. http://answers.yahoo.com/question/index?qid=20090215185329AA1tcHl, accessed 31 July 2011.
4. http://www.urbandictionary.com/define.php?term=French+mistake, accessed 31 July 2011. Posted by 'Mo T Juste', 21 September 2006. 318 'up' votes, 16 'down' votes.
5. The idioms 'closet' and 'closeted' are understood widely in the English-speaking world, and probably derive from the British code-language Polari. See Baker (2002a: 99) and (2002b: 67).
6. See especially *The Gold Diggers* films that fetishize wealth and prosperity.
7. For a discussion of hyper-stereotypes, see Gray (2006: 64).
8. *Blazing Saddles* is peppered with the word 'nigger.' Brooks has discussed the use of this word in many interviews, see Daly (2000). 'The French Mistake' sequence includes the normally homophobic slurs 'sissy Marys' and 'faggots.'
9. Consider the frequent Hitler routines such as 'Hitler on Ice' and 'Springtime for Hitler.'

8.   Conclusion

1. See Reeder (2004) for criticism of *The L Word*.

Bibliography

Abramovitch, Seth (2012). 'Lana Wachowski Reveals Suicide Plan, Painful Past in Emotional Speech,' *Hollywood Reporter* (November 2).

Achtenberg, Ben and van Dongen, Helen (1976). 'Helen van Dongen: An Interview,' *Film Quarterly* 30.2: 46–57.

Ades, David (2009). 'Angela Morley 1924–2009,' *Robert Farnon Society*. http://www.rfsoc.org.uk/amorley.shtml.

Adorno, Theodor and Eisler, Hans (2007). *Composing for the Films*. With a new introduction by Graham McCann (New York: Continuum; first published 1947, Oxford University Press).

Agawu, Kofi (1993). 'Schubert's Sexuality: A Prescription for Analysis?' *19th-Century Music* 17.1: 79–82.

Agel, Henri (1965). *Robert Flaherty* (Paris: Éditions Seghers).

Aguila, Justino (2006). 'Santaolalla in Oscar's Spotlight: The Multifaceted Composer, Performer and Producer is Nominated for his Brokeback Mountain Score,' *Orange County Register*. Santa Ana, CA (February 17).

Alexander, Thomas Kent (1967). 'San Francisco's Hipster Cinema,' *Film Culture* 44 (Spring; essay dated June 22, 1966).

Altman, Rick (2001). 'Cinema and Popular Song: The Lost Tradition,' in *Soundtrack Available: Essays on Film and Popular Music*, ed. Pamela Robertson Wojcik and Arthur Knight (Durham, NC and London: Duke University Press), 19–30.

Altman, Rick (2004). *Silent Film Sound* (New York: Columbia University Press).

Ammer, Christine (2003). *Unsung: A History of Women in American Music* (Portland, OR: Amadeus Press).

Anderson, Melissa (2002). 'Candied Glam: The Cultural Cachet of Candy Darling,' *Quarterly Review of Film & Video* 19.1: 59–69.

Araki, Gregg (2008). Director commentary on *The Living End* (DVD).

Associated Press (2009). 'Actor, comedian Dom DeLuise dies at 75.' Updated May 5, 2009. No byline. http://today.msnbc.msn.com/id/30581493, accessed July 2011.

Audissino, Emilio (2015). Correspondence with author (9 March).

Bailey, Derek (1992). *Improvisation: Its Nature and Practice in Music* (Bosyon, MA: Da Capo Press).

Baker, Paul (2002a). *Fantabulosa: A Dictionary of Polari and Gay Slang* (London: Continuum).

Baker, Paul (2002b). *Polari: The Lost Language of Gay Men* (London: Routledge).

Bandy, Mary Lea (1998). 'Ballet of the Roughnecks: Notes from Helen Van Dongen's Production Diary of Robert Flaherty's *Louisiana Story*,' *MoMA* 1.3: 6–9.

Baron-Cohen, Simon and Harrison, John E. (eds.) (1997). *Synaesthesia: Classic and Contemporary Readings* (Oxford and Cambridge, MA: Wiley-Blackwell).

Barrera, Sandra (2005). 'Sound Thinking Latin Grammy Nominee Gustavo Santaolalla Matches Traditional Music With the Very Contemporary,' *Daily News*, Los Angeles Newspaper Group, Los Angeles, CA (October 19).

Barsam, Richard (1988). *The Vision of Robert Flaherty: The Artist as Myth and Filmmaker* (Bloomington: Indiana University Press).

Bauer, Jerry (1980). 'Mel Brooks, a revealing dialog with the world's funniest man,' *Adelina Magazine* (February). http://www.brookslyn.com/print/Adelina1980/Adelina1980.php, accessed June 2011.

BBC (2011). 'Wales Music: Shirley Bassey – As I Love You.' http://www.bbc.co.uk/wales/music/sites/shirley-bassey/pages/as-i-love-you.shtml.

Bell, Arthur (1979). 'Playboy Interview: Wendy/Walter Carlos,' *Playboy* (May).

Benderson, Bruce (2014). *Against Marriage* (Los Angeles: Semiotext(e)).

Benshoff, Harry (1997). *Monsters in the Closet: Homosexuality and the Horror Film* (Manchester: Manchester University Press).

Bering, Jesse (2013). *Perv: The Sexual Deviant in All of Us* (New York: Scientific American/Farrar, Straus & Giroux).

Berman, Greta (1999). 'Synesthesia and the Arts,' *Leonardo* 32.1: 15–22.

Bernstein, Mary and Taylor, Verta (eds.) (2013). *The Marrying Kind? Debating Same-Sex Marriage within the Lesbian and Gay Movement* (Minneapolis, MN: University of Minnesota Press).

Berry, Chris (2007). 'The Chinese Side of the Mountain,' *Film Quarterly* 60.3: 32–37.

Bethke, Erik (2003). *Game Development and Production* (Plano, TX: Wordware Publishing).

Bilski, Emily D. and Braun, Emily (2005). *Jewish Women and Their Salons: The Power of Conversation* (New Haven, CT: Yale University Press).

Bird, John (1999). *Percy Grainger* (New York: Oxford University Press).

Bolton, Matthew (2013). 'The Ethnics of Alterity: Adapting Queerness in *Brokeback Mountain*,' in *Queer Love in Film and Television: Critical Essays*, ed. Pamela Demory and Christopher Pullen (New York: Palgrave Macmillan), 257–68.

Braheny, John (1990). 'Interview: Danny Elfman,' *Los Angeles Showcase Musepaper*. http://www.bluntinstrument.org.uk/elfman/archive/JohnBraheny1990.htm, accessed August 22, 2014.

Brasseaux, Ryan André (2009). 'The Backstory on *Louisiana Story*,' *Louisiana Cultural Vistas* (Spring): 20–29. http://www.nxtbook.com/nxtbooks/leh/lcv-spring09/.

Brett, Philip (1983). *Benjamin Britten: Peter Grimes*. Cambridge Opera Handbooks (Cambridge: Cambridge University Press).

Brett, Philip, Wood, Elizabeth, and Thomas, Gary C. (eds.) (2006). *Queering the Pitch: The New Gay and Lesbian Musicology*, 2nd edition (New York: Routledge).

Brocka, Q. Allan (2011a). Facebook post (March 12).

Brocka, Q. Allan (2011b). Facebook post (May 9).

Brockes, Emma (2004). 'Mein camp,' *The Guardian* (September 27). http://www.guardian.co.uk/film/2004/sep/27/theatre.usa, accessed June 7, 2011.

Bronski, Mark and Bronski, Michael (1999). 'Gods and Monsters: The Search for the Right Whale,' *Cinéaste* 24.4: 10–14.

Brooks, Mel (unknown). 'Mel Brooks on *Blazing Saddles* [3/4]' (Interview). http://www.youtube.com/watch?v=Danxt1y8EvM, accessed 24 April 2011.

Brooks, Xan (2012). 'Lana Wachowski opens up about transgender decision,' *The Guardian* (September 7).

Brookslyn: A Mel Brooks Fan Site. http://www.brookslyn.com/print/print.php#int, accessed July 2011.

Brown, Blain (1996). *Motion Picture and Video Lighting* (Burlington, MA: Elsevier Science).

Brown, David (2007). *Tchaikovsky: The Man and his Music* (New York: Pegasus Books).

Brown, Julie (2010). 'Carnival of Souls and the Organs of Horror,' in *Music in the Horror Film*, ed. Neil Lerner (New York: Routledge), 1–20.

Brown, Royal S. (1994). *Overtones and Undertones: Reading Film Music* (Berkeley, CA: University of California Press).

Buckland, Fiona (2001). *Impossible Dance: Club Culture and Queer World-Making* (Middletown, CT: Wesleyan University Press).

Buhler, James (2014). 'Gender, Sexuality, and the Soundtrack,' in *The Oxford Handbook of Film Music Studies*, ed. David Neumeyer (New York: Oxford University Press), 366–82.

Buhler, James, Neumeyer, David, and Deemer, Rob (2010). *Hearing the Movies: Music and Sound in Film History* (New York: Oxford University Press).

Burlingame, Jon (2009a). 'Music arranger Angela Morley dies,' Variety.com (January 18). http://variety.com/2009/film/news/music-arranger-angela-morley-dies-1117998739/.

Burlingame, Jon (2009b). 'Obituaries: Angela Morley,' *Variety* (January 26), 54.

Burlingame, Jon (2009c). 'SCL mourns Angela Morley,' *News: Quick Notes* (The Society of Composers & Lyricists). https://www.thescl.com/SCL_mourns_ANGELA_MORLEY/print.

Burton, Tim (1995). *Burton on Burton*, ed. Mark Salisbury (London: Faber & Faber).

Butler, Judith (1988). 'Performative Acts and Gender Constitution: An Essay in Phenomenology and Feminist Theory,' *Theatre Journal* 40.4: 519–31.

Butler, Judith (2006). *Gender Trouble: Feminism and the Subversion of Identity* (London: Routledge).

Byrne Bodley, Lorraine (2008). 'Late Style and the Paradoxical Poetics of the Schubert-Berio *Renderings*,' in *The Unknown Schubert*, ed. Barbara M. Reul and Lorraine Byrne Bodley (Aldershot: Ashgate), 233–50.

Carey, Melissa and Hannan, Michael (2003). 'Case Study 2: The Big Chill,' in *Popular Music and Film*, ed. Ian Inglis (London: Wallflower), 162–77.

Carlos, Wendy (2000). 'On Prurient Matters.' http://www.wendycarlos.com/pruri.html. Revised and edited November 2000. Accessed September 23, 2014.

Carlos, Wendy (2001). 'Rachel Elkind-Tourre.' http://www.wendycarlos.com/rachel.html. Updated July 17, 2001. Accessed September 23, 2014.

Carlos, Wendy (2014). 'Ouch! A Shortlist of the Cruel.' http://www.wendycarlos.com/ouch.html, accessed September 23, 2014.

Chambers, Ross (2005). 'The Queer and the Creepy: Western Fictions of Artificial Life,' *Pacific Coast Philology* 40.1: 19–35.

Chion, Michel (1990). *L'Audio-Vision* (Paris: Editions Nathan).

Chion, Michel (1995). *La musique au cinema* (Paris: Fayard).

Chion, Michel (2010). *Le Son: traité d'acoulogie*, 2nd edition (Paris: Armand Colin).

Christopher, Robert J. (ed.) (2005). *Robert and Frances Flaherty: A Documentary Life, 1883–1922* (Montreal: McGill-Queen's University Press).

Clark, Suzannah (2011). *Analyzing Schubert* (Cambridge: Cambridge University Press).

Clarke, Dominic (2014). 'Trans in the Mainstream: The State of Trans Representation and Why *Transamerica* Remains So Important,' *Indiewire* (July 22).

http://blogs.indiewire.com/bent/trans-in-the-mainstream-the-state-of-trans-representation-and-why-transamerica-remains-so-importart-20140722.

Clover, Joshua and Nealon, Christopher (2007). 'Don't Ask, Don't Tell Me,' *Film Quarterly* 60.3: 62–67.

Conrad, Ryan (ed.) (2010). *Against Equality: Queer Critiques of Gay Marriage* (Lewiston, ME: Against Equality Publishing Collective).

Cook, Bernie (2002). 'Interview with Callie Khouri, December 19, 2002,' in *Thelma & Louise Live! The Cultural Aftermath of an American Film,* ed. Bernie Cook (Austin, TX: University of Texas Press, 2007), 168–90.

Cook, Nicholas and Everist, Mark (eds.) (1999). *Rethinking Music* (New York: Oxford University Press).

Cook, Page (1968). 'Franz Waxman,' *Films in Review* 19.7.

Cooper, Peter (2006). 'Parton's Plea for Tolerance,' *USA Today* (February 23).

Copland, Aaron (1941). *Our New Music* (New York: McGraw-Hill).

Copland, Aaron (1949). 'Tip to Moviegoers: Take Off Those Ear-Muffs,' *New York Times Magazine.*

Copland, Aaron (1957a). 'Film Music,' in Copland, *What to Listen for in Music* (New York: McGraw-Hill), 202–10.

Copland, Aaron (1957b). *What to Listen For in Music,* revised edition (New York: McGraw-Hill Book Company).

Corra, Bruno (1912). 'Abstract Cinema – Chromatic Music,' in *Futurist Manifestos,* ed. Umbro Apollonio (New York: Viking Press, 1973), 66–70.

Coulthart, John (2008). 'A Clockwork Orange: The Complete Original Score,' *feuilleton* (July 10). http://www.johncoulthart.com/feuilleton/2008/07/10/a-clockwork-orange-the-complete-original-score/.

Cox, Christopher (2009). 'Interviews: Annie Proulx, The Art of Fiction No. 199,' *Paris Review* 188 (Spring).

Creekmur, Corey K. and Doty, Alexander (eds.) (1995). *Out in Culture: Gay, Lesbian and Queer Essays on Popular Culture* (Series Q) (Durham, NC: Duke University Press).

Crick, Robert Alan (2002). *The Big Screen Comedies of Mel Brooks* (Jefferson, NC: McFarland & Co.).

Cullen, Dave (ed.) (2007). *Beyond Brokeback: The Impact of a Film* (Livermore, CA: WingSpan Press).

Cullen, Dave (ed.) (2011). *The Ultimate Brokeback Forum.* http://www.davecullen.com/forum/, accessed 26 September 2011.

Curtis, James (1998). *James Whale: A New World of Gods and Monsters* (Boston: Faber & Faber).

Dallin, Leon (1974). *Techniques of Twentieth Century Composition,* 3rd edition (Dubuque, IA: William C. Brown).

Daly, Steve (2000). 'You've Got Mel,' *Entertainment Weekly* 529 (March). http://www.brookslyn.com/print/EntWeekly-5-00/EntWeekly5-00.php, accessed August 1, 2011.

Darrach, Brad (1975). 'Interview with Mel Brooks,' *Playboy Magazine* (February). http://www.brookslyn.com/print/PlayboyFeb1975/PlayboyFeb1975_part1.php, accessed July 9, 2011.

Darter, Tom and Armbruster, Greg (eds.) (1984). *The Art of Electronic Music* (New York: Quill / A Keyboard Book / William Morrow).

Davis, Richard (1999). *Complete Guide to Film Scoring* (Boston: Berklee Press).

De Coulteray, George (1965). *Sadism in the Movies*, trans. Steve Hult (New York: Medical Press of New York).

Donnelly, K. J. (2014). *Occult Aesthetics: Synchronization in Sound Film* (New York: Oxford University Press).

Doty, Alexander (1993). *Making Things Perfectly Queer: Interpreting Mass Culture* (Minneapolis, MN: University of Minnesota Press).

Doty, Alexander (2000). *Flaming Classics: Queering the Film Canon* (New York: Routledge).

Dowell, Pat, Rapping, Elayne, Cross, Alice, Schulman, Sarah, and Grundmann, Roy (1991). 'Should we go along for the ride? A Critical Symposium on *Thelma & Louise*' (Special Section), *Cinéaste* 18.4: 28–36.

Dubowsky, Jack Curtis (2011). 'The Evolving "Temp Score" in Animation,' *Music, Sound and the Moving Image* 5.1: 1–24.

Dubowsky, Jack Curtis (2014). 'Savvy Orchestration: Easy Listening and Film Scoring.' Paper presented at the Music and the Moving Image Conference (May 31), New York University.

Duralde, Alonso (2008). '*The Living End* Lives Again,' *The Advocate* (May). http://www.advocate.com/printArticle.aspx?id=22247, accessed June 8, 2011.

Dyer, Richard (ed.) (1977, 1980). *Gays & Film* (London: British Film Institute).

Dyer, Richard (ed.) (1984). *Gays & Film*, revised edition (New York: New York Zoetrope).

Dyer, Richard (2002). *The Culture of Queers* (New York: Routledge).

Easton, Dossie and Hardy, Janet W. (2009). *The Ethical Slut: A Practical Guide to Polyamory, Open Relationships & Other Adventures* (2nd edition) (Berkeley, CA: Celestial Arts).

Eastwood, Rainy (1996). Handsome Boy correspondence and Deal Memo (24 October).

Ehrbar, Greg (2002). '"Put One Note in Front of the Other": The Music of Maury Laws,' in *The Cartoon Music Book*, ed. Daniel Goldmark and Yuval Taylor (Chicago, IL: A Cappella Books), 193–200.

Einstein, Alfred and Mendel, Arthur (1941). 'Mozart's Choice of Keys,' *Musical Quarterly* 27.4: 415–21.

Elfman, Danny (1990). 'An Open Letter from Danny Elfman,' *Keyboard Magazine* (March).

Elfman, Danny (2000). Composer commentary track on *Edward Scissorhands 10th Anniversary Edition* (DVD) (USA: Twentieth Century Fox).

Elfman, Danny (2013). *Edward Scissorhands* (Full Score) (California: Omni Publishing).

Elley, Derek (1978a). 'The Film Composer: 3. John Williams, part 1,' *Films and Filming* 24.10: 20–24.

Elley, Derek (1978b). 'The Film Composer: 3. John Williams, part 2,' *Films and Filming* 24.11: 30–33.

Eraso, Carmen Indurain (2001). 'Thelma and Louise: "Easy Riders" in a Male Genre,' *Atlantis* 23.1: 63–73.

Evans, Brian (2005). 'Foundations of a Visual Music,' *Computer Music Journal* 29.4: 11–24.

Evans, Edward G. (1950). 'An Investigation of Harmonic Tension' (Dissertation) (Cleveland, OH: Western Reserve University).

Farmer, Clark (2008). '"Every Beautiful Sound Also Creates an Equally Beautiful Picture": Color Music and Walt Disney's Fantasia,' in *Lowering the Boom: Critical Studies in Film Sound*, ed. Jay Beck and Tony Grajeda (Urbana, IL University of Illinois Press), 183–98.

Fikentscher, Kai (2000). *'You Better Work!' Underground Dance Music in New York City* (Middletown, CT: Wesleyan University Press).

'Filmtracks: *Batman* (Danny Elfman)' (1997, 2011). *Filmtracks*. Written 29 August 1997, revised 2 June 2011. http://www.filmtracks.com/titles/batman.html, accessed 26 August 2014.

Fisher, Fred, Rose, Billy, and Raskin, Willie (1927). 'Fifty-Million Frenchmen Can't Be Wrong' (New York: Shapiro, Bernstein & Co.).

Flaherty, Frances Hubbard (1937). *Sabu, the Elephant Boy* (London: J. M. Dent).

Flaherty, Frances Hubbard (1960). *Odyssey of a Film-Maker: Robert Flaherty's Story* (Urbana, IL: Beta Phi Mu).

Flinn, Caryl (1992). *Strains of Utopia: Gender, Nostalgia, and Hollywood Film Music* (Princeton, NJ: Princeton University Press).

Fox, John (2009). *My Musical World* (Durham, CT: Eloquent Books).

Fox, Pamela (1998). 'Recycled "Trash": Gender and Authenticity in Country Music Autobiography,' *American Quarterly* 50.2: 234–66.

Freed, Richard (1973). Liner notes. LP. *The Contemporary Composer in the USA. Virgil Thomson Louisiana Story (Suite)*. TV-S 34534. (USA: Turnabout Vox Productions, Inc.).

Freedman, Carl (2007). 'Post Heterosexuality: John Wayne & the Construction of American Masculinity,' *Film International* 5.1: 16–31.

Fritz, Ben (2010). 'Movie projector: *Social Network* looks strong; *Let Me In* and *Case 39* will struggle,' *Los Angeles Times* (September 30). http://latimesblogs.latimes.com/entertainmentnewsbuzz/2010/09/movie-projector-social-network-looks-strong-let-me-in-and-case-39-will-struggle.html, accessed August 18, 2013.

Galeyev, B. M. (2007). 'The Nature and Functions of Synesthesia in Music,' *Leonardo* 40.3: 285–99.

Gaughan, Gavin (2009). 'Obituary: Angela Morley, transsexual conductor and arranger best known for BBC radio comedy classics,' *The Guardian* (January 23).

Gerstner, David A. (2011). *Queer Pollen: White Seduction, Black Male Homosexuality, and the Cinematic* (Urbana, Chicago, and Springfield, IL: University of Illinois Press).

Gillies, Malcolm, Pear, David, and Carroll, Mark (eds.) (2006). *Self-Portrait of Percy Grainger* (Oxford: Oxford University Press).

Gilmore, Bob (2014). *Claude Vivier: A Composer's Life* (Rochester, NY: University of Rochester Press).

Glass, Ira (1998). 'Durrell Daniels Interview. This American Life Episode 104: Music Lessons,' original airdate WBEZ June 5. Transcript: http://www.thisamericanlife.org/radio-archives/episode/104/transcript.

Gluck, Robert J. (2007). 'The Columbia-Princeton Electronic Music Center: Educating International Composers,' *Computer Music Journal* 31.2: 20–38.

Goldmark, Daniel (2005). *Tunes for 'Toons': Music and the Hollywood Cartoon* (Berkeley, CA: University of California Press).

Gorbman, Claudia (1987). *Unheard Melodies: Narrative Film Music* (Bloomington, IN: Indiana University Press).

Gorbman, Claudia (2007). 'Hearing *Thelma & Louise*: Active Reading of the Hybrid Pop Score,' in *Thelma & Louise Live! The Cultural Aftermath of an American Film*, ed. Bernie Cook (Austin, TX: University of Texas Press), 65–90.

Gorbman, Claudia (2012). 'Musical Worlds of the Millennial Western: *Dead Man* and *The Three Burials of Melquiades Estrada*,' in *Music in the Western: Notes from the Frontier*, ed. Kathryn Kalinak (New York and London: Routledge), 203–13.

Gramit, David (1993). 'Constructing a Victorian Schubert: Music, Biography, and Cultural Values,' *19th-Century Music* 17.1: 65–78.

Gray, Durian (2009). 'Remembering Sabu, "The Elephant Boy,"' *Sticky Rice: Gay Guide Asia and World*. http://www.stickyrice.ws/?view=tg_remembering.

Gray, Jonathan (2006). *Watching With The Simpsons* (New York: Routledge).

Green, Lucy (2007). *How Popular Musicians Learn: A Way Ahead for Music Education* (Farnham: Ashgate).

Greenberg, Harvey R., Clover, Carol J., Johnson, Albert, Chumo II, Peter N., Henderson, Brian, Williams, Linda, Kinder, Marsha, and Braudy, Leo (1991–1992). 'The Many Faces of *Thelma & Louise*,' *Film Quarterly* 45.2: 20–31.

Griffith, Richard (1953). *The World of Robert Flaherty* (London: Victor Gollancz).

Grimes, William (2009). 'Dom Deluise, Comic Actor, Dies at 75,' *New York Times* (May 5). http://www.nytimes.com/2009/05/07/movies/07deluise.html, accessed July 2011.

Gurza, Agustin (2006). 'The Oscars: The Composer. A back-breaker of an agenda; Nominated for his score to Brokeback Mountain, Gustavo Santaolalla long ago gained fame but still takes nothing for granted,' *Los Angeles Times*, Sunday Calendar; Part E. Calendar Desk (Los Angeles, CA: Tribune Publishing Company) (February 26).

Hagen, Earle (1971). *Scoring for Films* (New York: Criterion Music Corp.).

Halfyard, Janet K. (2004). *Danny Elfman's Batman: A Film Score Guide* (Lanham, MD: Scarecrow Press).

Halperin, David M. (2003). 'The Normalization of Queer Theory,' *Journal of Homosexuality* 45.2–4: 339–43.

Handley, William R. (ed.) (2011). *The Brokeback Book: From Story to Cultural Phenomenon* (Lincoln, NE: Bison Books/University of Nebraska Press).

Handzo, Stephen (1995). 'The Golden Age of Film Music,' *Cinéaste* 21.1/2: 46–55.

Hanke, Ken (2000). *Tim Burton: An Unauthorized Biography* (Los Angeles, CA: Renaissance Books).

Hanley, Robert (1976). 'Busby Berkeley, the Dance Director, Dies,' *New York Times* (March 15). http://www.nytimes.com/packages/pdf/arts/010909busby2.pdf, accessed July 2011.

Hart, Kylo-Patrick R. (2013). *Queer Males in Contemporary Cinema: Becoming Visible* (Plymouth: Scarecrow Press).

Hart, Lynda (1994). "'Til Death Do Us Part: Impossible Spaces in *Thelma & Louise*,' *Journal of the History of Sexuality*, Special Issue, Part 2: Lesbian and Gay Histories, 4.3: 430–46.

Hartz, Jason M. (2010). 'The Plow That Broke the Plains: An Application of Functional Americanism in Music' (dissertation, Ohio University).

'Have you heard it before? Herrmann vs Elfman' (2009). YouTube video, 0:59, posted by Zorba Movies (July 25). https://www.youtube.com/watch?v= ttV5C5evB7Y.

Haworth, Catherine (2012). 'Introduction: Gender, Sexuality, and the Soundtrack,' *Music, Sound, and the Moving Image* 6.2: 113–35.

Hayes, Dugan (2006). 'Noise Music As Queer Expression', *MIT Open Courseware* (Cambridge, MA: Massachusetts Institute of Technology). http://www.mitocw. espol.edu.ec/courses/special-programs/sp-406-sexual-and-gender-identities-fall-2006/assignments/, accessed September 26, 2011.

Healey, Jim (1995). '"All This For Us": The Songs in *Thelma & Louse,' Journal of Popular Culture* 29.3: 103–19.

Hemon, Aleksandar (2012). 'Beyond the Matrix,' *The New Yorker* (September 10).

Herdt, Gilbert (1989). 'Introduction: Gay and Lesbian Youth, Emergent Identities and Cultural Scenes, at Home and Abroad,' in *Gay and Lesbian Youth,* ed. Gilbert Herdt (New York and London: Haworth Press), 1–42.

Hess, John L. (1977). 'Goddard Lieberson, Who Fostered LP's at Columbia Records, Dies,' *New York Times* (May 30).

Holleran, Andrew (2006). 'The Magic Mountain,' *Gay & Lesbian Review Worldwide* 13.2: 12–15.

Hoover, Kathleen and Cage, John (1959). *Virgil Thomson: His Life and Music* (New York: Thomas Yoseloff).

Horton, Robert (2014). *Frankenstein* (New York: Wallflower Press).

Howe, Hubert S. Jr (1969). 'Recent Recordings of Electronic Music: Switched-On Bach by Walter Carlos; *The Nonesuch Guide to Electronic Music* by Paul Beaver; Bernard J. Krause,' *Perspectives of New Music* 7.2: 178–81.

Hu, Marcus (2012). Email correspondence with the author (25 June).

Hubbs, Nadine (2004). *The Queer Composition of America's Sound: Gay Modernists, American Music, and National Identity* (Berkeley, CA: University of California Press).

Inglis, Ian (ed.) (2003). *Popular Music and Film* (London & New York: Wallflower Press).

James, David E. (2009). 'L.A.'s Hipster Cinema', *Film Quarterly*, 63.1: 56–67.

Julien, Isaac and MacCabe, Colin (1991). *Diary of a Young Soul Rebel* (London: BFI Publishing).

Kalinak, Kathryn (1992). *Settling the Score: Music and the Classical Hollywood Film* (Madison, WI: University of Wisconsin Press).

Kalinak, Kathryn (2007). *How the West Was Sung* (Berkeley, CA: University of California Press).

Karlin, Fred (1994). *Listening to Movies: The Film Lover's Guide to Film Music* (New York: Schirmer).

Karlin, Fred and Wright, Rayburn (1990). *On the Track: A Guide to Contemporary Film Scoring* (New York: Schirmer Books).

Karlin, Fred and Wright, Rayburn (2004). *On the Track: A Guide to Contemporary Film Scoring,* revised 2nd edition (New York: Routledge).

Kassabian, Anahid (2001). *Hearing Film: Tracking Identifications in Contemporary Hollywood Film Music* (New York and London: Routledge).

Kassabian, Anahid (2013). 'The End of Diegesis as We Know It?' in *The Oxford Handbook of New Audiovisual Aesthetics,* ed. John Richardson, Claudia Gorbman, and Carol Vernallis (New York: Oxford University Press), 89–106.

Kearney, Christine (2012). 'Dolly Parton Talks Dreams, Love, Plastic Surgery,' *Reuters US Edition* (30 November) (New York: Reuters). http://www.reuters.com/article/2012/11/30/entertainment-us-books-dollyparton-idUSBRE8AT04C20121130.

Keightley, Keir (2008). 'Music for Middlebrows: Defining the Easy Listening Era, 1946–1966,' *American Music* 26.3: 309–35.

Kendall, Lukas (1995a). 'Danny Elfman: From Pee-Wee to Batman to Two Films a Year; Part 1 of 2' (Interview). *Film Score Monthly* 62 (October): 13–14.

Kendall, Lukas (1995b). 'Danny Elfman: Part 2' (Interview). *Film Score Monthly* 64 (December): 11–14.

Kendall, Lukas (1995c). 'Steve Bartek' (Interview). *Film Score Monthly* 64 (December): 14–16.

Kerman, Joseph (1980). 'How We Got into Analysis, and How to Get Out,' *Critical Inquiry* 7.2: 311–31.

Kerman, Joseph (1985). *Contemplating Music: Challenges to Musicology* (Cambridge, MA: Harvard University Press).

Kipling, Rudyard (1948). 'Toomai of the Elepants,' *The Jungle Books* 2: 145–72 (Garden City: Doubleday).

Kitses, Jim (2007). 'All that Brokeback Allows,' *Film Quarterly* 60.3: 22–27.

Klein, Howard (1965). 'Music of the Here and Now,' *New York Times* (July 18), X19.

Korsyn, Kevin (2003). *Decentering Music: A Critique of Contemporary Musical Research* (New York: Oxford University Press).

Kramer, Lawrence (1993). 'Schubert: Music, Sexuality, Culture,' *19th-Century Music* 17.1: 3–4.

Kramer, Lawrence (1998). *Franz Schubert: Sexuality, Subjectivity, Song* (Cambridge: Cambridge University Press).

Kun, Josh (2005). 'Against Easy Listening,' in Josh Kun, *Audiotopia: Music, Race, and America* (Berkeley, CA: University of California Press), 29–47.

LaBruce, Bruce (2011). Q & A. Frameline 35, the San Francisco International LGBT Film Festival, screening of biopic *Advocate for Fagdom* (2011). Dir. Angélique Bosio. Roxie Theatre, San Francisco, 22 June.

Lanza, Joseph (1994). *Elevator Music: A Surreal History of Muzak, Easy-Listening, and Other Moodsong* (New York: St. Martin's Press).

Larkin, Colin (ed.) (2006). *Encyclopedia of Popular Music*, 4th edition (Oxford: Oxford University Press).

Larson, Randall (1985). *Musique Fantastique: A Survey of Film Music in the Fantastic Cinema* (Metuchen NJ: Scarecrow Press).

Laws, Maury (2006). Interviewed by Rick Goldschmidt (April 19, 2003) on *The Daydreamer*, CD soundtrack bonus track (Percepto Records).

Leacock, Richard (2003). 'Letters Home: A Reading of Cinematographer Richard Leacock's Letters April 1946–June 1947 with Images from the Production.' DVD Extra in *Louisiana Story* (DVD) (Homevision).

Lehman, Frank (2013). 'Hollywood Cadences: Music and the Structure of Cinematic Expectation,' *Music Theory Online* 19.4. Society for Music Theory.

Leigh, Spencer (2009). 'Angela Morley: composer and arranger who worked with Scott Walker and scored *Dynasty* and *Dallas*,' *The Independent* (January 22).

Leland, John (2004). *Hip: The History* (New York: HarperCollins).

Lerdahl, Fred (2001). *Tonal Pitch Space* (New York: Oxford University Press).

Lerner, Neil (1997). 'The Classical Documentary Score in American Films of Persuasion: Contexts and Case Studies, 1936–1945' (dissertation, Duke University).

Lerner, Neil (1999). 'Damming Virgil Thomson's Music for *The River*,' in *Collecting Visible Evidence*, ed. Jane M. Gaines and Michael Renov (Minneapolis, MN: University of Minnesota Press), 103–15.

Lerner, Neil (2001). 'Copland's Music of Wide Open Spaces: Surveying the Pastoral Trope in Hollywood,' *The Musical Quarterly* 85.3: 477–515.

Lewis, George H. (1989). 'Interpersonal Relations and Sex-Role Conflict in Modern American Country Music,' *International Review of the Aesthetics and Sociology of Music* 20.2: 229–37.

Link, Stan (2010). 'The Monster and the Music Box: Children and the Soundtrack of Horror,' in *Music in the Horror Film*, ed. Neil Lerner (New York: Routledge), 38–54.

Lochner, James (2006). 'Petroleum, Politics and Prizes: Inside Virgil Thomson's Pulitzer Prize-Winning Score for *Louisiana Story*,' *Film Score Monthly* 11.4 (April).

London, Bette (1993). 'Mary Shelley, Frankenstein, and the Spectacle of Masculinity,' *PMLA* 108.2: 253–67.

Los Angeles Times (1992). 'H. W. Spencer: Composer and Arranger,' Obituary (September 22).

Love, Heather (2007). *Feeling Backward: Loss and the Politics of Queer History* (Cambridge, MA and London: Harvard University Press).

Luckman, Susan (1998). 'Rave Cultures and the Academy,' *Social Alternatives* 17.4: 45–49.

Lustig, Jessica (2005). 'So Danny Elfman Walks into Carnegie Hall ...' (Interview). http://www.americancomposers.org/elfman_interview.htm, accessed September 10, 2013.

Lustig, Milton (1980). *Music Editing for Motion Pictures* (New York: Hastings House).

MacDonald, Laurence E. (1998). *The Invisible Art of Film Music* (New York: Ardsley House).

Magee, Bryan (2000). *The Tristan Chord: Wagner and Philosophy* (New York: Metropolitan Books).

Mallinder, Stephen (2013). 'Foreword,' in S. Alexander Reed, *Assimilate: A Critical History of Industrial Music* (Oxford and New York: Oxford University Press).

Manvell, Roger and Huntley, John (1957). *The Technique of Film Music* (London and New York: Focal Press).

Matson, Michael (2013). Email correspondence with the author (14 September).

McClary, Susan (1991). *Feminine Endings: Music, Gender & Sexuality* (Minneapolis, MN: University of Minnesota Press).

McClary, Susan (1993). 'On the Steblin/Solomon Debate,' *19th-Century Music* 17.1: 83–88.

McClary, Susan (2006). 'Constructions of Subjectivity in Schubert's Music,' in *Queering the Pitch: The New Gay and Lesbian Musicology*, 2nd edition, ed. Philip Brett, Elizabeth Wood, and Gary C. Thomas (New York: Routledge), 205–34.

McKee, Alan (2000). 'Images of Gay Men in the Media and the Development of Self Esteem,' *Australian Journal of Communication* 27.2: 81–98.

Merritt, Russell (2008). 'Crying in Color: How Hollywood Coped when Technicolor Died,' *Journal of the National Film and Sound Archive of Australia* 3.2/3 (Australia: National Film and Sound Archive).

Miller, D. A. (1990). 'Anal Rope,' *Representations* 32: 114–33.

Miller, D. A. (2007). 'On the Universality of Brokeback Mountain,' *Film Quarterly* 60.3: 50–60.

Miller, Danny and Shamsie, Jamal (1996). 'The Resource-Based View of the Firm in Two Environments: The Hollywood Film Studios from 1936 to 1965,' *Academy of Management Journal* 39.3: 519–43.

Morley, Angela (1999). Guest Speaker appearance, American Society of Music, Arrangers & Composers (A.S.M.A.C.) (May 19), The Ventura Club, Sherman Oaks, CA. http://yost.com/humor/the-goon-show/angela-morley/.

Morley, Angela (2008). 'Angela Morley Career Autobiography.' http://www.ange-lamorley.com/site/bio.htm, accessed July 4, 2011.

Morris, Mitchell (2013). 'Calling Names, Taking Names,' *Journal of the American Musicological Society* 66.3: 831–35.

Mulvey, Laura (1975). 'Visual Pleasure and Narrative Cinema,' *Screen* 16.3: 6–18.

Munt, John (2013). Email correspondence with the author (7 September).

Murch, Walter (2001). *In the Blink of an Eye: A Perspective on Film Editing*, 2nd edition (Beverly Hills, CA: Silman-James Press).

Music and the Moving Image, Special Issue: 'Gender, Sexuality, and the Soundtrack' (6.2, 2012).

Musiker, Reuben and Musiker, Naomi (1998). *Conductors and Composers of Popular Orchestral Music* (Westport, CT: Greenwood Press).

Musto, Michael (2009). 'Dom DeLuise: Gay?' *Village Voice* (May 11). http://blogs.villagevoice.com/dailymusto/2009/05/dom_deluise_gay.php, accessed June 2011.

Muxfeldt, Kristina (1993). 'Political Crimes and Liberty, or Why Would Schubert Eat a Peacock?' *19th-Century Music* 17.1: 47–64.

Nathan, Sara (2012). '"I did write a suicide note addressed to my parents … it was just that I didn't belong": Transgender *Matrix* director Lana Wachowski on her childhood torment,' *Daily Mail* (October 24).

Needham, Gary (2010). *Brokeback Mountain* (Edinburgh: Edinburgh University Press).

Neumeyer, David and Platte, Nathan (2012). *Franz Waxman's Rebecca: A Film Score Guide* (Lanham, MD: Scarecrow Press).

New York Magazine (1979). 'Composer Changes More Than Tune' (April 2), 65.

New York Times (1984). 'Arthur Bell, 51, a Columnist, Homosexual Rights Activist' (Obituary) (June 4).

O'Neal, Sean (2014). 'Danny Elfman on Oingo Boingo, film scores, and the Beatles almost ruining *Batman*,' *AV Club*. http://www.avclub.com/article/danny-elfman-oingo-boingo-film-scores-and-beatles--210856.

Orbanz, Eva (1998). 'Step by Step,' in *Filming Robert Flaherty's Louisiana Story/The Helen van Dongen Diary*, ed. Eva Orbanz (New York: Museum of Modern Art), 91–115.

Ormiston, Craig (2011). 'Film Friday: The Project Triangle,' *Craig O's Blog: a daily random thought on life, business film and tech*. http://www.craigormiston.com/post/4086117420/film-friday-the-project-triangle, accessed August 12, 2011.

Ortmann, Otto (1933). 'Theories of Synesthesia in the Light of a Case of Color-Hearing,' *Human Biology* 5.2: 155–211.

Osterweil, Ara (2007). 'Ang Lee's Lonesome Cowboys,' *Film Quarterly* 60:3: 38–42.

Oteri, Frank (2007). 'Wendy's World,' *New Music Box*. http://www.newmusicbox.org/articles/wendys-world/.

Owen, Harold (1992). *Modal and Tonal Counterpoint* (New York: Schirmer Books).

Parish, James Robert (2007). *It's Good To Be the King: The Seriously Funny Life of Mel Brooks* (Hoboken, NJ: John Wiley).

Parker, Christine (2015). Email correspondence with the author (March 13).

Patterson, David W. (2004). 'Music, Structure and Metaphor in Stanley Kubrick's *2001: A Space Odyssey*,' *American Music* 22.3: 444–74.

Patterson, Eric (2008). *On Brokeback Mountain: Meditations about Masculinity, Fear, and Love in the Story and the Film* (Lanham, MD: Lexington Books).

Patterson, Nick (2011). 'The Archives of the Columbia-Princeton Electronic Music Center,' *Notes* 67.3: 483–502 (Music Library Association).

Paulin, Scott D. (1997). 'Unheard Sexualities? Queer Theory and the Soundtrack,' *Spectator* 17.2.

Peacock, Kenneth (1988). 'Instruments to Perform Color-Music: Two Centuries of Technological Experimentation,' *Leonardo* 21.4: 397–406.

Peake, Tony (2000). *Derek Jarman: A Biography* (Woodstock, NY: The Overlook Press).

Peirce, Kimberly (2014). Director Q&A, Outfest Screening of *Boys Don't Cry* (October 30). West Hollywood City Council Chambers.

People Magazine (2003). 'Nipped, Tucked & Talking Celebs You Always Thought Had "A Little Work Done" Are Opening Up About the Pain, the Pleasure and the Prevalence of Hollywood's Favorite Procedures,' *People Magazine* 60.9 (September 1).

Peraino, Judith A. and Cusick, Suzanne G., convenors (2013). Colloquy on 'Music and Sexuality,' *Journal of the American Musicological Society* 66.3: 825–72.

Perry, Kevin (2011). 'GQ&A: Gary Numan,' *British GQ* (December 7). http://www.gq-magazine.co.uk/entertainment/articles/2011-12/09/gary-numan-interview-dead-son-rising.

Picart, Caroline Joan S. (2000). 'Visualizing the Monstrous in Frankenstein Films,' *Pacific Coast Philology* 35.1: 17–34.

Pinch, Trevor and Bijsterveld, Karin (2003). '"Should One Applaud?" Breaches and Boundaries in the Reception of New Technology,' *Technology and Culture*, 44.3: 536–59.

Pinch, Trevor and Trocco, Frank (2002). *Analog Days: The Invention and Impact of the Moog Synthesizer* (Cambridge, MA: Harvard University Press).

Potter, Caroline (2014). 'Reverie: The Music of Angela Morley,' *A Sketch of the Past* (website). Posted July 30. http://asketchofthepast.com/2014/07/30/reverie-the-music-of-angela-morley/.

Poznansky, Alexander (1991). *Tchaikovsky: The Quest for the Inner Man* (New York: Schirmer Books).

Pramaggiore, Maria (1997). 'Fishing for Girls: Romancing Lesbians in New Queer Cinema,' *College Literature* 24.1: 59–75.

Prendergast, Roy M. (1977). *Film Music: A Neglected Art* (New York: New York University Press).

Prendergast, Roy M. (1992). *Film Music: A Neglected Art*, 2nd edition (New York: W. W. Norton).

Proptarts.com (2012). 'How to do Craft Services and Catering on a Low Budget.' http://www.proptarts.com/Craft_Service_101.html, accessed May 20, 2012.

Proulx, Annie, McMurtry, Larry, and Ossana, Diana (2005). *Brokeback Mountain: Story to Screenplay* (New York: Scribner).

Prout, Ebenezer (1899). *The Orchestra. Volume II: Orchestral Combination* (London: Augener).

Quirk, Lawrence J. and Schoell, William (1998). *The Rat Pack: Neon Lights with the Kings of Cool* (Dallas, TX: Taylor).

Ramey, Phillip (1972). 'Walter Carlos: Then, Now and In-Between,' Liner Notes. *Sonic Seasonings*. Walter Carlos. Columbia Records KG31234 (New York).

Rapée, Erno (1925). *Encyclopedia of Music for Pictures* (New York: Arno Press [1974 reprint]; New York: Mahony & Scheid Press [original 1925 edition]).

Raphael, Rina (2014). '5 style lessons we can learn from Dolly Parton,' *Today*. Posted May 15. http://www.today.com/style/5-style-lessons-we-can-learn-dolly-parton-2D79655017.

Rath, Derek (2005). 'The Sound of *Brokeback Mountain*,' interview with Gustavo Santaolalla. National Public Radio. First broadcast December 8. http://www.npr.org/templates/story/story.php?storyId=5044116, accessed August 28, 2013.

Reay, Pauline (2004). *Music in Film: Soundtracks and Synergy* (New York: Wallflower).

Reed, Christopher (2011). *Art and Homosexuality: A History of Ideas* (New York: Oxford University Press).

Reed, S. Alexander (2013). *Assimilate: A Critical History of Industrial Music* (Oxford and New York: Oxford University Press).

Reed, Susan (1985). 'After a Sex Change and Several Eclipses, Wendy Carlos Treads a New Digital Moonscape,' *People* 24.1 (July 1).

Reeder, Constance (2004). 'The Skinny on the L Word,' *Off Our Backs* (January–February): 51–52.

Reul, Barbara M. and Byrne Bodley, Lorraine (eds.) (2008). *The Unknown Schubert* (Aldershot: Ashgate).

Reynolds, S. and Press, J. (1995). *The Sex Revolts: Gender, Rebellion, and Rock 'n' Roll* (Cambridge, MA: Harvard University Press).

Rich, B. Ruby (1992). 'New Queer Cinema,' *Sight and Sound* 2.5: 30–37.

Rich, B. Ruby (2003). 'Two for the Road,' *The Advocate* 883: 48–49.

Rich, B. Ruby (2005). 'Film & Music: Film: Hello Cowboy: Ang Lee's award-winning gay western is the most important film to come out of America in years, says B. Ruby Rich,' *The Guardian* (September 23).

Rich, B. Ruby (2007). 'Brokering *Brokeback*: Jokes, Backlashes, and Other Anxieties,' *Film Quarterly* 60.3: 44–48.

Rich, B. Ruby (2013). *New Queer Cinema: The Director's Cut* (Durham, NC and London: Duke University Press).

Richter, Nicole (2013). 'Trans Love in New Trans Cinema,' in *Queer Love in Film and Television: Critical Essays*, ed. Pamela Demory and Christopher Pullen (New York: Palgrave Macmillan), 161–86.

Rigney, Melissa (2003). 'Brandon Goes to Hollywood: Boys Don't Cry and the Transgender Body in Film,' *Film Criticism* 28.2: 4.

Rohter, Larry (2008). 'His Film Scores Are Spare, His Tango Newfangled,' *New York Times*. Dateline Buenos Aires (August 15).

Rollins, Peter C. and O'Connor, John E. (eds.) (2009). *Hollywood's West: The American Frontier in Film, Television, and History* (Louisville, KY: University Press of Kentucky).

Rorem, Ned (1994). *Knowing When to Stop: A Memoir* (New York: Simon & Schuster).

Rosar, William H. (1983). 'Music for the Monsters: Universal Pictures' Horror Film Scores of the Thirties,' *Quarterly Journal of the Library of Congress* 40.4: 390–421.

Rosen, Judith (2007). 'Carlos, Wendy,' *Oxford Music Online*. http://www.oxfordmusiconline.com.ccl.idm.oclc.org/subscriber/article/grove/music/47301.

Ross, Alex (2010). *Listen to This* (New York: Farrar, Straus & Giroux).

Rotha, Paul (1983). *Robert J. Flaherty: A Biography* (Philadelphia, PA: University of Pennsylvania Press).

Ruby, Jay (1980). 'A Re-examination of the Early Career of Robert J. Flaherty,' *Quarterly Review of Film Studies* 5.4: 431–57.

Russell, Mark and Young, James (2000). *Film Music* (Boston: Focal Press).

Russo, Vito (1981). *The Celluloid Closet: Homosexuality in the Movies* (New York: Harper & Row).

Santaolalla, Gustavo (2006). 'The Weight of Victory Can Be Too Heavy,' *New York Times* (February 28).

Saunders, John (2001). *The Western Genre: From Lordsburg to Big Whiskey* (London: Wallflower).

Schewe, Elizabeth (2014). 'Highway and Home: Mapping Feminist–Transgender Coalition in *Boys Don't Cry*,' *Feminist Studies* 40.1: 39–64.

Schubart, Christian Friedrich Daniel (1806). *Schubart's Ideen zu einer Ästhetik der Tonkunst* (Vienna: Bey J. V. Degen).

Schubert, Franz (1894–1895). 'Ellen's Gesang. III. Hymnean die Jungfrau,' *Franz Schubert's Werke, Serie XX: Sämtlicheeinstimmige Lieder und Gesänge, No. 474* (pp. 90–91) (Leipzig: Breitkopf & Härtel, Plate F.S. 833). Reprinted: New York: Edwin F. Kalmus, n.d. (after 1933). Study Score No. 1088 (#16400).

Schuckmann, Patrick (1998). 'Masculinity, the Male Spectator and the Homoerotic Gaze,' *Amerikastudien/American Studies* 43.4: 671–80.

Schumach, Murray (1964). *The Face on the Cutting Room Floor: The Story of Movie and Television Censorship* (New York: William Morrow).

Scordo, Lizbeth (2012). 'Dolly Parton Talks Lesbian Rumors, Plastic Surgery, and Looking Like the Town Tramp on "Nightline",' *US Magazine* Celebrity News (November 28). http://www.usmagazine.com/celebrity-news/news/dolly-parton-talks-lesbian-rumors-plastic-surgery-and-looking-like-the-town-tramp-on-nightline-20122811.

Sikov, Ed (2002). *Mr Strangelove: A Biography of Peter Sellers* (London: Sidgwick & Jackson).

Siskel, Gene (1977). 'No kidding, Mel Brooks is a serious filmmaker,' *Chicago Tribune* (November 6).

Slocum, J. David (2007). 'An Outlaw-Couple-on-the-Run Film for the 1990s,' in *Thelma & Louise Live! The Cultural Aftermath of an American Film*, ed. Bernie Cook (Austin, TX: University of Texas Press), 122–45.

Slowik, Michael (2012). 'Why Max Steiner Was Wrong, Or: Re-recording and the Hollywood Film Score, 1929–1931,' conference paper, Society for Cinema and Media Studies, Boston, MA. Panel S3, March 25.

Smelik, Anneke (2000). 'Gay and Lesbian Criticism,' in *Film Studies: Critical Approaches*, ed. John Hill and Pamela Church Gibson (Oxford: Oxford University Press), 133–44.

Smith, Jeff (1998). *The Sounds of Commerce: Marketing Popular Film Music* (New York: Columbia University Press).

Smith, Jeff (2001a). 'Popular Songs and Comic Allusion in Contemporary Cinema,' in *Soundtrack Available: Essays on Film and Popular Music*, ed. Pamela Robertson Wojcik and Arthur Knight (Durham, NC and London: Duke University Press), 407–30.

Smith, Jeff (2001b). 'Taking Music Supervisors Seriously,' in *Experiencing the Soundtrack*, ed. Philip Brophy (Sydney: Australian Film, Television and Radio School), 125–46.

Smith, Jeff (2012). 'Nostalgia Panel Respondency,' conference paper, Society for Cinema and Media Studies, Boston, MA. Panel N3 (March 24).

Smith, Jeff (2013). 'What Exactly Is a Partial Cue? Jurisdictional Conflict in Warner Bros. Films of the Early Sound Era,' paper presented at the SCMS Seattle 2013 H16 Annual Conference (March 7).

Snyder, Blake (2005). *Save The Cat! The Last Book on Screenwriting You'll Ever Need* (Studio City, CA: Michael Wiese Productions).

Solomon, Maynard (1989). 'Franz Schubert and the Peacocks of Benvenuto Cellini,' *19th-Century Music* 12.3: 193–206.

Solomon, Maynard (1993). 'Schubert: Some Consequences of Nostalgia,' *19th-Century Music* 17.1: 34–46.

Solomon, Maynard (2004). 'Schubert: Family Matters,' *19th-Century Music* 28.1: 3–14.

Stanfield, Peter (2002). *Horse Opera: The Strange History of the 1930s Singing Cowboy* (Urbana and Chicago, IL: University of Illinois Press).

Steblin, Rita (1983). *A History of Key Characteristics in the 18th and Early 19th Centuries* (Ann Arbor: UMI Research Press).

Steblin, Rita (1993). 'The Peacock's Tale: Schubert's Sexuality Reconsidered,' *19th-Century Music* 17.1: 5–33.

Steiner, Fred (1974). '"Black-and-White" Music for Hitchcock's Psycho,' Part I. *Film Music Notebook* 1.1 (Sherman Oaks, CA: Film Music Society).

Sternfeld, Frederick W. (1948). '*Louisiana Story*: A Review of Virgil Thomson's Score,' in *Film Music Notes: Official Organ of the National Film Music Council* 8.1 (September–October) (New York).

Stewart, Colin (2011). 'Praise for Dolly Parton's Extreme Surgeries,' *Orange County Register* (February 11; updated August 21, 2013) (Santa Ana, CA: Freedom Communications). http://www.ocregister.com/articles/extreme-287988-parton-praise.html.

Stilwell, Robynn J. (2007). 'The Fantastical Gap between Diegetic and Nondiegetic,' in *Beyond the Soundtrack: Representing Music in Cinema*, ed. Daniel Goldmark, Lawrence Kramer, and Richard Leppert (Berkeley, CA: University of California Press), 184–202.

Stranieri, Vyvyan (2010). *Tim Burton Education Kit* (Australian Centre for the Moving Image).

Stryker, Susan (2006). '(De)Subjugated Knowledges: An Introduction to Transgender Studies,' in *The Transgender Studies Reader*, ed. Susan Stryker and Stephen Whittle (New York: Routledge), 1–18.

Stryker, Susan (2008). *Transgender History* (Berkeley CA: Seal Press).

Sturken, Marita (2000). *Thelma & Louise* (London: BFI Modern Classics / BFI Publishing).

Sturtevant, Victoria (2007). 'Getting Hysterical: Thelma & Louise and Laughter,' in *Thelma & Louise Live! The Cultural Aftermath of an American Film*, ed. Bernie Cook (Austin, TX: University of Texas Press), 43–64.

Subotnick, Morton (2012). 'A Conversation with Morton Subotnick,' Library of Congress annual Founder's Day Concert (November 9). http://www.loc.gov/today/cyberlc/feature_wdesc.php?rec=5927, accessed April 13, 2015.

Suchy, Patricia A. and Catano, James V. (2010). 'Revisiting Flaherty's Louisiana Story,' *Southern Spaces* (27 April). http://www.southernspaces.org/2010/revisiting-flahertys-louisiana-story.

Swan, Rachel (2001). *Boys Don't Cry* (Review). *Film Quarterly* 54.3: 47–52.

Symons, Alex (2012). *Mel Brooks in the Cultural Industries: Survival and Prolonged Adaptation* (Edinburgh: Edinburgh University Press).

Taylor, Ken (2014). 'Wendy Carlos Biography.' http://www.musicanguide.com/biographies/1608003925/Wendy-Carlos.html (Net Industries).

Taylor, Robert Lewis (1949a). 'Profiles: Moviemaker: I. Education for Wanderlust,' *The New Yorker* (June 11).

Taylor, Robert Lewis (1949b). 'Profiles: Moviemaker: II. Hudson Bay to Samoa,' *The New Yorker* (June 18).

Taylor, Robert Lewis (1949c). 'Profiles: Moviemaker: III. Tamu and Sabu,' *The New Yorker* (June 25).

Tchaikovsky, Peter Ilyich (1892; 1987 edition). *Nutcracker Suite in Full Score* (New York: Dover Publications).

Tellenbach, Marie-Elisabeth (2000). 'Franz Schubert and Benvenuto Cellini: One Man's Meat,' *The Musical Times* 141.1870 (Spring): 50–52.

Thomas, Tony (1973). *Music for the Movies* (Cranbury, NJ: A. S. Barnes and Co).

Thomas, Tony (1991). *Film Score: The Art & Craft of Movie Music* (Burbank, CA: Riverwood Press).

Thomson, Virgil (1948). *Louisiana Story* (score for orchestra) (not published; held at the Library of Congress, Washington, DC).

Thomson, Virgil (1966). *Virgil Thomson* (New York: Alfred A. Knopf).

Thornton, Sarah (1996). *Club Cultures: Music, Media and Subcultural Capital* (Middletown, CT and London: Wesleyan University Press).

Timm, Larry M. (2003). *The Soul of Cinema: An Appreciation of Film Music* (Upper Saddle River, NJ: Pearson Education).

Tommasini, Anthony (1997). *Virgil Thomson: Composer on the Aisle* (New York: W. W. Norton).

Troche, Rose (2014). Email correspondence with the author (21 October).

Turner, Guinevere and Troche, Rose (1995). *Go Fish: The Full Original Screenplay* (Woodstock, NY: Overlook Press).

Twitchell, James B. (1983). '"Frankenstein" and the Anatomy of Horror,' *The Georgia Review* 37.1: 41–78.

Tyler, Parker (1972). *Screening the Sexes: Homosexuality in the Movies* (New York: Holt, Rinehart, & Winston).

Urban Dictionary (2011). 'French Mistake.' http://www.urbandictionary.com/define.php?term=French%20Mistake, accessed July 10, 2011.

Vachon, Christine (2006). *A Killer Life* (New York: Simon & Schuster).

Vachon, Christine with Edelstein, David (1998). *Shooting to Kill: How an Independent Producer Blasts Through the Barriers to Make Movies That Matter* (New York: Avon Books).

Välimäki, Susanna (2013). 'The Audiovisual Construction of Transgender Identity in *Transamerica*,' in *The Oxford Handbook of New Audiovisual Aesthetics*, ed. John Richardson, Claudia Gorbman, and Carol Vernallis (New York: Oxford University Press), 372–88.

van Dongen, Helen (1998). '*Louisiana Story*: Notes During the Production,' in *Filming Robert Flaherty's Louisiana Story/The Helen van Dongen Diary*, ed. Eva Orbanz (New York: Museum of Modern Art), 21–74.

Warner Bros. Inc. (1974). *Pressbook: Mel Brooks' Blazing Saddles*.

Waxman, Franz (2012). 'History of Motion Picture Music,' in *The Routledge Film Music Sourcebook*, ed. James Wierzbicki, Nathan Platte, and Colin Roust (New York: Routledge).

Webster, James (1993). 'Music, Pathology, Beethoven, Schubert,' *19th-Century Music* 17.1: 89–93.

Wentz, Brooke (2011). Interview by email (May).

Whiteley, Sheila and Rycenga, Jennifer (eds.) (2006). *Queering the Popular Pitch* (New York and London: Routledge).

Whitesell, Lloyd (2013). 'Compromising Positions,' *Journal of the American Musicological Society* 66.3: 835–39.

Whitfield, Irène Thérèse (1939). *Louisiana French Folk Songs* (Louisiana: Louisiana State University Press).

Whitmer, Mariana (2012). *Jerome Moross's The Big Country: A Film Score Guide* (Lanham, MD: Scarecrow Press).

Wilson, Pamela (1995). 'Mountains of Contradictions: Gender, Class, and Region in the Star Image of Dolly Parton,' *The South Atlantic Quarterly* 94.1: 109–34.

Winter, Robert S. (1993). 'Whose Schubert?' *19th-Century Music* 17.1: 94–101.

Woods, Paul (ed.) (2007). *Tim Burton: A Child's Garden of Nightmares* (London: Plexus).

Wright, Steven H. (2006). 'The Film Music of Danny Elfman: A Selective Discography (Review).' *Notes*, Second Series 62.4: 1030–42.

Yacowar, Maurice (1981). *Method in Madness: The Comic Art of Mel Brooks* (New York: St. Martin's Press).

Yahoo! Answers (2011). http://answers.yahoo.com/question/index?qid=2009021 5185329AA1tcHl, accessed July 10, 2011.

Young, Elizabeth (1991). 'Here Comes the Bride: Wedding Gender and Race in *Bride of Frankenstein*,' *Feminist Studies* 17.3: 403–37.

Young, Elizabeth (2008). *Black Frankenstein: The Making of an American Metaphor* (New York: New York University Press).

Yumibe, Joshua (2009). '"Harmonious Sensations of Sound by Means of Colors": Vernacular Color Abstractions in Silent Cinema,' *Film History* 21.2: 164–76.

Zador, Leslie (1971). 'Movie Music's Man of the Moment,' *Coast FM and Fine Arts* (June): 31.

Zekas, Rita (1994). 'Bible belter out to out Bert and Ernie,' *Toronto Star* (January 30), C2.

Film and music sources

Age of Consent, The (1984). (LP). Bronski Beat. MCA-5538 (Universal City, CA: MCA Records).

Blazing Saddles: Original Motion Picture Soundtrack. CD reissue with booklet. La-La-Land Records. LLLCD1072. (p) 1974, 2008 Warner Bros. Entertainment.

Brooks, Mel (1974). 'The French Mistake' (music and lyrics by Mel Brooks). *Blazing Saddles Original Motion Picture Soundtrack*. CD reissue with booklet. La-La-Land Records. LLLCD1072. (p) 1974, 2008 Warner Bros. Entertainment.

Eating Out: Drama Camp, a.k.a. *Eating Out 4* (2011). (DVD). Dir. Q. Allan Brocka (USA: Ariztical Entertainment).

Edward II (1991). Dir. Derek Jarman (UK: BBC Films).

Edward Scissorhands (1990). Dir. Tim Burton (USA: Twentieth Century Fox).

Fellini Satyricon (1969). Dir. Federico Fellini (Italy: PEA).

Home Alone (1990). Dir. Chris Columbus (USA: Twentieth Century Fox).

Hot Horny & Born Again (1993). (CD). Glen Meadmore (USA: Pervertidora).

Hours and Times, The (1991). Dir. Christopher Munch (USA: Antarctic Pictures).
Hustler White (1996). Dir. Rick Castro and Bruce LaBruce (Germany: Jürgen Bruning Filmproduktion).
L.A. Zombie (2010). Dir. Bruce LaBruce (Germany: Wurstfilm).
Living End, The (1992). Dir. Gregg Araki (Canada: Cineplex Odeon).
Lomax, Alan and Lomax, John (1999). *Cajun & Creole Music: The Classic Louisiana Recordings 1934–1937*, 2 vols. (CD) (Cambridge, MA: Rounder Records).
Looking for Langston (1989). Dir. Isaac Julien (UK: British Film Institute).
Louisiana Story: The Reverse Angle (2008). Dir. Tika Laudun (Baton Rouge: Louisiana Educational Television Authority, Louisiana Public Broadcasting).
Morris, John (1974, 2008). *Blazing Saddles: Original Motion Picture Soundtrack*. CD reissue with booklet. La-La-Land Records. LLLCD1072. (p) 1974, 2008 Warner Bros. Entertainment.
Music for the Movies: The Hollywood Sound (DVD) (1995). Dir. Joshua Waletzky (Sony Classical Film & Video; Kultur Video, 2007).
Night of the Lepus (1972). Dir. William F. Claxton (USA: A. C. Lyles Productions).
Peirce, Kimberly (2009). *Boys Don't Cry*, DVD Director Commentary (USA: Fox Searchlight Pictures).
Philips (1958). *London Souvenir: A Musical Souvenir of London Town – Wally Stott and His Orchestra*. Stereo LP with gatefold and booklet. SAL 3432 (London: Philips).
Poison (1991). Dir. Todd Haynes (USA: Killer Films).
Reservoir Dogs (1992). Dir. Quentin Tarantino (USA: Miramax Films).
Riot Acts: Flaunting Gender Deviance in Music Performance (2010). Dir. Madsen Minax (USA: Outcast Films).
R.S.V.P. (1992). Dir. Laurie Lynd (USA: Frameline Distribution).
Rudolph the Red-Nosed Reindeer (1964). Dir. Larry Roemer (Rankin/Bass Productions).
Sergeant, The (1968). Dir. John Flynn (USA: Warner Bros./Seven Arts).
Shallow Hal (2001). Dir. Bobby Farrelly and Peter Farrelly (USA: Twentieth Century Fox).
Social Network, The (2010). Dir. David Fincher (USA: Columbia Pictures).
Song of Bernadette (1943). Dir. Henry King (USA: Twentieth Century Fox).
Swoon (1991). Dir. Tom Kalin (USA: Killer Films).
Together and Apart (1988). Dir. Laurie Lynd (USA: The Cinema Guild).
Traditional (1934a). 'Je m'endors,' performed by Jesse Stafford, recorded 1934 by John and Alan Lomax (Archive of Folk Song 17a2, Library of Congress).
Traditional (1934b). 'Creole Blues,' performed by Wayne Perry, recorded 1934 by John and Alan Lomax (Archive of Folk Song 20a3, Library of Congress).
Young Frankenstein (1974). Dir. Mel Brooks (USA: Twentieth Century Fox).
Young Soul Rebels (1991). Dir. Isaac Julien (UK: British Film Institute).

Index

Whale, James 174–5, 177, 181,
184, 187–9, 206–7, 235n1,
236n15
Whitfield, Irene Thérèse 35–6,
39–45
Wierzbicki, James 50, 230n1
Wilder, Gene 209, 221
Williams, John 8, 105, 118, 126,
128, 201–2, 233n14
Wonder Woman 118
Wood, Robin 173

Woods, Robert 68–70
word painting 152

Young, Neil 89–90, 154
Young Frankenstein 175, 195, 209,
212, 216, 218, 222
Young Soul Rebels 52, 60, 62–5, 225

Zimmer, Hans 98, 131, 135, 138,
141–2, 193
zombies 53, 79

CPSIA information can be obtained
at www.ICGtesting.com
Printed in the USA
LVOW04*1943010316

477330LV00013B/1204/P